Ava Helen Pauling

Portrait of Ava Helen Pauling by Alice Neel. Photograph by Ms. Lida Moser. Courtesy of Alida Anderson Art Projects, LLC.

Ava Helen Pauling

PARTNER, ACTIVIST, VISIONARY

Mina Carson

OREGON STATE UNIVERSITY PRESS • CORVALLIS

The paper in this book meets the guidelines for permanence and durability of the Committee on Production Guidelines for Book Longevity of the Council on Library Resources and the minimum requirements of the American National Standard for Permanence of Paper for Printed Library Materials Z39.48-1984.

Library of Congress Cataloging-in-Publication Data
Carson, Mina Julia.
  Ava Helen Pauling : partner, activist, visionary / Mina Carson.
    pages cm
  Includes index.
  ISBN 978-0-87071-698-0 (alkaline paper) -- ISBN 978-0-87071-699-7 (e-book)
1. Pauling, Ava Helen. 2. Pauling, Linus, 1901-1994--Marriage. 3. Women political activists--United States--Biography. 4. Political activists--United States--Biography. 5. Pacifists--United States--Biography. 6. Social justice--United States--History--20th century. I. Title.
  CT275.P47895C27 2013
  973.91092'2--dc23
  [B]
                        2012044618

First published in 2013 by Oregon State University Press
Printed in the United States of America

Oregon State University Press
121 The Valley Library
Corvallis OR 97331-4501
541-737-3166 • fax 541-737-3170
    http://osupress.oregonstate.edu

Dedication:

To Lyn and Ricky

Table of Contents

Acknowledgments

Writing the life of Ava Helen Miller Pauling has been a peculiarly local and unexpectedly personal project. Every day I walk past the building where Ava Helen and Linus Pauling first met. Every day I look out over the quadrangle through which they strolled or hurried to get to their classes. My History Department office is in the old Home Economics Building, where Ava Helen took many of her courses at Oregon Agricultural College.

Living and working in Corvallis since 1989, I had heard of Linus Pauling many times. He is a beloved and honored alumnus, as well as a native son of Oregon. Early in my years at Oregon State University, I served on the Ava Helen Pauling Peace Lecture committee. Until several years ago, that was my only contact with the woman whose life I have the privilege to narrate in this book. Then one day, Linda Richards, a gifted graduate student in the History of Science, mentioned to me in passing that nobody had yet used the Ava Helen Pauling portion of the Pauling Papers. Aha!

Working in the OSU Special Collections, which houses the Ava Helen and Linus Pauling Papers, is as close to archival heaven as any scholar is likely to reach. Cliff Mead, Chris Petersen, and other staff members and students over the years have created a model environment to house the sprawling archive and host visiting researchers. My own visits have been frequent and simple: just a stroll across the campus. And because these professionals are pioneers of the digitized archive, anybody with a computer connection can access in most cases document-level records in the collections. In addition, the website offers narratives and chronologies, hundreds of photos, scanned and transcribed documents, and video records of special events celebrating Pauling's and other researchers' places in the history of science. Special Collections at OSU is a gift to the curious.

Cliff Mead presided over the creation of this collection, collaborating with Linus Pauling to deliver, house, and catalogue the thousands of shelf feet of documents, books, and memorabilia that Linus and his family so generously gave to OSU. Cliff introduced me to the archive and became my guide and cheerleader in writing about Ava Helen. When he retired,

Chris Petersen took on day-to-day leadership during the year that I was finishing my research. Besides profiting from his knowledge about the Paulings, I have been lucky enough to collaborate with Chris on several oral history interviews and a day of talking with and filming Linus Pauling, Jr., interacting with the students at Linus Pauling Middle School in Corvallis. Trevor Sandgathe, also on the Special Collections staff, wrote the first narrative of Ava Helen Pauling's life, an invaluable orientation as I plunged into the papers. Thanks also to Larry Landis, Karyle Butcher, Faye Chadwell, and Anne Bahde of the Valley Library. I have built up many debts and friendships at the library over the years, and I would prefer to name more names, but I will resist.

The Pauling family personifies generosity. Dr. Linus Pauling, Jr., flies from Honolulu to Oregon to participate in events that carry his father's name. In this, he follows a practice of selflessly honoring his father begun several decades ago when he stepped in and helped stabilize the Linus Pauling Institute when it was floundering. Now the institute is flourishing in a new building integrated with science teaching and research programs on the Oregon State University campus.

I have been privileged to meet Linus on at least four occasions over the last few years. He has generously shared his memories of his parents and his own early life. His participation has enriched this account immeasurably. He and I have different perspectives on his mother, appropriately, but his intimate knowledge has pushed me to complicate my picture of her place in the world. He responded immediately and at length to my plea for additional details about his mother's last days, though the memories had to be painful. He is an extraordinary person; I have deep affection for him and gratitude for the opportunity to get to know him a bit.

I was also fortunate enough to talk with Cheryl Pauling, Kay Pauling, and Grace Pauling in the course of preparing this biography, and I owe them thanks not just for their time, but for their honesty and insights.

Thanks also to Therese Graf Tanalski, who wrote to me about her memories of Linus Pauling's interactions with her father, Samuel H. Graf, at OAC, and her own friendship with Ava Helen and Linus Pauling during the time they spent at the University of California at San Diego.

Ingrid Ockert, another Pauling scholar, shared her research and conclusions with me. She knows the archive at least as well as I do. In the last weeks of this project, she located precious documents and photographs that have greatly enhanced this story. And again, my thanks and appreciation to Linda Richards, whose ideas readers will find throughout the manuscript, and whose enthusiasm for Ava Helen Pauling and her colleagues in WILPF made me take those episodes very seriously. I have been fortunate to meet these two scholars in the early stages of what will undoubtedly be rich careers. Tom Hager, Pauling biographer *par excellence,* listened to me ramble on about one patch of difficulty I was having. Rambling is therapeutic, and I worked it out. Thanks, Tom.

Linda and I traveled to Paris together to present linked papers on the American women of WILPF at the third Women of the World conference at Université Paris 13 in November 2011. Thanks to Fatma Ramdani and the other organizers for hosting that conference and our stay in the city the Paulings loved so much.

I am also grateful for the financial support of the Oregon State University Special Collections Resident Scholar Program and the Horning Endowment.

Thanks too to the staffs of the Schlesinger Library on the History of Women at the Radcliffe Institute for Advanced Study at Harvard University, the Lamont Library at Harvard University, and the Swarthmore College Peace Collection, for their help and hospitality.

Both the faculty and the students of the OSU History Department have listened to bits and pieces of this research over the years; I thank them for their patience and good questions. I have also had the opportunity to present papers to local audiences, including the OSU Library, the Academy for Lifelong Learning, and the OSU Women's Network, who have listened critically and compassionately and sent me in some new directions. Joel Miller, interim minister at the Unitarian Universalist Fellowship of Corvallis, offered me insights about Unitarian humanism in the Paulings' generation.

Eric Beasley, Marcianne Koetje, and the rest of the staff at Linus Pauling Middle School—I would so like to name you all!—have not only nurtured my own kids, but have also actively and deliberately created a forum for local youth to learn about and apply the values the Paulings represented, in science, peace, and community building. Linus and Ava Helen would be proud and delighted to have their names associated with such a school.

Judy Ball generously read the entire manuscript and gave me valuable feedback and advice. Other friends have put up with me, encouraged me, reassured me, and done all the things friends do to help one through the days and the years. They are Mina McDaniel, Laurie Childers, Michael Everett, Shannon Guthrie, Bill Veley, Shelley Willis, Ed Dee, Carol Jauquet, Rebecca Sanderson, Dianne Erickson, Lois Pettinger, Marilyn Walker, Marilyn H. Walker, Kim Walker, Pam Walker, Claudia Keith, Marjorie Goss, and Paul VanDevelder. I have left out names, not on purpose, but because it is what one does at my age. You know who you are; I will make it up to you.

My beautiful children certainly did not help me complete this book, but they do complete my heart.

Introduction

Ava Helen Pauling is that elusive figure in historical memory, the wife of a celebrity. Only her last name is still recognized. Yet by the end of her life she had an address book that embraced the world and she could dash off a letter to any number of political leaders, academics, peace activists, writers, and artists, and expect the favor of a reply. Proud to be Linus Pauling's wife, lover, consultant, housekeeper, dietician, and co-parent, she also parlayed her intimacy with him into the status of change agent. She was the one who persuaded Linus that it wasn't enough to do brilliant chemistry if the world was tumbling toward annihilation. She coached one of the twentieth century's most gifted science teachers into teaching citizens about the linkages between atomic weaponry, health, and social justice.

But Ava Helen Pauling had her own career as an activist first for civil rights and civil liberties, and then against nuclear testing, and finally for peace, feminism, and responsible stewardship of the environment. In the 1940s Ava Helen[1] devoted time to the Los Angeles American Civil Liberties Union. In the 1950s she became a leader of the venerable Women's International League for Peace and Freedom. In 1961 she joined the brand new Women Strike for Peace. She spoke; she marched; she traveled both with Linus and by herself. She and Linus sponsored, circulated, and delivered petitions against nuclear testing, gathering thousands of signatures each time. They organized an international conference of scientists in Oslo in 1961 to oppose nuclear testing and nuclear proliferation. In 1963, after the U.S. and the Soviet Union signed a partial nuclear test ban treaty, Linus Pauling won the Nobel Peace Prize for 1962. Many believed Pauling was a dangerous radical who should not be encouraged. Many others, who knew the couple, believed that Ava Helen should have been the co-recipient.

Ava Helen made international headlines in May 1964 after she was turned back at the Netherlands border, as Dutch officials tried and failed to block the Women Strike for Peace from staging a silent march outside the NATO ministerial conference.[2] (She persisted and Dutch officials, embarrassed, finally relented.) She loved the new organization; it suited her democratic, inclusive, direct, and slightly mischievous style. About the same time, and before the founding of the National Organization for Women in 1966, she began speaking out on women's issues, and the dilemmas of well-educated women choosing early marriage over professional careers — as she had done in 1923.

As she elaborated her own set of ideals and colleagues, Ava Helen Pauling perfected a style of activism that wove together the strands of her multiple networks. Initially her political personality was polite, cautious, and group oriented, though she did not shy away from what she saw as a necessary confrontation. After their Pasadena garage was vandalized in 1945 to intimidate the Paulings into firing their Japanese American gardener, the sheriff warned her that others who had opposed the internment of Japanese Americans had suffered even worse attacks. "Sheriff," she asked him in her sweet voice, "are you threatening me, or are you protecting me?"[3]

> *When I first saw Ava Helen Miller, in a chemistry class in 1922, I was impressed not so much by her attractive appearance as by her obvious intelligence and sprightly manner. As the decades have gone by I have continued to be grateful to the gods of chance that my good judgment or good luck led to my having such a brilliant, thoughtful, interesting, conscientious, ethical, reliable, consistent, and exciting companion for fifty-seven years — and I hope for many more to come.*
> — Linus Pauling to Beatrice Rowland, 17 May 1980

Though Ava Helen Pauling's own activist career is well worth narrating, it is a richer story when told as the saga of the partnership — romantic, marital, and political — of two strong spirits who survived not only the sexual and parenting tensions of their early adulthood, but also the threat of destructive competition and cross-cutting pressures in middle age. In an interview in the early sixties, Ava Helen Pauling remarked that many people had asked if she and Linus ever quarreled. "Well, of course we do," she replied to these phantom questioners. "We have the very hottest of arguments at times. To live with someone with whom one always agreed would be unbearable. Surely one would have to be a nincompoop and the other a tyrant. Or possibly both could be liars?"[4] Ava Helen was not always sweet, to Linus, or to her coworkers, or to her children. She knew how to get things done; she had expectations; she persisted. She was the executive around the house, and that could be hard on the children and sometimes on Linus. But she also worried about what Linus wanted, and what Linus thought. Partly the woman in charge; partly the trailing spouse — it was a dance, and she did it for decades.

The Paulings' marriage was a life's work. They were two Oregon teenagers who fell in love at college in the early 1920s. When Linus graduated from the Oregon Agricultural College and headed off to the California Institute of Technology to study chemistry, Ava Helen quickly shook off her intention to earn a college degree. Their passion would not be put off. At the end of a year of anxious separation, they married and she joined him in Pasadena. Ava Helen believed that if Linus was truly a genius, her calling was to nurture and protect that genius.

> *Well, a month after we had been married, we were in western Washington, a little town called Dayton, Washington. I was working on paving a road there; I was a paving engineer. And my wife said, "We'll go on a picnic on Sunday." There was a little creek that ran though the south end of this small town and had trees. So we went on a picnic. She got the hotel that we lived in to make some sandwiches for us and we got a book from the library on intelligence tests. So on the picnic we gave each other these intelligence tests, with largely mental arithmetic. I found she could do all of these things faster than I could and more accurately, too. But here we were already married. It was too late for this knowledge to be of any value to me."*
> —Typescript, Linus Pauling interview with "Samantha" S., 1990.

The seed they planted by conspiring to downplay Ava Helen's intellectual capabilities did not sprout in any obvious way until the 1960s, when she admitted her regret that she had undervalued herself by not finishing college. But she had not lived a life of cultural deprivation; in most ways her profile did not match the frustrated alcoholic housewife of Betty Friedan's *The Feminine Mystique*, parts of which Ava Helen would publicly criticize. She read carefully and thoughtfully, as she had been taught in her excellent Salem, Oregon, high school, and in two years at OAC. She took notes on lectures, meetings, political speeches, and stray thoughts. She did crossword puzzles and played word games. She read newspapers and magazines. She joined a book club as a young matron in Pasadena. She tried to understand her husband's work, assisted in his lab, and traveled with him.

This is the key to understanding the Pauling marriage and grasping the price that they, and to an extent their children, paid for their nearly sixty-year partnership. Ava Helen's devotion to Linus meant that he always came first. Her identity for the first twenty years of their married life was as his wife. Though she was intelligent, curious, and creative—qualities he valued in her and did not, at least initially, intend to quash—she found her vocation and satisfied her intellectual cravings, at least for a while, in shadowing him and his career. Thus when their first baby was not yet a year old in 1926, when Linus won a Guggenheim and planned to study quantum mechanics in Europe, she decided to leave the child with her mother in Portland, Oregon, and accompany Linus to Germany unencumbered by a baby. The fellowship kept the couple away from the United States for almost eighteen months, and their son grew from eleven months to two and a half years in the care of his grandmother.

This choice is difficult for many of us to wrap our heads and hearts around. But our shock at her willingness to leave a small child to follow her husband—an unforced decision, since Linus assumed that they would bring the baby to Europe—helps us understand her compulsions and priorities. Though she came of age in a period of "scientific" child development, which militated against too much physical affection and attention to the child, she was not of a social class that consigned child rearing to servants. We can't really understand her decision only by examining its cultural context. Leaving her mother with the baby and a sheet of instructions on how to raise him, Ava Helen embarked on what was to that point the most important educational journey of her life. Pasadena had been more cosmopolitan than Corvallis, Oregon; Munich was more cosmopolitan than California. With husband Linus she could walk through the door to a larger culture; with baby Linie she would be bound to a life both more confined than, and separate from, her husband's. Many years later, she became a strong advocate of publicly funded nursery schools and day care. Though she was unable at the time to articulate and justify her need to have children *and* to have time away from them, she made that happen.

Nonetheless, Ava Helen was a dutiful and energetic mother. She bore four children in twelve years. She prided herself on her knowledge of child development, nutrition, and education. She took on the duties of childcare so that Linus could work at the university and then in the evening in his study. The division of labor was no surprise; the couple had discussed it in their prenuptial correspondence, and Ava Helen entered the marriage expecting to be a fulltime wife and mother. Though Linus, Jr., as the oldest, had the most precarious childhood in material terms, all the children had bicycles, pets, friends, parties, and holidays. The younger three grew up with both a swimming pool and a flock of chickens. The family developed routines and rituals. Ava Helen believed strongly that she and Linus encouraged their four children to follow their own tastes, ideas, and dreams. In retrospect, though, the outcomes don't fully square with the ideology and the intention.

The Paulings' marital tensions grew out of the twin and often conflicting pulls of two vital kinds of work for Linus Pauling, and also out of the Paulings' trying to live chronically at a fever pitch of global engagement while Linus pursued his core passion in science and Ava Helen took on a series of troubled caretakers at their Big Sur ranch, the grown children's turbulent personal lives, and an ever vaster correspondence, as well as grocery shopping, cooking dinner, entertaining family, friends, and colleagues, and confronting the health challenges of later middle age. By his early forties Linus was a public figure , famous for his brilliant scientific theories and, within a few years, his outspoken political convictions. Both before and after winning the Nobel Prize for Chemistry in 1954, Pauling spent much of his energy fending off attacks by state and federal legislators and agencies attempting to prove that he was a Communist. After winning the Nobel Peace Prize, and in partnership with Ava Helen, he spoke out against atomic proliferation, nuclear reactor plants, racism, the Vietnam War, and government repression of dissent. Ava Helen genuinely enjoyed her husband's success, and her own intense participation in his collegial and political life. But being the wife of a celebrity brought constant pressures and challenges, from her worries about lovely women he met on his travels to the need to be on guard all the time against attacks on him.

In the mid-1960s, as Ava Helen was pursuing an increasingly full schedule as a social justice lecturer in her own right, Linus Pauling turned a corner in his research projects. His preoccupation with the powers of vitamin C, growing out of his interest in orthomolecular medicine, turned into a red flag to the bull of the American medical establishment, and became one more way in which the Paulings taunted the increasingly vulnerable institutions of mainstream America: the AMA, the Kennedy, Johnson and Nixon administrations, California higher education officials.[5] For several decades the Paulings had occupied that liminal area between liberal bourgeois comfort and left-liberal Cold War *dis*comfort. Once again, their private and public lives shook together as doctors pooh-poohed Vitamin C and American consumers swept the shelves clean, and as the Nixon administration expanded the Vietnam War while ever-larger swathes of the American populace took to the streets in protest. Linus Pauling fought recurrent sinus infections with Vitamin C; by the late 1970s, Ava Helen was battling stomach cancer with much larger doses of the same therapy.

It is crucial to tell the story of Ava Helen's life as it was embedded in her marriage of almost sixty years, and her position as the hub of the family wheel. That story is dynamic, as are most lives. She never questioned her marriage or her devotion to Linus (whom she called Paddy). But as she got older, she questioned the decisions of her earlier adulthood, and that questioning made her a second-wave feminist a bit ahead of the wave.

Ava Helen Pauling was not initially a feminist. In a notebook of reflections on life and reading, written in 1927, at the end of the eighteen Guggenheim months, she wrote, "If a woman thinks honestly & clearly, she must soon reach the conclusion that no matter what life work she chooses it could be done better by a man, and the only work in which this is not the case is the work involved in a home with children. In this way she contributes truthfully and substantially to the career of her husband and through her children to the improvement of the world."[6]

Was this Ava Helen's way of girding up her loins for life in Pasadena with a toddler and a work-driven husband? At that time she had not articulated an alternate blueprint for her future. She genuinely believed that she was on the path meant for her, the path through husband and children to her own "improvement of the world." But this conviction would change over time. And she took the actions and decisions that altered her own blueprint long before she was able to own, or own up to, a revised set of priorities and ambitions.

In an interview with Lee Herzenberg in 1977, when she was seventy-four, Ava Helen Pauling reflected on the time she began to question her choices in life. She dated these questions back to the 1940s and 1950s, when she became active with women's groups for peace and against nuclear testing. The coming of the second European war had pushed both the Paulings into increased activism. They joined the Union Now movement, which gained steam in 1940, and preached the necessity of the United States joining Britain in fighting fascism. Ava Helen also helped in the work of sheltering British children from Nazi bombing by bringing them to America. This was certainly the period in which, though she did not devalue her husband's scientific work as his main joy, she began to question that work as the driver of *their lives together*. Increasingly she saw, and said, that *perhaps* she could have had a different kind of life if she had started younger, if she had valued her own mind. Looking back, in the 1977 interview, she hints that as she became a woman activist she began reflecting on what women might want and need that was different or distinct from what men needed, and also on why women did not more actively oppose war and nuclear fallout.[7]

In her earlier interviews in the late 1950s and first half of the 1960s we see that her liberal feminism was already somewhat developed. In 1963 she characterized herself as a "modern feminist."[8] By 1964 her positions on the status of women were well articulated, and they implicitly questioned some of her own life choices. "Why do so many girls need the emotional security they think an early marriage will bring?" she asked poignantly. "Why has the number of women who take advanced study decreased? ... Why do so many women in this country make a career of research in beauty aids rather than researching these questions?"[9] By 1965 she had delivered several versions of her talk, "The Second X Chromosome: The Study of Woman."

Paired with marital tensions was the unusual passion and equality that defined this union. The equality sprang from Ava Helen's expectation of a determining voice in family decisions and also from Linus's mellow approach to his most intimate relationship. The couple's romantic and physical passion was buoyed by genuine love of each other's companionship and, as the years went by, the ability to anticipate, parry, and laugh at each other's jibes. They were each other's best straight men.

Telling Ava Helen's life from *her* perspective — to the extent that is possible — rather than from Linus's or from those of colleagues, children, friends, and admirers, brings her contribution to the "whole world" into focus. Many of her papers disappeared after her death, misplaced or destroyed by family members appropriately vigilant about her privacy or their own. But still, she left much of herself — her ideas, her beliefs, her daily reflections. Family members also generously shared her correspondence, her manuscripts and interviews, her random household papers, her travel itineraries, her calendars: all the detritus that allows us to glimpse how a person *really* lived and what she *really* valued. We have hundreds of family photographs, from Ava Helen's and Linus's childhoods to their last years together. Even her photographs are poignant. Her face is lit up in most of her portraits and snapshots over the years. She smiles, she laughs, she teases the camera, she ponders her companions' remarks. She was "nice" in the way that twentieth-century women were taught to be nice; but she was also a strong executive. Richard Morgan, Linus's younger cousin, adored Ava Helen. He also told Linus's biographer that he sensed she was artful, that she was always *on*.[10]

She was complicated. She charmed the world. "I discussed politics with the prime minister, and gardening with the king," she noted in a diary of the Paulings' trip to Stockholm where Linus received the Nobel Prize for Chemistry in 1954. Telling the story of this complex, effective person should allow her to emerge as her own woman, an activist, reformer, and idealist, while complicating the rich narrative of her life as spouse and mother, grandmother, hostess and housewife.

CHAPTER 1

The HIM Book: 1903 to 1923

Some day I will figure out which volume my love occupies and how much it weighs.
— Ava Helen Miller, June 1922[1]

Like many people without money, I grew up with very little self-confidence.
— Ava Helen Miller, November 1979[2]

They lived happily ever after.

Many twentieth-century women were brought up to expect or hope for this joyous culmination, as they were taught to merge their identities with those of their husbands: their childhoods just a prelude to "happily ever after." In previous centuries, married women had sacrificed their legal identities along with their fathers' names. By the 1920s, when this particular love story unfolded, state property laws had been moving away from "coverture" for a hundred years. But it would be almost another century before most American women assumed a cultural as well as technical right to autonomy within marriage.

This love story was a little different. To be sure, the two Oregon adolescents who met in college and married a year and a half later looked a lot like their peers at the Oregon Agricultural College. Both of their families were middle class, at least in aspiration, but lived often on the brink of respectability: both were mother-headed households challenged to make ends meet. While Ava Helen Miller followed at least three siblings to Oregon Agricultural College, and lived with family members in a house near campus, Linus Pauling broke away from his doting and needy mother to follow his passion for chemistry down the Willamette Valley from Portland. Both young people were bright,

Left: Ava Helen in 1914, approximately ten years old.

Below: The Miller girls in 1912. Annotations by Linus Pauling.

Right: The Miller girls in a family car. Ava Helen is on the left.

naïve, and used to hard work when they arrived on the Corvallis campus, Linus Pauling in 1917 and Ava Helen Miller in 1921.

Born in 1903, Ava Helen Miller was the tenth child in a family of twelve. Her father, George Richard Miller, had emigrated from Hamburg, Germany. He was a teacher and then a farmer in Beavercreek, Oregon, a rural hamlet southeast of Portland.[3] Apparently he took up a 160-acre plot in pursuit of some landed dream. He was also a liberal Democrat with socialist ideas.[4] Ava Helen's mother's parents had migrated to Oregon by covered wagon. Nora (Elnora) Gard, one of their daughters, became a suffragist. As would happen for her sixth daughter, Ava Helen, Nora met her future husband as a student in his class.[5] They married in 1886. George Miller was almost thirty and Nora Gard just eighteen. Ava Helen inherited her father's eyes and absorbed his ideas. Some of the sisters remembered Ava Helen as her father's special pet.

The many Miller children learned to argue politics around the dinner table. They also learned to work the farm. George was hard on the children, probably very hard. There is an unverified family story of the sheriff coming out to the Four Corners farm and warning Nora Gard Miller that if he heard any more about the sons being abused, he would arrest her husband.[6] Miller may also have been rough with the daughters—all, according to family legend, except Ava Helen. When Ava Helen was nine, her parents divorced and her father left the household and eventually also Oregon. Special pet or not, she recorded starkly as a college student: "My father went out of my life when I was nine years of age. I don't remember much about him."[7] Ava Helen saw him at least once more, in March 1926, when she and Linus passed through Chicago on the way to Germany for Linus's Guggenheim year.[8] Her father had just remarried and lived with his second wife, Minnie, for about twelve years. Minnie Miller died in 1938, and George Richard Miller in 1949.[9]

Milton Miller dressed for track.

Sometime after her parents' divorce, her family left the farmhouse and moved to nearby Canby, so the children could attend school. The youngest three girls were the "little girls" together. Despite a broad age range, the family seems to have been tightly knit, at least during Ava Helen's childhood, and the long line of girls took many opportunities to pose for snapshots. They were strikingly pretty, with deep-set eyes, and their four brothers were conventionally handsome. George and John Miller were significantly older. Clay and Milton were still at home when Ava Helen was a little girl, and the family built outings around their high school activities. She remembered later that for some reason she hated Milton running track, and at the age of nine she cried whenever she attended a meet "and also cursed Mr. Ralston [Milton's coach] with all of the profane words of a 9 year old vocabulary."[10] During the Great War, both Clay and Milton enlisted in the army and shipped out to France, as did her brother-in-law Walter Spaulding. They all came home again.

Ava Helen excelled in her schoolwork. She and nineteen classmates finished eighth grade in the spring of 1918; she delivered the graduation essay and sang a solo. After grammar school she moved to Salem and lived at her sister Nettie's house, so she could attend Salem High School. She had already begun studying piano in Canby. Her Salem piano teacher persuaded her to offer a recital in the spring of her first year of high school; she received a polite notice in the Salem paper.

Though she was known by family and friends as "Ava Helen" for most of her life, the cover of a pocket notebook from her junior or senior year of high school is signed, simply, "Ava Miller." On both sides of the lined pages, she jumbled notes from the classes she was taking at the time: English, Spanish, chemistry, math, and possibly history. (There are notes on the political functions of coffee houses in English history, probably taken in a classroom lecture.) Many pages are ripped or cut out of this slender book, and the notes are random. She developed early her lifelong habit of taking notes on whatever paper was at hand: old calendars, spiral notebooks, the backs of letters, hotel stationery.

She seems to have been close to at least one teacher in Canby or Salem, Winifred Helen James, who taught English 7 and 8. In 1921, perhaps to commemorate her high school graduation, Miss James gave her an inscribed copy of a guided journal called *The HIM Book*, in which Ava Helen later recorded fragments of her life that, pasted together, offer poignant glimpses

Ava Helen and her Canby, Oregon, middle school classmates. Ava Helen is third row up, third from left.

Ava Helen with girl friends in her senior year at Salem High School, 1921.

into her girlhood world.[11] Her notes suggest a lively, flirtatious disposition. There were plenty of boys to write down in *The HIM Book*, even if some were cousins. She called her brother-in-law, Walter Spaulding, with whom she lived on Court Street in Salem during her high school years, "spoiled, selfish and narrow-minded," and remembered that they had had one "very bad fight" in which Walter had apparently handled her roughly. She intervened on Nettie's side in the couple's frequent arguments, and later told Linus that Walter had treated her sister badly (whether he physically abused her is unclear).[12] On the other hand, she felt constrained to call him "good-hearted," and conceded that he was good to her when she lived under his roof.[13]

Ralph Hamilton, Wallace Griffith, and Keith Brown also found places in Ava Helen's HIM records. She filled in this book on the occasion of her engagement to Linus Pauling, and the intent was to show her beloved these bits of her heart. Thus the mischievous little notes of teasing and false regret: "He joined the navy during the war," she wrote of Claire Haines of Canby, "and I have ever felt happy to think I refused to kiss him good-by which perhaps took a bit of conceit out of him. [Haines was] married in 1921."[14] On the back of a photograph of Haines she wrote in retrospect: "my heart's first flutter."[15]

There were limits to her teasing. Deeply in love almost from their first acquaintance, she wrote of Linus, "I learned Chemistry from him. We studied Love together." And farther down: "I want to see him in my son."

The Spaulding household in Salem, however uncomfortable at times, was probably lively and certainly close to the state's political heartbeat. Her sister Nettie was secretary to one of the Oregon Supreme Court justices, so there was a direct link to affairs in the capital, and 1630 Court Street, the Spaulding home, was just a few blocks' stroll from the Supreme Court building and the State Capitol. Ava Helen carried her father's Democratic politics into her adolescence; of a family friend, an admired physician, she wrote: "We quarreled about politics. He is a Republican." During their courtship, Ava Helen confided to Linus that her childhood had been full of "terrors." We have only his response to that confession, and the terrors go unnamed. She may have been referring to the terrors on the farm before George Miller left, or they may have been the Spaulding family quarrels, which seem at times to have gotten physical.[16] Linus swore in return that they would never frighten their own children.

Ava Helen graduated from Salem High School in three years. She was class president her senior year. For her senior class picnic at Silver Creek Falls that spring she helped organize the food for a class of one hundred twenty-five. She dared to kiss a boy for the camera. She was a girl of fun and will, as well as a sense of duty.

Ava Helen followed the family path to Oregon Agricultural College in the fall of 1921. The General Catalogue lists four of Nora Gard Miller's children as enrolled in 1921-22: Milton Marion Miller, a senior in agriculture; Clay Carl Miller, a junior in agriculture; Mary Maxine Miller, though younger than Clay, a class ahead of him as a senior in home economics; and Ava Helen Miller, a freshman in home economics. Five Miller children were past college age in 1921, and two were younger. Lulu Gorgo Miller, the daughter just ahead of Ava Helen, was not enrolled at OAC.[17] Nora Gard Miller maintained a house in Corvallis, at 15th Street and Washington, to house several if not all of her OAC-enrolled children.[18]

Like most women at OAC at that time, Ava Helen enrolled in more courses than a twenty-first-century student might imagine juggling: clothing and textiles, hygiene, physical education, Spanish, French, social ethics, general chemistry, library practicum, technical English, food chemistry, food selection and preparation, child care, and introduction to economics.[19]

Located in Corvallis, a town at that time of 6,500, Oregon Agricultural College in 1921 enrolled five thousand students taught by two hundred fifty faculty members. Students could choose a wide range of extracurricular activities, including athletics, theater, journalism, and music. Campus "rook" traditions, in which freshmen wore beanies or ribbons, were policed

Nora Miller in front of the house she maintained for her children on S. 15th Street in Corvallis, 1924

by upperclassmen, to whom the first year students had to defer. There was no smoking on campus, and no crossing the lawns. Students were expected to attend athletic events, but the men were not allowed to "fuss" — that is, to take women to the games as dates. Some students joined fraternities and sororities. Student publications and photos suggest a lively, fluid social life.

In contrast to the University of Oregon in Eugene, at the southern tip of the Willamette Valley, OAC was the land grant college and its program offerings leaned toward agriculture, business, engineering, vocational education, and home economics. Though the sciences and humanities were organized into departments, they were also relegated to service offerings, no degree being available in those disciplines. In the fall of 1922, recognizing OAC's growing attractiveness to out-of-state and

Formal portrait of Ava Helen Miller, 1922.

international students, the college for the first time charged non-residents a higher tuition. The brick and frame buildings clustered around a well-groomed campus. The original thirty-five-acre site established in 1887 had grown to three hundred fifty to accommodate the agricultural programs.[20] The Willamette Valley had been a garden spot since the days of the Oregon Trail. Beyond Corvallis, "the glens and gorges of the Coast Range," as the General Catalogue gushed in 1923, "… the distant splendor of the Cascades, …with their wealth of trees and the perennially snow-capped peaks — Hood, Jefferson, and the Three Sisters — present a constant panorama of picturesque mountain scenery."[21]

Home economics majors took two full years of chemistry. Freshmen took general chemistry; organic chemistry came in either the freshman or sophomore year, followed by two terms of food chemistry. The faculty often scrambled to staff class sections in the larger courses. On the first day of the winter term of 1922, the young women in General Chemistry 102 were startled to see a tall, thin young man stride into the Science Hall classroom and stand at the instructor's desk. Nobody knew who he was. Both Paulings

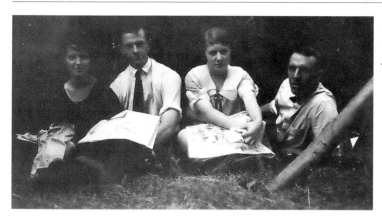

Ava Helen, Linus, and two friends, 1922.

remembered some details of that day the same way. Linus Pauling, the new student instructor, ran his finger down the list of students and asked Miller, Ava Helen, what she knew about the properties of ammonium hydroxide. "I don't know how it happened, just good luck I picked that name," he joked years later during an interview for the popular science program NOVA. "Who knows? I might have been married to Emilia Bauersocks if I happened to pick that name."

"Allegra Magreal," his wife interjected as if they had often shared this joke.

"Allegra Magreal. Yes," Pauling laughed.[22]

Ava Helen found herself thinking about this instructor. "We thought it was interesting that he had his black curly hair parted in the middle," she reminisced. She and her friends looked forward to the next class with this young instructor because he was so "knowledgeable." Linus Pauling began stumbling over himself when he dealt with Miss Miller. At first she caught no special signs of interest from him — and she was watching for them — but suddenly there was a note from the instructor in her lab notebook, oddly referring to an incident in recent years where another instructor had been reprimanded for taking an inordinate interest in one of his students. Pauling asserted that he did not want to be caught out for the same offense. Bridling at Pauling's awkward gambit — though she had been grilling one of his fraternity brothers about him — Ava Helen walked up to him after class and said that she expected him to teach her chemistry and nothing else. A few weeks later they took their first walk across campus with each other. To his horror, as they crossed a creek Linus elbowed Ava Helen's nose, bumping her hard enough to bring blood. It hurt, but gave her one more thing to tease him with.

Left: Linus Pauling in his OAC freshman beanie.
Right: Ava Helen and Linus at Linus Pauling's graduation from OAC, 1922.
Far right: Ava Helen Miller in 1922.

The courtship developed quickly. His compunctions had flown away, judging from the notes he and Ava Helen passed back and forth on her homework. "I simply can't remember this producer gas," she wrote on one assignment in May 1922. "I'm very, very sorry. Please don't think I'm not bright."

"I don't," responded her avid beau. "In addition to having all your other endearing qualities, you are the brightest of girls, sweetheart."[23]

In the 1920s there were fewer ethics codes or social prohibitions against these liaisons.[24] From the beginning Ava Helen called herself Linus's "little girl," and given her petite stature and his premature status as an academic authority at the age of twenty-two, it is not surprising that their early communication took the comfortable form of male dominance and female compliance.[25] But that relationship model was complicated by Ava Helen's underlying willfulness and Linus's unique brand of sensitivity.

Though Linus Pauling did take his own intellectual promise seriously, his private writings also reveal self-doubt and modesty. An underage freshman, ready to enter college before he finished high school, he questioned himself

 in his journal a month before entering OAC in the fall of 1917. He compared himself to a friend, also getting ready to attend OAC: "big, manly Paul Harvey, beside whom I pale into insignificance. Why should I enjoy the same benefits the [sic] he has, when I am so unprepared, so unused to the ways of man?"[26] In fact Linus Pauling loved college and relished his independence from his widowed mother, Belle, who had been loath to part with him. As a sophomore, just seventeen years old, Pauling started to make a mark in his chemistry and math classes.[27] The summer after his second year he earned good money on a road-paving crew, surveying the paving, and sent the money home to his mother to keep for his college expenses. At the end of the summer Belle surprised her son with an empty bank account; she had hijacked his money for household expenses. He could not return to OAC. It seemed the road crew was his fate. Years later he admitted to his son Peter that his desperation that fall—and his very real hunger—had probably led to a lifetime of anxiety about money.[28]

In late fall he got an offer out of the blue to teach quantitative chemistry at OAC, and he leaped at the opportunity. Instead of learning to drive the steamroller that he had overturned the summer before, he was elevated over his peers as an instructor at the age of eighteen.[29] Not enrolled formally in classes that fall, Pauling had the opportunity to forge ahead in his chosen discipline and learn to teach at the same time. Among other courses, he began teaching the home economics chemistry sequence. By the time he strode into Ava Helen Miller's classroom in the winter of 1922, he was a veteran even though just a senior, five months from graduation.

Ava Helen Miller must have found it exciting to date her instructor. Though he had arrived at OAC as a sixteen-year-old naïf, he had already kissed a girl (Gwendolyn, for the "first" and "last" time, "thanks be," he wrote obliquely).[30] He may have kissed a few more along the way (of Irene Sparks he wrote, during the fall of his freshman year, "She is the girl for me").[31] Pauling's reflections on college life and his own intellectual growth were naïve, optimistic, and full of youthful grandiosity. His junior year entry into the College Orator contest reflected his fascination with nothing less than the evolution of the earth and humanity with it. On the latter, he was reserved. "We are not the flower of civilization," he wrote. "We are but the immature bud of a civilization yet to come. We are children of the dawn, witnessing the approach of day."[32]

The sweethearts spent many hours together between March and May, beginning to develop the private language that suffused their letters for the next fifty-nine years. They made plans to attend the Prom in May. Linus graduated with an A average, delivered the class oration in June, and accepted the California Institute of Technology's (Caltech's) generously supported admission offer. In a last stab at professional propriety at the end of spring term Chemistry 103, Linus arbitrarily lowered Ava Helen's grade, so nobody would think he favored this lively young freshman, now his fiancée.[33] She resented that for years afterward.[34] In one of his first letters to her, sent in early May from his mother's home in Portland, he expressed surprise that there hadn't been more of an uproar about the young couple's announcement of their engagement. "No one seems at all worried or anything," he wrote. "My dear mother hasn't evinced the curiosity I expected—it may be because I talked of you so much during spring vacation."[35]

As a senior Pauling was quite clear about what he wanted to do—Chemistry—and where he was going—to graduate school at Harvard, Berkeley, or the new California Institute of Technology—until his infatuation with Ava Helen briefly threatened to derail his life project. Occasionally he wavered. "Up until the time you came into my life," he told her, "my work was sufficient for me."[36] Perhaps he should marry her right away, work for a while to save money for graduate school, and follow his dream later? He worried about her being idle or anxious; he nursed some guilt at keeping her waiting while he followed his passion. Their mothers wanted nothing to do with an early wedding. Nora Gard Miller wanted this daughter to finish college. Belle Pauling probably wanted no interference with her own claim on Linus's earnings, but she argued that he needed to go to graduate school and get his Ph.D. before he committed himself to this marriage. She did tell Linus's sisters and cousins what a "sweet" girl Ava Helen was.[37] The young couple was determined to marry, but complied with their mothers' wishes and laid plans for several years away from each other.

As early as June 1922, just a few months after they had begun to date, they were sharing intimate details. Linus wrote not just about his reading, but also about his finances, his diet, his sunburn, and his conviction that he was getting broader across the chest. "When I stand in my birthday suit in front of my big mirror my chest seems larger than it used to be. My hips are broad compared with my waste [sic], but not compared with my chest. I have a number of rather fine dark hairs on my chest too—perhaps some day I'll be all fuzzy. I don't think so, though, and I don't care to be."[38]

From Linus's work site in Warrenton, Oregon, that summer of 1922 Ava Helen received daily letters from her doting and busy fiancé. When he wasn't doing his paving inspector work for the state highway department, he was reading French and working physical chemistry problems supplied by his soon-to-be Caltech mentor, A. A. Noyes. A special office for the paving inspector had yet to be built at Astoria, and Linus got to oversee that project. She read letters filled with cheerful reflections on his co-workers, his chemistry problems, his hopes for the future, his successful attempt to secure a loan from his Uncle Jim ("The Miller girls are splendid women and I am quite sure this particular one will make you a good helpmate," Linus quoted his uncle), and his overflowing love for her ("you are the dearest girl in the world").[39] Although we have few of Ava Helen's letters to Linus from this period, his own daily letters respond to hers in detail.[40] She wrote to him about her financial worries, and he reassured her that he would share his loan and his earnings with her. For the first time in his life he felt free to spend or save the money he earned, without accounting to his mother for every dollar. A loan of $1000 from uncle Jim Campbell was earmarked for his mother and sisters, so Linus could move on to graduate school without lingering worries for them.[41] To his future wife he reported that he had "never become intimate with my family." Despite his mother's high expectations of his dutiful obedience, and his own guilty feelings as he tore away, he kept a large part of his inner life barricaded away from them.[42] Once he admitted to her that he did not help them much financially, whereas his sister Pauline did.[43]

He was eager to protect her, too, from the careless comments of their friends, who suggested that a long separation might lead to Linus looking at other girls. "Being apart won't make us forget each other, sweetheart— nothing can separate us in spirit."[44] They spent the July 4 weekend together that summer, and other evenings every so often. By the end of July, Linus's restlessness had issued in a new plea to his beloved: Would she consider marrying *this* September, rather than waiting another year, or two, or three?

This query came out of the blue. The prolonged separation ahead while he completed graduate school in California and she slogged through OAC was suddenly intolerable. But more pressing even than their families' reluctance to bless a precipitate union was the money question. Linus knew that he must do his graduate work. As he saw it, the only way to assure her lifelong happiness was for *him* to be "out-of-the-ordinary."[45] Though this sounds hilariously narcissistic now, there was wisdom in his reasoning. He needed his work to be happy: to be complete. He reassured her that, if he had to choose, he would choose her over his chemistry, but this was not always the tune he played, and fortunately for him, Ava Helen did not want him to make that sacrifice. For the next fifty years she hewed to the same standard. She relied on him to be extraordinary. The time would come when she would look back with regret at having failed to seize that kind of ambition for herself. But she did not begrudge him his fame, won by brilliance, persistence, and her own household management. She thrived on his fame.

In the summer of 1922, Linus tried to figure out how much money they would need to live together in Pasadena as he pursued his graduate studies and she continued her education at one of the California universities. How much of a loan would they need to supplement his $600 stipend?[46] He wondered if she would be willing to share a house with his OAC friend Paul Emmett, who would also attend Caltech, and Paul's mother. He worried that they would not be able to afford a piano for Ava Helen. He knew they could hardly afford the wedding they hoped for. As he wrote, he started to talk himself out of what he knew was an impractical scheme. Yet he waited anxiously for her reply. Touching back to the vivid everyday world, he asked her about the crabs he had sent over from the coast. He returned to his fantasy. "A few days ago this would have seemed like the wildest dream. Now it seems not improbable. I'm not building my hopes high, tho, sweet. I wish you could talk it over with your mother."[47]

Before she answered he rushed a second letter into the mail. He called himself "careless" for proposing an early marriage. "Dear heart, I so abhor mediocrity. I want our life to be wonderful." He knew he must devote his energies to graduate study and somehow simultaneously carry out this agonizing long-distance courtship.[48]

Ava Helen wrote back to Linus and offered a plan. They could get ahead financially if she got a job to supplement their income while he studied. He nixed that idea. "You are not equipped for work you like nor can you make a great deal."[49] During the last week of July Linus's feelings racketed around like a pinball. He brought himself to the point of believing that they would certainly marry, and even planned the day of the event and the honeymoon (a night in a hotel).

Then he spoke to his mother. Onto his longing Belle poured all the cold water she could chill. Why didn't Ava Helen's family finance her schooling? Why hadn't she worked over the summer? Why couldn't she work in Oregon over the coming year? What if something went wrong in his graduate studies? What kind of gratitude would an early marriage show for the "sacrifices" his family had made for him? Surely he owed them the Ph.D. (an interesting assertion from the woman who had begrudged him his bachelor's studies). What if poverty embittered the young couple? What if they had a baby? What if one of them fell ill? Further, the Emmetts could not provide a suitable place to live in Pasadena. Mrs. Emmett disapproved of Paul even dating before he finished his graduate work. And they too were struggling financially.

It was a litany of disasters that only a mother's mind could marshal. Linus's dreams were shattered. He had planned to write to Ava Helen's mother, but now he even gave up that step.[50] "Dear heart, I believe now that perhaps it would be unwise of us to be married. ... I think that my rather blind enthusiasm has caused me to forget things."[51] Now repeatedly he asked her not to tell either of their mothers that he was helping her out financially. The young man's agony and the irresolution of life in two places resonates through the correspondence. Even his mother had to admit that she had "never seen a couple so completely gone on each other."[52] However, Linus's unquenchably cheery disposition provided ballast. While he was being pulled apart by irreconcilable desires, he was also enjoying crab fritters, mayonnaise, malted milk, and Ava Helen's candy. His appetite was healthy and his taste for his chemistry problems unabated. He made friends easily at the work site and enjoyed his neighbors across the hall and the woman who ran the restaurant where he ate most meals. He was not a man waffling in his love or evading his beloved, but he believed in the future and could face disappointment in the present. "We are making our small sacrifice now so that our gift to the world may be perfect."[53]

And Ava Helen was a woman who, for all her little-girl flirtatiousness, could cut to the heart of the matter. "It hurt me a little," Linus admitted in a letter a few days later, "that you thot it was just because of my mother's wishes that we aren't married." He wrote that he would do whatever Ava Helen wished — though he did not see how he could resign his assistantship or manage his loans. She had acutely assessed his dependence on Belle's good opinion, and perhaps used it to poke him after her disappointment. But she also stuck to her sensible belief that they needed to minimize their financial dependence, and she too resigned herself to waiting for marriage.[54]

In early September Linus detoured through Corvallis on his way to stay with his family in Portland for a few days before taking off with Paul Emmett for their big adventure at Caltech. "They are too dense to ask if I had been to see you, and I'm not going to tell them outright."[55] He planned to circle back through Corvallis one more time. There is an unusual break in the daily letters between September 6 and September 16, so the couple probably spent a few days together in that period of time, either in Corvallis or perhaps Portland. "Did you get to Corvallis all right? Did you cry because your bad boy left you?" Linus wrote on the 16th.[56]

Her fiancé's description of his trip to California, and his lyrical portraits of Pasadena, the mountains, and the coast, suggest one compelling reason the

Paulings made their lifelong home in California. From the beginning Linus was entranced by the state's natural beauty and its architectural charms. Housing was expensive, though. He stayed in a hotel while he waited to move into the Emmetts' new house, bought for $6500, which struck Linus as very high.[57] "Our house is a beautiful little place, as are all of them here. Pasadena is lovely—there are all kinds of palms—some forty feet tall and some three feet thru. There are orange groves a hundred feet from our house, and all the way to school, and there are palms in front of the house. It is all beautiful. The pepper trees are delicate lacy things. I'm enclosing some leaves," he wrote, sending her a bit of his new world; "—they may lose their odor, tho."[58] He fantasized all year about how they would hike the hills together, and perhaps have their own little house.

The dense sheaf of letters from Linus to Ava Helen between June 1922 and their wedding date a year later, and the few surviving notes from Ava Helen back to her lover, make it clear that when the couple spent time together, they were completely engaged with each other. They were sexually involved from very early in the relationship, and their letters use a private language that is not difficult to decode. "I uy and uy and uy oo," wrote Linus repeatedly.[59] "I uz oo, with all my heart," he wrote in a variant that seems to have carried the explicit translation of sexual intercourse. Their letters refer to rare face-to-face meetings and previous letters. Linus apologizes a number of times for "hurting" Ava Helen, and the context leaves no doubt that the "hurt" was sexual in nature. The couple educated themselves as best they could. Ava Helen turned to women friends like "Pebbles," a sorority woman at OAC. "She is good to tell you things," wrote Linus. "Your mother should have told you. I have never learned anything in the right way, except by reading. Our last Sunday was beautiful, sweet. I'm so glad you were not hurt. I didn't know you were before."[60]

The couple read intensively, braving the cultural bombshells exploding in the postwar period. Pauling urged Freud and Havelock Ellis on his fiancée. He recommended William J. Robinson, *Woman: Her Sex and Love-Life*, which he told Ava Helen was intended for girls by "the foremost American authority on sex matters."[61] He confessed that Robinson's instruction had allayed a number of his own fears about his sexual and romantic needs and attitudes. "For example, I love you with all my heart and mind and soul, and yet I can leave you and work all the harder at my vocation because of my love." He had worried about enjoying his work in the midst of the great love affair of his life; he had also perhaps been feeling a bit guilty for dwelling on their sex life. Robinson reassured him. "Also, I have found that boys naturally think of sexual matters." Despite his worries, he believed that he and Ava Helen were "perfectly united."[62] Robinson wrote for the "average case," and Pauling was certain that he and Ava Helen were "above the average," as witness his extreme sensitivity and faithfulness to her. ("The average man isn't very good. I'm surely glad we found each other young," he wrote, though it isn't clear whether he was more worried about his turning bad or Ava Helen's meeting some other man who was not "very good.") Robinson also asserted that men loved their sweethearts more as sexual intimacy increased, "contrary to your mother's opinion." Linus reported to Ava Helen that Robinson recommended "uzzing" (probably not Robinson's term) three times a month.[63] Specific recommendations for sexual intercourse during pregnancy followed. In a rapturous conclusion to this long confessional letter, Linus dwelled on Ava Helen's "beautiful pure white little body" point by point. "Sweet girl, my one desire is to make myself better for you." With a nod to humor in the midst of these sentimental passages, he signed himself "Linus, who is Ava Helen's husband, and who loves Ava Helen, and who will always be good and true to Ava Helen, who deserves the goodest and truest man in the universe (that's Linus: the egotistic cuss, he's always saying high-flown things about himself)." In a final burst of adoration, he concluded: "Kisses, dear, and hugs, and tongue-touches, and uzzes, and wee Ava Helens and Linuses, and gentle gentle uzzes, and perpetual happiness and content."[64]

Ava Helen wrote back in the same frank, fond tone. This couple was learning sexual negotiation. On the one hand she exclaimed, "Pooh! I'm not scared to tell you one thing! How could you hurt me way down there?" But she also remarked that he'd better not get used to waking at four in the morning (as he reported in one letter), because they had already reached "a little gentleman's agreement about uzzing every night." She teased him that she would get "a little electric sign board" for "those mornings" to warn him away with the message: "No uzzing allowed."[65]

Linus Pauling and Ava Helen Miller were probably unusual among college youth in 1922 in their frank intimacy, their easy and passionate sexuality, even in an era of sharply increased cultural openness about sex. Pauling's discussion of Robinson, along with his familiarity with Freud, Dostoevsky, Shaw, Upton Sinclair, and other modernist writers, puts him in a literate class that was, truly, "above the average," as he proudly judged himself and his beloved.[66] In her now-classic study of 1977, *The Damned and the Beautiful: American Youth in the 1920s*, Paula Fass concluded that college students were indeed experimenting with sex, but in a peer-conscious and graduated set of behaviors that focused on "dating and petting," in her terms, usually stopping short of sexual intercourse. "The young first sanctioned eroticism and then imposed degrees and standards of acceptability."[67] In *Campus Life* (1987), Helen Lefkowitz Horowitz agrees, adding that dating became another way to establish social standing in the collegiate pecking order.[68] In this still marriage-oriented erotic culture, Linus and Ava Helen jibed with their peers nationally. In their relatively guilt-free enjoyment of intercourse, they may have been unusual, at least during their courtship in small-town Oregon in the early 1920s. But perhaps not. In her classic study, *Woman's Body, Woman's Right*, Linda Gordon cites several studies of premarital intercourse among women born between 1900 and 1909, which found that the percentage of women who had engaged in sex before marriage shot up from about a quarter of women born in the previous decade to around half of women questioned in Ava Helen's birth cohort.[69] Marilyn Yalom summarizes a long-term study by physician Clelia Mosher of forty-five middle-class married women between 1892 and 1920. A third of them reported regular orgasms in intercourse, with many more averring some measure of satisfaction with an active sexual life.[70]

And forty-one of the forty-five in Mosher's study used birth control. By the 1920s, well-read college graduates would have been aware of the work of Margaret Sanger and others in advocating legalized birth control. After World War I, public practice rapidly outstripped the laws, and information about limiting birth, as well as other sexual issues, circulated more widely. William J. Robinson, Linus's favorite sexuality mentor, was also a national leader in birth control advocacy, both for eugenic reasons (to limit births among the financially and genetically challenged) and for reasons of marital health and happiness.[71] As for Linus Pauling and Ava Helen Miller, we do not know how they avoided pregnancy. Aware as they were of contemporary theories of sexuality and marriage, it is tempting to believe they would also have been up to date on the technology of birth control.[72] It is hardly surprising that this issue is not reflected in the correspondence. Though frank, their sexual talk was also coded.

Certainly Linus was fascinated with eugenics and firmly convinced that birth control was vital to the progress of humanity, as birth limitation would presumably allow "better" humans to prevail against poor, ill-educated families. He chimed in with Havelock Ellis on preventing conception "if the heredity is poor. Our children will have good heredity won't they, honey?"[73] He remarked later that a national system of clinics would be best, to instruct the poor and prevent "the breeding of crowds of sick, deformed, ignorant and unintelligent foreigners doomed to poverty and a life devoid of happiness." He remarked that those clinics wouldn't affect the practices of the "more intelligent and desirable classes," who knew what to do already.[74] Despite this chauvinistic outburst, he understood that regulating or outlawing birth control would ultimately degrade his own union with Ava Helen. "Think how funny it would be, dear, for us to live our lives together and uz each other only about three times."[75] He entertained a dark fantasy in which, without any control, they would either have countless babies, or no intercourse. "We would be irritable, and our life would be ruined." He reassured her that she had nothing to fear in marriage—that they would not have children until she was ready. Meanwhile he longed for her, but swore he would not "uz" her again until their wedding night, to make it even more lovely.[76]

This is one of our best insights, oblique as it is, into the young couple's use of birth control—at the very least their intention to use birth control in their future life together. In terms of their methods, we may guess that it was some combination of rhythm, withdrawal, and condoms, those being the most commonly available methods of avoiding pregnancy at the time. A diaphragm or "pessary" might have been difficult for Ava Helen to secure before the couple was married; afterward it may have been easier for her to approach her physician or pharmacist.

It is hard to imagine where the young couple found space to experiment and explore each other's bodies. One letter from Linus during his first year in California hints that Ava Helen's mother's house was one such place; he recalls her brother Clay catching them under a blanket, "with my uzzer up by yours … And then we had to part," he concludes, without apparent anxiety or remorse.[77] After a January visit, he wrote, "I feel so sorry for your little uzzer. I'll be so careful with you, dear. Perhaps your uzzer is lonesome, dear wife. I feel that our love—we were so full of love, weren't we?—may have had something to do with it."[78]

Any guilt in the love letters centered not on their rare nights of secret intimacy, but on their separation during this year of intensive courtship. Linus described a trip with the Emmetts over to the beach, then said he would not travel with them again, because he was happier doing his work, "for when I am doing it I feel that I am bringing you closer to me."[79] Linus continued to formulate plans to marry in a year and allow Ava Helen to finish college in California. Though there was no university for her in Pasadena, she might attend Occidental, five or six miles away. However, they would need a car for that. "I'll try to get a better position next year; perhaps at the end of it we will be better off."[80] She reported getting A grades in organic chemistry. She had been the best student in his classes the year before, and indeed by the spring of 1923 Linus asked her whether she too planned to be a scientist.[81] Caltech was out of the question; it did not admit women undergraduates until 1970—one year after Princeton and Yale, as undergraduate coeducation swept the nation.[82] Linus also considered taking a job in industry, but decided that in the short run that wouldn't bring them any more money—probably a relief, since his heart was in academia. "I think, dear, that the best thing is for me to remain here for a while. I'll do more teaching, taking fewer subjects and less research, and get as much of a salary as I can."[83]

Not just for Linus, but also for Ava Helen, passion was cut with common sense. In November she assured him that they made the right decision to wait. "We would have been so engrossed with Love that French and Calculus would have suffered." She argued that they might not have had the "will power" to "do as we should"—young minds and young bodies were "plastic," and she feared simply watching him and loving him rather than engaging in the duties of life.[84]

Yet her ambivalence emerged in the form of teasing remarks, perhaps at some level meant to make Linus jealous. At OAC that fall, she took organic chemistry, both French and Spanish (an intriguing forecast of her later international orientation), Food Selection and Preparation (her worst subject, though she became quite a good cook), and gym. Organic chemistry was probably her most successful subject after French; she proudly reported that "crazy Mr. Quigly," who taught the course, told her she was the best student in the section. "Mr. Quigly talks to me lots. He is nice. I like him. ... He tells me lots of funny things that happened when he was in school. I love you, darling." She told Linus that she was trying to work up the courage to tell Mr. Quigly that her "husband" was a chemist; but her admiring remarks about her chemistry instructor followed by the *non sequitur* declaration of love for her fiancée suggest a splitting of energy and attention.[85]

Ava Helen had been brought up to believe in her role as a helpmeet. "Lonely, lonely laddie boy, whose 'loaf-giver' I am," she wrote, affectionately, in October 1922, referring to Ruskin's definition of cookery. "My dearest wish is that you will find every meal perfect in appointment, in service, in delectability, in taste, and in nutrition."[86] Her own academic excellence was fun, stimulating, charming, but beside the point. "I'll never be in the lime light now for I don't ever see any one, and I have absolutely no ambition in those directions. I shall be always a fine, clean, noble woman who is willing to do anything for her husband." Again, though, in the next sentence she berated a classmate for her stupidity. "You shouldn't have passed her last year, and I told you she didn't deserve it. If she deserved a D, I surely should have had an A. I'm going to tell Doc Scott too some day. Just wait till he sees my Organic grade."[87] This was one of the first digs at her future husband for downgrading her performance in the spring, to avoid the appearance of favoritism. The B in general chemistry rankled for years.

Ava Helen was both mischievous and frank. "Mary is playing the piano," she reported in her letter that evening, "which is driving me nearly crazy. She is picking out by the one-finger method 'By the Waters of Minnetonka.' It sounds like the 'Trickles of the Lost River.'"[88] (In a later letter she complained of Mary's overuse of the loud pedal. Linus sympathized.[89]) Contrasting another instructor with the pleasing Mr. Quigly, she wrote, "I nearly die in Mr. Thurber's class, cause he is so dead and I want to say so badly what it is and he just creeps along. I bet if I put a tack on his chair, it would take him ten minutes to realize it was there and fifteen to get up."[90] When Linus lorded it over her, saying "smart" things or speaking angrily to her, she let him know and he apologized, abashed.[91] She chided him for unfair characterizations of her in his letters. At the same time, she got in digs at him for his independent life in California. "The other thing you said," Linus wrote, his Achilles heel getting the best of him, "is that I was incorrect in saying I'd do what you wish, for I won't unless I also desire to. … I am deeply hurt dear. Even though you believe it, will you please, sweet Ava Helen, never say it again to me?" But he moved on. In the next paragraph he was discussing the glories of scientific discovery, and the joy of sleeping without pajamas between them.[92]

The couple also worked on the intersection of their belief systems and intellectual styles. He assumed that she shared his passion for chemistry and the astonishing scientific stew that was Los Angeles in those days. In February he sent a clipping from the Los Angeles Sunday *Times* detailing Arnold Sommerfeld's lectures on quantum physics ("Mighty Atom's Secrets Are Wrested from It").[93] A few days later he referred casually to the time when she would get her Ph.D., though usually he wrote of her simply finishing her bachelor's degree.[94] Like other liberal intellectuals, he despised the Ku Klux Klan and deplored the influence of religious fundamentalists in American culture.[95] He usually assumed that she shared these ideas.

He did lecture her occasionally on the logical fallacy of believing in an omnipotent God and believing that God is good (for a "good" and omnipotent God would not permit senseless human suffering).[96] In addition, they had a long exchange on faith healing, which her brother-in-law Walter Spaulding was pursuing for some physical ailment. Pauling rejected the idea that faith healing or spiritual healing had any basis except pure chance. Ava Helen took offense, seemingly more at his lecturing her than at his reasoning. He backpedalled. "Sweet, you mustn't think that I think I am superior to you, for it isn't true. It hurts me to have you think so. I used to think I was superior to most everyone; it is somewhat of a surprise to find that you far out-distance me in many ways."[97]

Still, he stuck to his position and couldn't resist recommending scientific authorities to bolster his skepticism. "Dear, if you think much of this divine healer read quite a bit on psychology, psychoanalysis and suggestion. I can see no reason why Christ or God would allow one man to make a few scattered partially successful cures. Why is not disease [done?] away with? If Christ or God intended to relieve the world," he pursued his relentless and fruitless logic, "is not the most simple way to merely relieve it, systematically and justly, [rather than] let a man make a few scattered haphazard cures? The mystery is great. I like to ignore all pedantic questions and merely live happily in the faith (or the assumption) that the duty of man is to help mankind to progress."[98]

Ava Helen pretended to give in, writing to him, "as usual I'll have to call off my pet war dogs and call myself defeated." Linus protested her wording.[99] She bridled at his apparent assumption that she and he would merge when they were married. He hastily reassured her. "Your reasoning is very good in regards to our having our own individualities. All I want is that we should help each other to understand things. If we talk clearly and unreservedly of everything we won't have foolish differences of opinion, in our religious beliefs, for example, instead of trying to convert each other to our own ways, we shall seek as far as we can together."[100]

Pauling was easily offended by what he perceived as poor manners. Maybe this was a defensive reaction to his lower-middle-class social status, or maybe he was genuinely repulsed. The Emmetts' practice of licking their knives at dinner disgusted him. "I shudder at the things they do." He and Paul Emmett shared a bed, usually sleeping in shifts, and he assured Ava Helen that when they were both in it, he kept way over on his side so as not to touch Paul. "He is careless about his person—he is very untidy," reported Linus primly.[101] In March he expatiated on poor Paul's shortcomings: "It drives me wild—he swishes water through his teeth, and eats with his knife, and says 'these cheese,' and leaves half the buttons on his vest unbuttoned—I surely am odd."[102] He confided that he read a letter carelessly left on the department stenographer's desk, from his professor, Fulton, at OAC. Fulton had said that Emmett was "probably better" than Pauling at mathematics, and "led the class in physical chem." To his credit, Pauling admitted that his indignation crumbled when he realized that assessment might well be true. "I know I have a tendency to place myself higher than I belong."[103] Still, it probably rankled that the uncouth Paul had been appraised as intellectually superior to himself.

By March the couple was actively planning their wedding, which would take place at Nettie's house in Salem, although throughout the spring the location remained tentative as Linus waited to hear if his grandmother might be able to attend. Ava Helen completed her winter term at OAC and did not enroll for spring term. She spent a week at her sister's Salem house on Court Street, and then returned to Corvallis.[104] Pauling planned to work for the Oregon Highway Department again over the summer. His Caltech professors were trying to figure out how to ease the young couple's financial worries while being fair to other students. Linus shared his excitement at having Ava Helen join him in California. The beautiful state continued to grow on him. "It hasn't been too warm, and the flowers are in bloom, and the orange trees, and calla lilies in everyone's yard. I love you, dear. Next year at this time we'll go for little trips in our old Ford, and we'll camp out on the desert, and sleep together in our sleeping bag, which will hold us close to each other."[105] At the end of April he consummated the deal with his major professor, Caltech chemist Roscoe Dickinson, to buy his old Ford for fifty dollars.[106]

Ava Helen too seems to have been excited, and with her anticipation came heightened irritability and insecurity. Far away in California, Linus escaped the constant pressures of family bearing down on Ava Helen from all sides, although he continued to defend himself against his mother's accusations that he was an undutiful son.[107] He commented that she seemed "quite vacillating" about her own mother: "one day you write telling me how bad she is, and the next day how lovely she is." He concluded wistfully: "I hope you won't have the bad days with me."[108]

Ava Helen complained not just about her own mother but about his as well. After a visit involving the two mothers — hardly a simple encounter — she wrote: "She was too peevish at me, and I don't care. I am getting tired of trying to get along with people. From now on she has to get along with me and I'm not going to waste any more tears crying about it either. My whole life has been an endeavor to get along with somebody and I'm sick of it."[109] She was not yet twenty years old, and a month away from marriage.

CHAPTER 2

Becoming Mrs. Pauling

I think of the biggest sweetest most beautiful thing in the universe, and Ava Helen's love is that thing. My love is just beside it, holding it tightly and caressing it.
—Linus to Ava Helen, [February 5, 1923]

Time passes awfully slowly when you are not with me, dear love.
—Linus Pauling to Ava Helen Pauling, September 30, 1940[1]

Linus tempted fate on the way to his wedding in June 1923. Ava Helen was oblivious until he arrived, miraculously safe and sound, just before the ceremony. Hurrying to reach Nettie's home in Salem a few days before the ceremony planned for June 17, Linus decided to drive through the night. He had no long distance experience, having taught himself to drive after buying his car in April. In the middle of the night he missed a curve in the Siskiyou Mountains and rolled the car into a ditch. A piece of the crushed roof gashed his leg. He bandaged his own wound while waiting for help.[2] In the morning a motorist found the young man and his wreck by the side of the road. Somehow Linus limped the car to Salem. Twenty-five years later he would undergo a similar night of lonely, scary waiting; this time his youth and ardor carried him through.

Ava Helen, meanwhile, enjoyed the traditional pre-wedding rituals. Linus had given her a Delta Upsilon pin to mark their engagement the previous year. He also gave her a diamond set in white gold and a large cedar chest—the latter perhaps more intimate and significant to the couple than the jewelry, because it would contain their bedding. Despite their disapproval of this early marriage, the mothers of the bride and groom each gave the couple presents, as did Ava Helen's sisters and many Oregon

Linus and Ava Helen Pauling on their wedding day, Salem, Oregon, 1923.

friends. A pie plate and a sterling pie knife, a crocheted bed set, linen pillow cases, a picture of Oregon scenery, and ten dollars were among the couple's trove in the pre-wedding shower.

Nettie's house offered a satisfying stage for a June wedding. The family engaged a Presbyterian minister to preside; this perhaps reflected the religious preferences of the Miller family. The house was filled with pink and white roses, with blue flowers at the altar. Ava Helen's sisters and nieces formed the bridal party. Her brother Clay gave her away. (Ava Helen had not seen her father in ten years. He did not attend the wedding.) Linus's boyhood friend Lloyd Jeffress, now a psychology student at Berkeley, stood as best man. The Pauling and Miller clans turned out for the ceremony. The newspaper reports highlighted Ava Helen's vivaciousness, her popularity at Salem High School, and her theater activities at OAC. The Salem paper noted Linus as a "Delta Epsilon [sic] man," a graduate of the "Agricultural college."

The couple's "wedding journey to various points in Oregon" turned into a night in Corvallis, followed by Ava Helen's trailing Linus to some of his postings as a paving-plant inspector in Washington and Oregon for one more summer. When she wasn't with Linus in some roadside town, she spent time with his hard-to-please mother in Portland. That summer was Ava Helen's farewell to Oregon. Except for scattered visits to their extended families in Portland, the Paulings' move to Pasadena that fall marked the beginning of their long life together in California. Linus began his second year at Caltech, while Ava Helen kept house in a small rental near campus.

During his first year in graduate school, Pauling had learned x-ray crystallography from Roscoe Dickinson and become intensely interested in quantum theory. He met Arnold Sommerfeld, visiting from Germany. Biographer Robert Paradowski reports that some of Pauling's crystal

Ava Helen, Linus, and family members at their wedding, 1923.

models at that point were better than Sommerfeld's. During his second year, after his marriage, he took a heavy course load and continued to impress his mentors with his acuity. He also introduced himself to G. N. Lewis, Noyes's old colleague and now rival for recruiting youthful talent at Berkeley. When Lewis showed some interest in taking Pauling on for a post-doctoral fellowship after he took the Ph.D., Noyes prepared to take measures to retain this prodigy after graduation. After he received his Ph.D. in the spring of 1925, Pauling was on his way out the door to Berkeley when Noyes figured out a way to keep him at Caltech to finish some of his crystallography work.[3]

A year into their marriage, Ava Helen sat down with her *HIM Book* to complete the record of her engagement. "It is not strange that I didn't write a diary during my engagement," she wrote. "Why waste time on a lifeless thing like a diary, when the most wonderful man is with you, and you are so busy living life?" Here Ava Helen remembers her engagement as a time spent "with" Linus, though the couple was separated most of that long

*Ava Helen and Linus
Pauling at Corona del
Mar, 1924*

year. But now she felt, on a dark day in Pasadena in 1924, she would revisit those months in her head, and write about her "thoughts and feelings" at the time. "We are engaged and are delightfully, ecstatically happy," she began. "We feel a little doubtful as to how this news will be received for we have known" — and then the account breaks off.[4] Perhaps the sun came out; perhaps Linus came home from the lab; perhaps somebody knocked on the door. Perhaps it was too hard to think about their defiance and doubt as they pondered how to tell their families that they just couldn't wait any longer to be married.

In the first months of marriage she took on the identity of wife. Not only was that culturally expected, but also the couple had grown so close during their courtship that it would be surprising if Ava Helen had chosen to differentiate herself from her role in the couple. But unlike many other wives, who stayed at home or planned on early parenthood, Ava Helen accompanied Linus to lectures and department social events as well as to the laboratory. She recorded results for him and occasionally wrote love notes in the margins of his lab notebooks. She did not look for a job or continue her formal college education. Years later she remarked that she had been able throughout her marriage to take whatever courses interested her, without pursuing a degree. Linus had discovered before they married that it would have been difficult for Ava Helen to enroll in a California college or university near Pasadena. Moreover, Linus's graduate stipend was just enough to pay basic expenses, not to support additional tuition and commuting costs. During their engagement the couple had corresponded about Ava Helen's working for pay, and Linus had dismissed the possibility as more expensive than remunerative. It is not clear what conversation they had about this issue after they married. Having excelled in chemistry and organic chemistry at OAC, Ava Helen tried to keep up with Linus's work in these first years. During their engagement, Linus had entertained the idea that Ava Helen should finish her college degree, and in the throes of his longing for her he periodically offered to give up his graduate fellowship in order to allow her to finish at OAC. But he had charted his course, and he must have hoped that his beloved would see things his way — which she did. In one burst of generosity, he offered to take a job in Corvallis at least for a couple of years, but then backed off concluding that "our success in making our home and rearing our beautiful children depends on you and my job" — decisively outlining the roles that the couple would fill for the next twenty years.

On March 10, 1925, not quite two years after the Paulings married, Ava Helen bore their first child, named after his father, Linus Carl Pauling. Like many mothers, Ava Helen may have been too busy, or overwhelmed, to reflect on the experience except in ephemera we no longer have. But her priorities became clear in the winter of 1925-26, eleven months after Linie's birth. When Linus *père* sought a Guggenheim to go to Germany to pursue his burning interest in the new field of quantum physics, Ava Helen planned to go with him. Further, she intended to travel without the baby. Little Linus could stay with Ava Helen's mother in Portland while the couple spent the year in Europe. Linus later remembered protesting in "shock," but he yielded as Ava Helen argued that the journey would be hard on the baby and would keep them from doing the things they longed to do in Europe.[5]

The two-day train ride from Pasadena to Portland confirmed her judgment. "It was difficult traveling with the baby," Ava Helen wrote frankly on the first page of the travel diary she and Linus kept jointly that year.[6] Her blunt assessment resonates with generations of parents, and also remains one of the baby's only appearances in the records of that year. Ava Helen left her mother — who had raised twelve children — with a sheet of commands on child rearing. In peremptory language that might have amused Nora Gard Miller if it did not annoy her, Ava Helen instructed her to tie one-year-old Linus to his potty chair every morning at 9:30 after his orange juice. "Defecate" and "urinate" were the appropriate words for the activities Linus should engage in there. The toddler should not be allowed to masturbate, but he should not be shamed, either, or told "untrue" stories about the "evil effects" of touching himself. "The prevailing stories are entirely false and harmful." It is not clear if Ava Helen had some reason to think that her mother believed those stories, or if she was just exercising her modern home economics training, or both. Her mother should keep Linus's genitals "scrupulously clean and unchafed — (use plenty of oil and powder)," she suggested helpfully. "Next teach Linus that his hands are to hold toys, food, etc., but not to pick or rub his ears, eyes, nose, or genitals. If it is necessary, hold his hands until he sleeps." This is clearly an instruction from a woman in her twenties, unbothered by bending over a child's bed as he wriggled toward sleep. "Be sure his clothes are comfortable — and lastly consult a doctor." This was a long section on a matter that was supposed to be underplayed. Ava Helen also issued instructions for social training. Linus Jr. should never be asked to perform in public, whether it be shaking an adult's hand or repeating nonsense syllables.

Top: Linus Pauling reading with Linus, Jr., on his lap, 1925.

Below: Ava Helen with Linus, Jr., 1925.

His grandmother should also refrain from talking about Linus in front of him: "Besides being very disgusting to any one of intelligence, it is also very bad for him, and it will develop habits and traits which you will have to punish for later." These were not specified. The performance ban seems quite humane, except that the reason was not to spare the child telling social

Family portrait with Linus, Jr., 1926.

lies, but to avoid fostering "boldness" that might also, presumably, have to be punished later.[7]

After four days in Portland, to allow baby Linus to make the transition from his parents' care to his grandmother's, Ava Helen and Linus reboarded the train and headed east through Washington, where the wild currant was already in bloom, and then through endless tunnels in the snowy mountains. The Pullman was their introduction to the luxuries of train travel. "We missed the Baby awfully," Ava Helen noted the second day.[8]

A stop in Chicago brought a brief reunion with Ava Helen's long-lost father—an event that Linus recorded years later, but that appears nowhere in Ava Helen's notes about that "coldest and ugliest" city. Perhaps those words captured what must have been an emotionally confusing meeting, scrambled into a few minutes before their train was scheduled to depart for New York.[9] A wintry visit to Niagara Falls, where the spray "froze and fell on us in little ice beads," pleased them much more. "I should have liked staying longer," Ava Helen wrote. The New York Central carried them into a Manhattan sunrise. Later that day they went up in the Woolworth Building,

Ava Helen with a camera, aboard a ship during the 1926-27 European trip.

at fifty-seven stories the tallest building in New York before the 1930s. "Ava Helen was very frightened," Linus noted, though she did like seeing men playing handball on a nearby roof forty floors above street level. They walked Broadway that night and agreed that while the lights were "extensive," they were not "overwhelmed" by the prospect. They went to a cabaret and criticized the performers. Their careers as world travelers had begun.[10]

The Paulings' education in cosmopolitan living continued as they drank their first beer and wine aboard the ship to Europe. Seasick the second day, and tossed by an ocean storm on another night, overall they had a happy voyage with assorted table companions: a German baron, a Portuguese consul, and several Italians who invited them to visit ashore.

They planned to spend the first few months traveling, before Linus began his fellowship work in Munich. Eager to snare this talented young scientist before G. N. Lewis at Berkeley wooed him away, Linus's chairman, A. A. Noyes, had first helped Pauling secure a National Research Council fellowship, and then pushed him toward one of the early Guggenheim fellowships, which would allow Pauling to study quantum theory with its pioneers in Europe. To allow all this to happen before Lewis captured Pauling, Noyes had propelled the Paulings out of the country even before the official Guggenheim announcement, giving them an extraordinary gift of money to travel through Italy and the Mediterranean countries on their way to the Institute of Theoretical Physics in Munich.[11] So here they were, dining with minor aristocrats and officials, preparing to tour the sights that their middle-class American education had taught them to revere.

Though they were not church goers, the Paulings shared an American Protestant-inflected prejudice against Catholics and the Roman Catholic hierarchy. Of the tippling, talkative priest who traveled with them, she wrote acidly that she suspected Christ wouldn't like him.[12] The shipboard Italians, commented Ava Helen, were "friendly, carefree, and rather noisy, but also charming." The Paulings' youthful eugenics reading showed in their reactions during their tour of southern Europe and northern Africa. In Madeira, begging children besieged them, and she suggested that it was a shame there were so many of them. Cruising past Gibraltar, the Paulings discovered English tea biscuits and squid, and loved them both. "Filthy but picturesque," Ava Helen decided about Algiers, echoing generations of European and American travelers.[13] She repeated the sentiment in Naples. Her aversion to the "public excretory system" does not seem as coy after her instructions for Linus, Jr.'s toilet habits and vocabulary. Again, the Paulings' cultural Protestantism emerged with her verdict on the Neapolitans: "vivacious, gay and, I'm afraid, rather indolent."[14]

The Paulings were stunned by the Museo Nazionale. "The statues, both bronze and marble, were perfect and marvelously beautiful." The other tourists did not appreciate what they were seeing: "We saw some Americans 'do' the entire museum in about an hour — too bad such persons are permitted to enter. We are going to go again this week."[15] The Oregon-bred Paulings leaped into their adventure. Unlike some of their peers in the postwar "Lost Generation," Ava Helen and Linus did not seek escape from their home culture or creative inspiration from the art and monuments of Europe. But as with those other expatriates, their European journey opened their eyes and changed their lives. They made picnics of bread, cheese, and oranges and occasionally drank wine with lunch; they strolled the marketplace as well as the temples and museums; they chatted in French and Italian with Italian men and boys on the train, and ate little cakes offered to them on one occasion, and an entire lunch another time when they forgot to carry their own food.

Ava Helen had a terrifying thrill like her ascent of the Woolworth Building when she and Linus hiked seven miles up Vesuvius, through orchards and over lava flows, to find that the mountain top was spouting pink smoke and red-hot rocks. At Pompeii they boldly chased away the guides and explored on their own. They delighted in their long afternoon poking through the ruins, and returned the next morning. They missed their train back to Naples, but got a cabdriver to take them to the next stop and hopped on. Rome impressed them with its relative cleanliness. Though they left no comments about the trains running on time (perhaps because of their mishap in Pompeii), Ava Helen wrote that in Rome there was "no begging as a result of Mussolini."[16]

Ava Helen's judgments became increasingly bold, simple, and sure. She was knocked back by the Borghese Gallery, with its incalculable wealth of Titians, Van Dycks, and Correggios. "Titian's 'Sacred and Profane Love' is so beautiful one wants to weep and it is misnamed, I think, for I can't see how either figure could be profane. I can understand now why masters are masters." She was glad to hear that an American's offer of six million for the "Sacred and Profane Love" was rejected; she found it "such a pity" that Napoleon had taken much of the collection for the Louvre.[17]

Ava Helen observed people as well as art. She guessed that Italians must be born with "a definite sense of the beautiful and artistic," from the settings for the animals in the zoo to the way people dressed every day. "There are few incongruities and almost no monstrosities in the way of clothes," though in the Italian way of life in general, "there are … many faults and things which need correction." In addition, some of their compatriots continued to rankle as Ava Helen began positioning herself as a refined citizen of the world. "We were made quite angry by the ill breeding of some Americans who were crowding to get in the elevator. One actually asked Linus to let her daughter in front of him. Linus did, of course, although it is a common thing for some of the American women to act as if they were the only important ones."[18]

She also experienced art as a representation of the body. "One can see by comparison with these lovely nude feminine bodies how ugly one is. Too bad!" She was disgusted by the Vatican's decision to put fig leaves and paint draperies over nudes in the classic paintings of Michelangelo and other masters. "To my mind all this shows that the 'order of the cloth' is not as saintly or as pure as it would seem." On a train ride from Pisa to Venice, she struck up a conversation with a twenty-nine-year-old bride. "She grew quite intimate with me … and asked all kinds of funny questions about sexual matters. I was surely surprised. She seems to be a nice girl." An Italian caretaker at the Venetian prison pressed Linus and Ava Helen about "Indians and Negroes" in the United States. "He seemed to think that we deliberately murdered all of them." Her first zoo delighted her and brought home to her in a humorous way the interrelatedness of all creatures. "It was interesting to note that the monkeys are more popular than any other thing in the zoo—Evolution! *N'est-ce pas?*"[19]

On the way home from St. Peter's, they followed a crowd to see Mussolini pass by in his car. In a bizarre episode, he had just been shot by an English woman, Violet Gibson (first rumored to be Polish); the bullet passed through his nose. The Italians claimed excitedly, "God saved Mussolini!" Ava Helen thought of the would-be assassin. "I hate to think of what will happen or is happening to the poor, foolish, inflamed Polish woman. Poor thing!"[20] They commented on the Fascist shirts and listened to the tales told by Italian citizens about the "dreadful turmoil" after the Great War. A Fascist leader in Florence persuaded the Paulings that "Mussolini does seem to have straightened it out."[21]

By the time they reached Florence, Linus had tired of travel and was aching to get back to work. Ava Helen complied. "He, poor boy, is tired of this inactivity [an interesting characterization of their strenuous travel] and would like going on to Munich. ... He is an angel to me, and we have bushels of fun together. He does everything for me."[22]

In Munich the Paulings rented a small apartment near the Institute at the University of Munich. They saved a snapshot of the street with a blue ink arrow pointing to their room on the second floor of the building. Linus would work under the general direction of Arnold Sommerfeld, the director of the Institute. As Thomas Hager has written, Sommerfeld's scientific contributions included his mathematical brilliance and his genius at mentoring young physicists. He was also an intensely handsome figure in his late fifties, stocky and powerful looking, with receding grey hair and a generous moustache. A year after the Paulings' return to Pasadena, Sommerfeld visited them there. There is a striking photograph in the Pauling collection that shows Sommerfeld standing over Ava Helen, who sits on the desert brush with arms wrapped around her knees. Though little Linus is a foot away, seated by her side in the sand, the image is still startlingly erotic.

Ava Helen would have been unlikely to allow herself to be attracted to any man other than Linus, but she flirted effectively throughout her life. She prided herself on being accepted as one of the Americans at the Institute, though she wrote lightly, "I fear I don't lend much to the department."[23] In

Left: The Paulings' room in Munich, marked with an arrow, 1927. Inscription on the back of the picture notes that the building was destroyed during World War II.
Right: Ava Helen, Linus, Jr., and Arnold Sommerfeld in Coachella Valley, California, in 1928.

the United States, and perhaps in Germany, a woman might be accepted as a social peer if she could hold her own in conversation without challenging her husband's professional status. Petite, vivacious, and clearly devoted to her husband, Ava Helen brought unalloyed femininity to her interactions with men and thus expanded her own and Linus's social worlds.

The events that Ava Helen chose to record may also have been dictated by some sense of what was appropriate to notice and to feel. Visiting the Stuttgart home of one of Linus's colleagues, Ava Helen commented in a diary entry, "Ilis wife was visiting his mother and I combed Linde's [the daughter's] hair." The children then saw the Paulings off at the train and gave Ava Helen some violets.[24] The note about the children is conventionally sentimental. If there was pervasive whispered criticism of Ava Helen's mothering in the family, she may have been particularly anxious to believe in her own maternal instincts.

Ava Helen's mother sent regular updates on Linus, Jr., growing from a baby to a toddler in Portland. Linus and Ava Helen sent her $75 per quarter to support her care of Linie, who would be two and a half when the Paulings returned in September 1927. They had been scheduled to return after a year abroad, but Linus secured a six-month extension of his Guggenheim. The supplementary Guggenheim money arrived in April, when the Paulings were literally down to their last twenty *pfennige*. They hopped a train for a trip to Stuttgart, Heidelberg, Mannheim, Köln, and then on to a week in Holland (the maximum time allowed without a visa). They took the train all the way along the Rhine, and Ava Helen had time alone with Linus to explore castles and cathedrals.

She also enjoyed visits with German and Dutch scientists, which often involved meeting their wives and children and sometimes being grilled on American fashions. Frau Mark in Mannheim asked Ava Helen "if it were the mode to be fat or thin in America. Amusing!"[25] Ava Helen observed in Holland that the women were more fashionable than in Germany — "much more bobbed hair." As always, she accompanied Linus on his laboratory visits, including one in Eindhoven where lunch was served "with all the physics men" right in the laboratory, and "poor Linus" had to give a colloquium directly afterward, dirty shirt and all.[26] That summer they moved from Munich to Zurich, where Linus spent a frustrating month trying to get a personal audience with Erwin Schrodinger; he had to satisfy himself with attending Schrodinger's weekly seminars. Stops in Paris and London on the way home rounded out the year and a half abroad — the Paulings' Grand Tour.

The European sojourn was a formative time for Linus Pauling's chemistry career. He confessed to Robert Paradowski years later that he had felt depressed during the early months in Europe. It was the first time, perhaps, since sneaking a look at the departmental letter about Paul Emmett, that he had felt intellectually inferior to other scientists, particularly young ones, like Wolfgang Pauli and Werner Heisenberg. Pauling's insecurity and Ava Helen's isolation put pressure on the couple's relationship, too, of course. Ava Helen was jealous of other women — in particular, one family story goes, their landlady. From this early period, her anxiety about his loyalty began to factor into her desire to travel with him, to stay close to him. Ironically and painfully, their sexual relationship may also have been compromised in these months by the difficulty of securing condoms in southern Germany.[27]

But Ava Helen's adventure in Europe was probably not predominantly a lonely, anxious one. She attended lectures at the university, and she learned to speak German. She wrote to a journalist many years later that she received the "major part of my education" during that year and a half in Germany.[28] Her confidence as a citizen of the world grew. Not quite ten years after the Great War, they spotted French and British soldiers in many of the towns along the Rhine: "very silly," Ava Helen commented.[29] Their year and a half in Europe also coincided with the height of the Sacco and Vanzetti controversy in the United States: the conviction of immigrant anarchists of murder during an armed robbery that became a *cause célèbre* worldwide. Aside from Ava Helen's shock that Linus had registered as a Republican for his first presidential election in 1924, this is the first hint we have of Ava Helen's intentional political influence on him. She condemned the trial as political and the work of the advisory committee appointed to review the death sentence as prejudiced. Linus had been reluctant to believe the worst of the justice system, but Ava Helen persisted until he agreed with her.[30]

She was awestruck by the art of Europe, the castles and mansions, the cathedrals with their treasures of art, manuscripts, jewels, and statuary ("to be holy does not mean lowly necessarily," she wrote wryly). Temperamentally outgoing, she helped to turn professional meetings into social encounters in the institutes and universities Linus visited. Returning to the United States meant returning to mothering a small child, keeping house so that Linus could work, raising a family on a budget, socializing with Linus's colleagues in a much less cosmopolitan setting and in a much more restrictive "faculty wife" role. It may not have been a wholly joyous homecoming for the young housewife.

Both Linus and Ava Helen passed family milestones during that journey. Ava Helen glimpsed her father for the first time since she was nine years old — and in the company of her new husband. Linus's mother died suddenly in Oregon in July 1926, after the Paulings had arrived in Germany. She had gotten increasingly ill, probably from the effects of pernicious anemia, and

Linus's sisters had been unable to cope with her needs. There was enough guilt to go around in a sad situation of financial stress and lack of medical clarity about diagnosis and treatment. Linus paid a price not only in self-imposed guilt for not being there, but also in recriminations from his sister Pauline, who took the distressing occasion to blame Linus for being out of the country and for not helping more with his mother while she was alive. Linus responded in sharp self-defense, but the very force of his words suggests that his sister's letter hit home. Lucile wrote placatingly, explaining that she had not sent a telegram because she was afraid to scare Ava Helen, who might panic if she saw a cable, fearing for the baby.[31] That is the generous side of the family story that Ava Helen had asked the sisters not to bother Linus with bad news from home while he was working in Germany. The sorrow and guilt may thus have become even more complicated by bitterness from Linus's family about Ava Helen's overprotectiveness.

As the Paulings established their married life in the late 1920s and early 1930s, the Depression changed the American landscape. As with most families, the Paulings' behaviors about money and budgeting can offer insights into their evolving priorities and values. In the early years of their marriage Linus kept careful lists of expenditures in his ubiquitous pocket notebooks. Probably to account for the gift money from Noyes, he kept a scrupulous list of even the smallest outlays in the early phase of their European journey, generally in the currency of the country. There were tips for waiters and chauffeurs, expenses for chocolate, bananas, and filberts, money for beggars, admission to monuments, and other small and large sums. Ava Helen teased Linus that when he had money he spent it, and certainly neither one of them avoided the small luxuries that made their lives pleasant.[32]

Back home, the Paulings seem to have passed the accounting chores back and forth. Their budget was initially tight on Linus's assistant professor salary. When they returned from Europe they rented a small house on Wilson Street. In 1931 they moved to a house owned by Caltech at 1245 Arden Road. It was almost twice as expensive at $90 a month, but there would be more room for their second baby, Peter, born that year. By then they could afford weekly "help."[33] They paid dues to the CIT faculty club, the Athenaeum. They subscribed to *Time* and became early patrons of Consumers Research. Ava Helen joined a book club. They covered the floors of their rented house with Persian rugs bought by installments from the Pashgian Brothers. They bought a radio, also on the installment plan, and rented a piano. Ava Helen had been able to play the piano in Germany; when Sommerfeld had learned that she was an enthusiastic musician, he had lent her a piano. Back in Pasadena, despite her growing responsibilities as mother and wife, Ava Helen still made time to play, at least during Linus, Jr.'s childhood.[34]

The Paulings also lent money to relatives. After one such loan, during the Depression years, Linus noted to Ava Helen, "After this, though, I think we'd better keep our money." She, too, feared that the loan had been precipitous. They made other small loans along the way, beginning a lifelong habit of sharing their good fortune, though carefully.[35] The early years challenged the Paulings to live a middle-class life on a working man's salary, and they both worried.

A modest assistant professor's salary would still have put the Paulings in a privileged position during the Depression years. There was never a hint that his position would become insecure. On the contrary, despite the self-doubt he experienced among the giants of quantum physics in Europe, Pauling was a rising star at CIT. But even at Caltech, the president asked the faculty to take a 10 percent pay cut in 1932, and the faculty complied. Linus objected, not to the austerity measure, but to President Millikan's

A page from Linus's family account book for 1926. Linus Pauling's handwriting.

assumption that it was the faculty and not the trustees who had the power to make that decision.[36]

Southern California would have been a strange place to observe the national crisis. On the one hand, as Kevin Starr has pointed out in his sprawling history of California, agriculture, the film industry, and defense contracting were key pieces of the state's economy that flourished relative to industrial and agricultural sectors elsewhere. On the other, labor battles, the forced expulsion of up to half a million Mexicans, and California's magnetism for drifters, dreamers, and refugees from the Dust Bowl created drama and cultural clashes that dominated the state's headlines throughout the decade.[37]

Though Linus had not been able to meet all the European quantum theory scientists, the time abroad had been fruitful as well as exciting, and back at Caltech he continued to collaborate by correspondence with the Dutch physicist Samuel Goudsmit and helped host Sommerfeld during his visiting professorship at CIT in 1928-29. Pauling's burgeoning reputation as a pioneer in joining quantum physics and chemistry commanded attention. Despite Noyes's strategic victory in keeping Pauling at Caltech, the young professor was invited to spend a month each year as a visiting lecturer at Berkeley. Linus enjoyed being courted, and this was his year for it; he was offered the Berkeley arrangement as Harvard was wooing him, and he wrote in delight to Ava Helen that even if they moved to Cambridge, he could expect to come back west every other year. At Berkeley, G.N. Lewis told Pauling that he had attracted more physicists to his lectures than any other guest. Linus expected that the month up north would bring a good fee, and perhaps a chance to spend some time as a couple. "When Linus starts going to school we may have to leave him during this month. Won't it be fun to go to Berkeley and live in a nice hotel apartment for a month every year?"[38] Apparently the adults-only European sojourn had suited him as well as his wife.

Pauling's genius in chemistry grew out of several core characteristics or habits of mind. One was his love of solving puzzles. Ava Helen shared this love, though obviously he would make a world-changing career out of it, while she settled for staying amused and keeping her mind sharp. When he could not manage the ridiculously complex mathematical calculations it would take to prove his theories of molecular structure, he went at the puzzle one crystal at a time, and then discerned some predictable patterns, which he disseminated in 1928 in a paper on predictions that became known as "Pauling's Rules." The other habit of mind was his love of the tangible, which kept him in chemistry despite the lure of physics., Linus began building paper models of molecules, sometimes with Ava Helen's help. These allowed him to visualize their structural characteristics.

Linus traveled east in April 1929 to visit Cambridge and explore the possibilities of a job teaching physical chemistry at Harvard. He was third in line for the position, which had been offered to Lewis and then to Richard C. Tolman, who had taught Pauling at Caltech. Ava Helen headed to Portland with Linus, Jr., to visit her mother and many siblings, while Paddy, as Ava Helen called him, boarded the train for the east coast. He had talked frankly with both Noyes and President Millikan before he left, and had left with assurances of a salary raise and, perhaps more importantly, freedom to travel every other year or so. The Caltech people knew that Harvard would offer a higher salary, but they could counter with promotion, new colleagues, research opportunities, and the possibility of department leadership ("Dr Noyes expects Tolman, Roscoe, + me to run the department after him; and Millikan expects me to—but of course this shouldn't determine our choice").[39] Pauling also consulted with Lewis about the Harvard position; his Berkeley mentor was coy, but clearly believed Pauling would do better on the west coast.[40] Certainly that's where Lewis wanted him.

During their long-distance courtship, Linus shared his life with Ava Helen through daily letters. The first trip to Berkeley in the spring of 1929, and then the two-week trip to Cambridge, reminded him of his loneliness away from her. "You mean everything to me, darling. You must tell me if you ever feel that you are dissatisfied, and we'll do something about it. I am perfectly happy with you."[41] Pauling was good at solitude; he could spend hours reading and more hours staring out the window, thinking. Throughout his life he could focus his mind on scientific problems and puzzles even when he was sick—in fact, especially when he was sick: the thinking relieved his frustration at being removed from the lab and the classroom. But he was forlorn when Ava Helen was not with him, and he filled the space between them with his dreams and reflections. He described the scenery in lyrical detail. As a western boy, he loved the big spaces and the flora of deserts and mountains. Already the deck was stacked against Harvard. "When I saw the joshua trees on the desert this morning I thought that we couldn't leave Pasadena for good."[42] Ava Helen agreed, responding in the same language of landscape. "When I saw how lovely California is on the train I thought that the advantages of Harvard would have to be very substantial ones in order to win us from Cal Tech. If you could only have seen the miles of flowers—lupine so blue and so profuse it looked like a blue lake."[43]

On the train Linus dreamed of a huge marble statue of a Roman emperor on his horse coming to life, and Ava Helen climbing the massive pedestal to get closer to the figure. As it became clear that she was in danger, he saw the statue's massive arm reaching out toward Ava Helen. "Here I have a feeling of rescue, but since I can't remember anything definite it may be only the relief of awakening."[44] It had been two years since they visited Rome; along with the possibility of uprooting the family to move east, they were thinking of returning to Europe the following year. The dream startled and interested Linus, though he drew no conclusions about its meaning. When Ava Helen shared her "bad" dreams (presumably about other men), he reassured her by analyzing the dreams as displaced anxiety about his being far away. He too had dreamed of "uz"ing another woman, but woke before "anything happened." "But wait till I catch you again, sweetheart! You'll not get off so easily."[45]

It is possible that the couple's erotic dreams, as well as the conciliatory affection that charges their letters during this period, was related to the strange triangular relationship they had formed with J. Robert Oppenheimer in the period after they returned to Pasadena, when Oppenheimer took up a visiting professorship at CIT. The three became close very quickly. As Thomas Hager writes, the friendship was both exciting and troubling for the naïve Pauling, whose intimacies had been relatively few. Oppenheimer started sending him poems and giving him gifts. Then, oddly, he moved on Ava Helen, inviting her to join him in Mexico when Pauling was away on a trip. When she told Linus what had happened, he broke off the friendship with Oppenheimer and scuttled the scientific collaboration they had imagined.[46] The next time Oppenheimer wooed one of the Paulings, it would be to get Linus to join what became known as the Manhattan Project. Linus turned him down.

Passing through Chicago, Linus described a stop much pleasanter than they had experienced three years earlier, in the bitter winter. The art institute drew him in. He strolled by Wedgwood pottery and paintings by Matisse, Van Gogh, and Gauguin. He offered to contact Ava Helen's father again on his way back through, if Ava Helen sent him the address. "His name is George, isn't it?"[47]

In Portland, Ava Helen reconnected with her family, Linus's family, and other intimates, particularly the Emmetts, Linus's boyhood friends. Her mother had been ill, and Ava Helen found the household din distressing. "The confusion here is shocking and dreadful. A radio (dreadfully cheap— Lu's) screams perpetually, every one talks raucously, and all in all there isn't much chance for a bit of ordinary quiet."[48] She felt uncomfortable and unwelcome among her siblings. "None of them are very nice to me except Mamma and Dickie and Pat. But I'm so different than they are," she wrote plaintively. "They never think that they aren't just perfect. Mamma really has made them hate us by being so loud in singing our praises. She is very loyal to you."[49] She hoped Linus would be home earlier than he had planned, in order to spring her from the family trap. "You'll laugh when you think how I wanted to come here sooner. You know I didn't really though."[50]

Motherhood weighed heavily on Ava Helen when Linus was away. She found little Linus puzzling and unpredictable. As a four-year-old, he was sometimes adorable, sometimes naughty, and always a force she felt needed to be reined in. "Linus [Jr.] and I sleep together, but in a big wide bed and I never touch him. He is always so surprised in the morning and chuckles." The aunts and grandmother were making a "fuss" over Linus; his behavior deteriorated, by her standards, and she had to be "very strict."[51] She longed to be home in Pasadena. She tried to resign herself to moving to Cambridge if that was what Linus thought they should do—particularly if it meant more money.

The Harvard offer was a milestone in Linus's reckoning with his changing place in the world of academic science. Ambivalent even before he arrived, he was frank with his Harvard hosts about his reservations, to the point that they asked him if he had another recommendation for the job. At the same time, he admired Harvard's growth and stability. He imagined himself just a cog in Harvard's three-hundred-year-old machine, with little fear of having to spend his time in administration. (Though he reported these as positive inducements, one may doubt, given his priorities at Caltech in those years, that he really wanted to be an obscure worker in the scientific vineyards.)

Linus was awestruck to find himself at the center of a dinner party with a group of notable scientists, most of whom were members of the National Academy. The food, starting with caviar, was excellent, the tablecloth lace. The numerous courses culminated in coffee and tobacco and good conversation. He learned that, if he took the post, his suite would include a large office and a private lab, as well as an assistant's room. At the moment he most seriously considered moving to Cambridge, he held out the vision to Ava Helen of hiring a maid and a "nurse girl" so that Ava Helen could work with him in his private laboratory. He regaled her with promises of concerts and lectures and the art gallery. "It is almost European in many ways."[52] But in the end, he decided, if he could not have the job at the rank of full professor he would not come. For a man barely four years out of graduate school, it was a breathtaking ambition, and it may well have been a way to deflect the Harvard offer by concluding that it just wasn't good enough. They would stay in Pasadena.

The Paulings took another major trip to Europe from May through September 1930. This time they took five-year-old Linus. For the older Linus, it was a richly rewarding trip, though it began with a disappointing month

Left: Baby Peter, Ava Helen, Linus, Jr., and Linus Pauling in front of their Arden Street home in Pasadena, 1931. Right: Linus, Jr., holding Peter on his shoulders, 1931.

in Manchester, England. There is no record of Ava Helen's experiences or responses. Traveling with a five-year-old precluded many activities the Paulings had enjoyed during the trip three years before. After Manchester, where Linus tried in vain to get W. L. Bragg (who had won the Nobel Prize in Physics in 1915) to pay attention to his questions or ideas, the family returned to Sommerfeld's Institute in Munich—their happy old haunt. Linus had time to work on the quantum mechanics of the chemical bond. More gratifying in the short run was Hermann Mark's agreeing to let him use the plan for an electron diffraction apparatus that could determine the structures of gas molecules.[53]

Meanwhile, Ava Helen was managing the first trimester of pregnancy with their second child. Peter Jeffress was born in Pasadena on February 10, 1931. At first they called the baby Jeff, but he became known as Peter all his life. During Linus's first sojourn at Berkeley after Peter's birth, Ava Helen's mother came to stay with the young family. Ava Helen and Linus wrote back and forth almost daily, trading professional gossip and news about the baby's development. Time and distance weighed on both of them, four hundred miles apart. Ava Helen reported further trouble with Linus, Jr., and felt guilty about her treatment of the little boy with whom she butted heads.[54] The older Linus read books, went to movies and floor shows with friends, and fantasized about making love to Ava Helen. They got away for one weekend together. "Don't you think we'd better arrange to go everywhere together after this?" Linus wrote. "I can't get along without you, sweetheart—it really is true."[55] Ava Helen managed the children and the house, chatted with her mother and friends, went to bed early and complained of feeling "weary" even though she believed she wasn't doing "anything to speak of."[56]

Pregnant again a year later with Linda (whom the couple named before she was born, confident that her small size meant that she was a girl), Ava Helen endured another long separation when Linus accepted a lectureship at the Massachusetts Institute of Technology (MIT) in Cambridge in the spring of 1932, directly after his month in Berkeley. She got away for one short visit to Berkeley, leaving Linie and baby Peter with her mother and their regular babysitter. She also may have visited Linus in Cambridge, because he writes of his anguish as he watched her train pull away. But it was impractical and probably uncomfortable to travel much ("I hope … that your nice fat tummy doesn't bother you too much"), so she waited in Pasadena for Linus's return. He wrote of his sexual longing for her and enumerated the glories of her body, revisiting the eroticism of their courtship letters.[57] "We are always going to have lots of fun, and travel places together, and see new things & meet new people, & each night I'll give you an uz and then hold you close." But for the moment she had to settle for dense descriptions of his travels.

Linus wrote to her of traveling down the Boston-New York corridor to Princeton and Yale, and finally New York. A colleague took him through the East Side tenement district, bustling with Jews ("mainly foreign") selling food and clothing. As Linus rode the train west across country he bombarded Ava Helen with telegrams full of private but hardly indecipherable sexual promises, including one to bring on labor through "unwonted activity." He arrived in Pasadena May 30; Linda was born May 31. The parents may have been amused by the newspaper's conviction that the family name was Paulino. Perhaps it brought back memories of their Grand Tour.

At least once in the 1930s Ava Helen left the children with Linus, when her mother fell ill in 1935. Linus had someone watching the children in the daytime, but came home to chaos in the evenings. He seems to have managed his children with a kind of benign amusement and sympathy, eating dinner with them, reading to them, even allowing them to take turns sleeping in the parental bed with him (the "Itzies" on one night, and young

Ava Helen with Linus, Jr., Linda, and Peter, 1934.

Linus on another).[58] This time with their father was highly unusual; he was generally at work or on the road, and when the family was together, Ava Helen was virtually always there.

Thus as Linus achieved his scientific breakthroughs on the nature of the chemical bond between 1930 and 1935, Ava Helen bore two children and entered a new phase of her marriage and her life. For the next ten years, she coordinated the household. This work was particularly hard when Linus was away, even though at home in Pasadena he spent relatively few hours with the family. Now she had not only active little Linus but also two babies, Peter and Linda, just a year apart. Financially, life became easier, as Linus fulfilled his ambition and became full professor at CIT in 1931 at the age of thirty. Another offer had come in from MIT, but Caltech moved swiftly to keep their young star. Pauling published his first two papers on the chemical bond in April and July of that year. In September he won the American Chemical Society's Langmuir Prize for a promising young chemist. Research funds and lecture honoraria padded the family budget, even after the 10 percent pay cut.

Excited by the intersection of quantum physics and chemistry in the late 1920s, and tackling the dilemma of the chemical bond by those lights in the early 1930s, by the later 1930s Pauling had moved to the interface between chemistry and biology. Pauling became a founder of what became known as molecular biology, as he followed up on the fascinating problems of immunology and the interactions of antibodies and antigens. When A. A. Noyes died in 1936, Pauling's colleagues suggested reluctantly that he be named acting chair of the chemistry division. Already there were hints of unrest, fears that Pauling would steer the division his own way and ignore the other scientists' priorities. Pauling turned down the first offer from Millikan, holding out not only for a higher salary, but also for a restructuring of the position that would indeed allow him to shape the division. He got both in 1938.

By then he and Ava Helen were the parents of four: Edward Crellin had been born five years after Linda, in 1937. Tellingly, Crellin, who was always called by his middle name, was named after the man who around that time gave Caltech what became known as the Edward Crellin Laboratory; Linus was a key player in that interaction.[59] With Linus's raise and promotion, the Paulings could afford to design and build their own house, out in the Pasadena hills on the new Fairpoint Street. There they lived, raised their children, and entertained colleagues and graduate students until Pauling left CIT in 1963.

The wide age range among the Pauling children ensured that they would later offer at least three different narratives of family life. Linus, Jr., was nearly out of the house when Crellin started school. As the oldest child, Linus remembers having to wear his Scout pants after he split the knee rather than buy a new pair. Despite having his parents to himself for five years, he has no fond and jealous memories of hoarding their love and attention. Instead he recalls a somewhat isolated boyhood, reading, wandering Pasadena by himself, and competing academically with more wealthy classmates at Polytechnic, the private school where the Paulings sent their children.[60] Caltech professors automatically received half-scholarships for their children, but the tuition was still a stretch for the family. When the Paulings moved from Arden Road to Fairpoint Street, in the hills over Pasadena, young Linus's blossoming social life became more difficult as he had to beg a ride or borrow a car from his parents. The younger children by contrast experienced Fairpoint Street as a move to the country. They kept chickens, played in the rocky hills, and swam in the pool.

The Paulings built family traditions. Up through Christmas Eve, while other households strung lights and set up trees, the Pauling home showed few signs of the holiday. Then, after the children went to bed with their ears full of Moore's "The Night Before Christmas," Ava Helen and Linus dashed around, putting up a tree, hanging swag, and wrapping presents. It was a practice that makes any parent gasp with disbelief. Since young Linus was so much older than his siblings, his father drafted him by the age of seven as a foot soldier in the Christmas Eve campaign. They would raid the Christmas tree lots in Pasadena after all the attendants had left for their own firesides, and choose the very best remaining tree, rope it onto the car, and head home. Linus, Jr., took the tradition seriously, as did the other children. In 1946, as a sophomore at Pomona, he captured the twenty-foot dormitory Christmas tree as it was about to be discarded, lashed it to the fender of the 1932 Ford, and brought it home triumphantly as the largest, most glorious tree ever in the Pauling living room. Mistletoe was the exception to the "no swag before Christmas" rule. The family made an outing of gathering mistletoe from the sycamore trees along the highway, cutting it, bundling it, hanging it from the rafters, and kissing each other and visiting graduate students under its pagan shelter.[61]

In June for a number of years, the family rented a house at the beach at Corona del Mar. There were also primitive camping trips into the Painted Canyon near the Salton Sea, times of family closeness when the older Linus had no other distractions. Ava Helen pulled together food, water, and bedding for the week, with Linus, Jr., helping as he got old enough. Sometimes they inveigled a visiting professor into the adventure, convinced they were offering him an experiential treasure.

Mealtimes were also family times. Ava Helen loved to cook and she was quite skilled at it. Her "Pauling omelettes," which Linus, Jr., accedes should have been called Miller omelets, were a "Yorkshire-pudding like concoction

The Paulings' house on Fairpoint Street, Pasadena.

Linda with her chickens, Peter in the wheelbarrow, at the Fairpoint Street house.

served with sugar and milk." Linus's Sunday morning contribution was waffles, which he made with "running criticism" from Ava Helen.[62] Particularly after Linus became division chair in 1938, she hosted Caltech functions. Teenager Linus, Jr., would be drafted to grind ingredients and do other muscle tasks. These were times of closeness between the two. There was dancing at the parties as well; both Paulings loved to dance and they passed on their pleasure to their children. Linus, Jr., was enrolled in a local cotillion to learn ballroom steps. Later, when folk dancing became popular, both the older Paulings and Linus, Jr., learned the dances. In 1950 Ava Helen broke her wrist when she tripped and fell during a folk dance party at the Fairpoint Street house.

Along with the new salary and the new house in 1938 came a new car, a Zephyr, to replace the family Ford. That '32 workhorse became first Linus, Jr.'s and then Peter's dating car. The boys would run the car up and down the long driveway when their parents were away.

Public and private crises

Twin crises, one private and one universal, changed the Paulings' lives in 1940. Ava Helen had always been more attuned to public affairs than Linus. But in the late 1930s the world's scientific communities hummed with alarm at events in Germany: the firing of Jewish academics and hints of expanding persecution. Deep in his science, busy all the time, Linus became aware of the European crisis through the fates of his international colleagues. Jewish academics were fired. There were hints of expanding persecution. As chairman, Pauling received pleas from vulnerable European scientists and their American sponsors to find places at CIT.[63] He cancelled his family's travel plans to travel to Europe in the summer of 1939. When Hitler invaded Poland on September 1, 1939, Pauling wrote to extend hope and comfort to his British friends and colleagues. Of course, even then he and many others underestimated the trials ahead. "I trust that now that the long-feared war is upon us you will find the actuality to be not so bad as the anticipation," he wrote to Leslie Sutton, a friend and colleague at Oxford. But he also offered aid in bringing Sutton's wife and children to the United States if that proved necessary.[64]

In 1940 American activists pursued divergent purposes, some lobbying to reinforce American isolationism, and some seeking ways to ally with the European democracies to oppose fascism. Both camps approached Pauling, who saw only one choice. The year before he had been deeply influenced by John Desmond Bernal's *Social Function of Science*, arguing that scientists must embrace their role in creating change for the public good, rather than acting as tools of an industrial order. Bernal's book helped change Pauling's thinking about his own social responsibility. But he disagreed with the neutrality stance of Bernal's followers in England and America.[65] Never a philosophical pacifist, in May 1940 he refused to sign a peace petition circulated by Arthur Compton of the University of Chicago: "I am a supporter of peace … On the other hand, the resolution carries the implication of nonresistance to the

Above: Ava Helen and Linus in Madison, Wisconsin, July 1939.
Right: Ava Helen, August 1939.

brutal attack by Germany on the principles of the freedom and security of the individual, including in particular the scientist who is devoted to the pursuit of truth. I can not subscribe to such a policy of nonresistance."[66]

Ava Helen and Linus together joined the Union Now movement, which called for the English-speaking democracies to merge in opposition to the rise of fascist regimes. Clarence Streit's book of the same name, published in 1938, went further, advocating something that looked a bit like the European Union of today. For the Paulings, Union Now offered the best response to Hitler and Mussolini, eschewing pacifism in favor of positive resistance to evil. Ava Helen volunteered with the Union Now office in Pasadena, and she began keeping a scrapbook in 1940, filling several volumes with clippings of editorials and meeting reports. In April of that year Linus gave his first non-scientific speech, in support of the Union Now movement, arguing that world government was inevitable and must be bent toward democratic rather than totalitarian ideals. By July Ava Helen had joined the Pasadena branch of the U.S. Committee for the Care of European Children, which hoped to facilitate the entry to America of refugee children from war zones.[67]

In September Linus accepted appointment to Division B of the new National Defense Research Committee, Vannevar Bush's brain child aimed at increasing scientists' involvement in defense related research, particularly weapons development. James B. Conant, who had tried to recruit Pauling to Harvard's Chemistry Department ten years before, was now president of Harvard and a defense preparedness activist. Pauling signed on to the division of bombs, fuels, gases, and chemical problems. The next month he visited Washington and made his first contribution to the war effort with a sketch for an oxygen detector to be used in submarines and planes. He returned to Pasadena feeling ill with a sore throat and a swollen neck, which he assumed would pass.

In March 1941 the Paulings traveled back east together, from bitterly cold Cambridge down to New York City, where Linus received the prestigious Nichols Medal, awarded by the New York section of the American Chemical Society. Linus's old friend Paul Emmett, now an engineering professor at Johns Hopkins, introduced him. In his acceptance speech Pauling joked about the edema that was now distorting his face to the point that his friends and colleagues remarked on it with curiosity and alarm. Just poison oak, he suggested, or a punishment for his and Ava Helen's distaste for the isolationist Senator Burton K. Wheeler.[68] But Pauling's condition was grave. Within a few days his frightened friends connected Pauling with Dr. Alfred Cohn; Cohn and his colleagues at the Rockefeller Institute for Medical Research examined Linus the next day and diagnosed him with glomerulonephritis, a fatal condition of the kidneys. They urged him to hurry back to the west coast to see Dr. Thomas Addis at Stanford University. Addis had been experimenting with dietary treatment of nephritis, and in the course of a two-week clinical stay and consultation he put Pauling on a strict low-protein diet (a treatment in direct opposition to the traditional regimen for the disorder, which had been aimed at suppressing the symptoms but turned deadly in its effects). Ava Helen became Addis's agent in Linus's recovery. Measuring, doling out, and recording Pauling's diet scrupulously for the next two years, Ava Helen insured that the routine would save her husband's life.

Addis also reinforced the Paulings' focus on the challenges of the postwar world. Linus had already corresponded with Addis on political matters before he became the San Francisco physician's patient. Twenty years older than the Paulings, Thomas Addis, Scots by birth, made his innovative medical career at Stanford from 1911 until his death in 1949. He became an advocate for Spanish refugees from the Franco regime in the 1930s, and a defender of the Soviet Union's advances in medicine. For these initiatives Addis became a target of his university's left-hunters. Even more nefarious, as a physician he supported national health care. He also made lifesaving advances in the treatment of nephritis and hemophilia.[69] In their two weeks together, Addis and Pauling worked rather like colleagues as Linus learned about the chemistry of kidney disease and the elements of his own disorder. Undoubtedly they talked politics, too, two interventionists staring into the cauldron of world events.[70]

After the initial diagnosis, Pauling stayed in bed for several months, a period of frustration and anxiety for him and the family. Ava Helen doggedly worked on developing a palatable diet of low-protein, low-salt food that would not kill her husband with culinary *ennui*. She reported regularly to Addis on Linus's progress. She had clearly been frightened. Relieved and happy, she wrote: "The gleam in the eye is better! His mental state is greatly improved too. He keeps planning text books; has written his report to the National Defense Council—Rockefeller Foundation etc. I am overjoyed to have him working and thinking of his work again just because it is the way he usually is."[71]

Linus's nephritis sharply intensified Ava Helen's day to day caretaking role in their marriage and stepped up the urgency both felt about staying together even when Linus was called away on business. Ava Helen's choice to travel with her husband rather than stay home with the children was not new, however. The Pauling adults had gone away together increasingly throughout the 1930s, as Linus's external lecture schedule became more hectic. When the Pauling parents were traveling, they left various colleagues and graduate students in charge of their sociable and rambunctious children. Crellin was only a few months old when Ava Helen joined Linus for an extended visit to Ithaca, New York, while Linus was a visiting professor at Cornell University. Lola Cook, their accustomed sitter, stayed with the children. Baby Crellin was having some feeding difficulties at the time. Ava Helen remarked in an oblique note to Linus that she loved him more than anything, "even Crellie but I love him so much that I try not to even remember he exists."[72] When Ava Helen returned to Pasadena, she reported to Linus that all the children had matured, that "the little baby" wasn't "little but a giant."[73]

By July 1941, the resilient Pauling was ready to travel again. Ava Helen enrolled the three younger children in Camp Arcadia and the couple hit the rails, this time to Chicago, Milwaukee, and northern Michigan, where they vacationed on Elk Lake with friends, cooking over a wood stove and lighting kerosene lamps in the evening. She continued to monitor every meal and report back to Addis. She also sent notes to the children. "Our dear Daddy continues to feel better and I am very encouraged," she wrote to them. "Are you all having a good time[?] You haven't spent all of your time writing to the Mamma and Daddy," she teased them.[74] Little Crellin was only four when he was sent to camp that summer.

Parenting decisions and dilemmas

Not surprisingly, Crellin learned early to ask for what he wanted and to dodge his siblings' bullying. "Please let me get right to the point," he wrote to his mother at the age of twelve, when his parents were away. "Tonight I was looking at an old *New Yorker* in the passpantry. It was 6:45. I had just finished taking the radiator off the roadster so Linda could get it fixed without the labor charge of taking it off. She snatched the *New Yorker* right out of my hands. When I tried to get it back, she threw me out of the house. I went in the other door and got it. ... She tried to get it back, but I started screaming. ... I have been armed with my scout knife ever since."[75]

In much of her writing about the children, Ava Helen expressed her ambivalence about motherhood. In a cluster of letters when Linus was at Cornell in 1937, Ava Helen revealed her heart and mind regarding the children. She loved them, but she worried about who they were becoming, and whether she and Linus were doing all they could to push them in positive directions. For these upwardly mobile denizens of academia,

The Pauling family with rabbits, 1941.

the traits that mattered were intelligence, ambition, self-direction, and independence. This was particularly true for the boys. When one of Linda's teachers suggested that their daughter let her mind wander in class, Ava Helen was less concerned.

In contrast, Ava Helen expressed much anxiety about Linus, Jr., at twelve: though clearly smart, he was "content to just get by." Apparently he had asked to play the accordion but had not accomplished much, and the parents had to return the accordion. She was startled and impressed when he held his own in a conversation about geography with a family friend, but neither she nor Linus conveyed to their eldest that excellence in history, politics, social relations, or literature was a worthy goal.[76] Peter, on the other hand, continued to be Ava Helen's golden boy. "He brings his books home and today he brought his arithmetic and did page after page. The whole book is too easy for him. It is astonishing what a good mind he has." Baby Crellin was "perfect" — no trouble at all.[77]

Ava Helen confessed at this time that she worried about her tendency to worry. She had become preoccupied with a holiday trip she had planned for when Linus returned that Christmas of 1937. So anxious that Linus would not have a good time, she lay awake several nights, and finally decided to cancel the trip. "I am angry though at another manifestation of what is wrong with me and which I don't seem able to change." This rare moment of introspection offers us some insight into how and why Ava Helen's world revolved around Linus, and perhaps into her tendency toward jealousy and possessiveness.[78] On the other hand, Linus was urging her to come back to Ithaca with him after the holidays. "Could you not get someone to do

Linus Pauling, Jr., at Flintridge School, Fall 1942.

the heavy work and leave Lola in charge of the children? I love you, girlie. I love the children, too, but I think that they can spare you for the month of January."[79]

As she watched the children grow, Ava Helen experienced some premonitions of difficulty: "Linda ... will need some managing when she is around thirteen. She'll need attention too and care."[80] She told Linus that Linda looked like an "angel" as she left for a party, and added, tellingly, "There are moments when one is happy to have children."[81] Her desire to be with Linus, and his urgent requests to her to travel with him, allowed the Pauling parents to bury their misgivings. The children's age range might have suggested that they could supervise each other, but as Peter and Linda got older, there were illicit parties and poolside gatherings. A sheet of rules left for Linda and Crellin in 1951 (when Linda was in college and Crellin barely in high school) provides a convenient inventory of the violations compiled in the previous decade. No starting the MG (that was Ava Helen's prized possession); no men or boys staying overnight; no trips outside Pasadena lasting longer than nine at night (with the exception of movies in Los Angeles!); the dog must be fed; no racing through the house; no wet or dirty feet; nobody in the parents' bedroom, and particularly no outsiders; no big parties; no alcohol. In an interview with Tom Hager years later, Linda Pauling laughingly confided that the young Paulings had made sure to break the rules systematically as soon as their parents had left.[82] Ken Hedburg, a graduate student pressed into baby-sitting service, recalls:

The Paulings lived in a wonderful large house — presently owned by Linda and her husband Barclay Kamb — which had two wings that, rumor has it, join at the tetrahedral bond angle. The Paulings had built a very nice swimming pool just below the house, a feature that made the baby-sitting task a real pleasure in the warm Pasadena summers. The children were a very lively bunch, and had a tendency (at least Linda and Peter did) to cruise through Crellin Laboratory and invite people up for swimming parties when their parents were away. There was one occasion, I believe it was during or just after such a party, when the senior Paulings came walking up the drive. I could only say, "But I thought you were in Europe!" I do not remember their response. I do remember, though, that it did not seem to matter to either Peter or Linda whether their parents were there or not. The Paulings must have been sorely tried now and then, for once Ava Helen spoke firmly through one of the windows, "Linda, can you get rid of those people, your father and I want to swim!" It was a very reasonable request: there were so many people that there was almost no room in the pool. We all left very quickly.[83]

After Peter and then Linda left for college, Crellin was the only child at home. For several years of high school he attended Chadwick, a new five-day boarding school. His letters home suggest a degree of assumed sophistication: "My woman situation is as bad as ever. The other S.O.B. likes her again, and is trying to corrupt me against her. He goes so far as to claim that she is not a virgin, but not by him. Such people should see a psychiatrist. The chances are damn near nil that he is right, and he is stupid enough to think I believe him."[84] But he did not like being sent away; he did not like feeling unwanted and in the way. With the toughness he had developed as the youngest Pauling, he lobbied his parents to let him come back to Pasadena for the last part of his senior year.[85]

The Pauling children experienced their parents' sexual attitudes and teachings in different ways. As a youth, Linus, Jr., felt limited openness between him and his parents. He remembers his father carrying the burden of sexual instruction as well as discipline. Sometimes Linus senior would sit down and reason with his children; other times he gave up and used a coat hanger, sometimes chasing the offender through the house. To the children the older Paulings seemed arbitrary, their rules bespeaking "strait-laced" attitudes: interesting considering their own active, persistent, and unconventional sexual life. Linus, Jr., remembers hiding, not confiding, his first romantic and sexual adventures during high school. He was bitter for years after being summarily denied the car on an important date night.[86]

Peter may have had similar experiences. As a child he had great energy and initiative; Ava Helen remembered wistfully years later, in more difficult times, that nobody could deflect young Peter from his projects. Like many siblings, the children could occasionally band together in solidarity against their parents' quirks. "Down here I was having a lot of fun," Linus, Jr., wrote wryly to Peter the summer the younger kids went to camp, "only now that Mom and Dad are home I am rapidly finding out all the things I didn't do and should have done, and all the things I did do and shouldn't have done."[87] For Linda and Crellin, Ava Helen was more often a confidante and source of advice and support, and they frequently wrote to her in detail of their sexual and romantic dilemmas as they came of age.

As a group, the Pauling children were bright, handsome, charismatic, active, talented, and just plain fun. Individually, each felt the burden of the Pauling legacy, and the complex family dynamics, in a different way. Ava Helen firmly believed that she and Linus had never imposed their values or preferences on any of the children, either in terms of what the children should believe or what they should become professionally. For the children—in particular the boys—it was as if their parents lived in a different world. Linus, Jr., was clearest about the message that his mother believed she was not sending. Being a research scientist was the pinnacle of professional achievement. Any other occupation was far down the status ladder. All three Pauling sons earned doctoral degrees (Linus an M.D.). Not one of them ever felt that he had met his mother's expectations.[88]

CHAPTER 3

"Let's make a rigid rule
that I go no place without you"

On a March morning in 1945, Peter dashed into the house and called his parents to come look at the garage. During the night vandals had done a thorough job. "Amricans [sic] die, but we love Japs. Japs working here!" they painted on the garage, along with a rising sun flag. "Jap" was painted on the mailbox.

The Paulings had agreed to hire one of two young Japanese-American men traveling from their internment at the Heart Mountain Relocation Center to Camp Shelby, where they would receive military training and join the 442nd Infantry Regiment, a Japanese-American unit currently fighting in the brutal Italian campaign. George Nimaki was to help Ava Helen with the gardening—something that before the war would have been normal in that Pasadena social group.

At first glance it might have seemed that the attack was also a backhanded tribute to Ava Helen's activism with the Los Angeles ACLU, which had fought the Japanese internment. But the nocturnal vandals also defaced the home of the Pasadena family that employed the other recruit. Ava Helen was angered by the sheriff's department response as well as by the original vandalism. The deputies seemed as curious about what the Paulings knew about their temporary employee as about who might have done the nasty graffiti. "[T]his was the sort of thing where anything could happen," she recorded the deputy as telling her: "that a house had been burned; even shots had been fired. I received the impression that the sheriffs were trying to intimidate me but this may be false … I pointed out that the patriot couldn't spell … but knew our name and spelled it correctly. " The Paulings told the deputies that they would continue to employ young Nimaki. Several days later they received a phone call. A boy's voice told Linus, "Get rid of that

Jap," and then hung up. Linus received even more explicit and threatening hate mail at his office, from another semiliterate "neighbor" who claimed to be part of a group that intended to burn their house, "tire" and feather his body, and cheer when some "jap" raped someone "near and dear to you."[1] Pauling had scheduled a trip to the east coast and wanted official protection for his family. It took the ACLU's high-profile intervention to secure surveillance for the time he was away.[2] Twenty-five years later Ava Helen still wondered how it was that information on their employment of the young Japanese man had spread so rapidly. A phone tap, perhaps? An informer in the Pasadena branch of the Committee for the American Way, which had been working against the Japanese internment?[3]

The garage vandalism turned out to be the first of many assaults on the Paulings—more often by government officials and journalists than by street thugs. In the first decade of the Cold War, they cut their way through a jungle of public attacks and private dilemmas that thickened as the Pauling parents moved deeper into middle age. Many couples their age would have been settling into the relative quiet of an empty nest. Instead, the Paulings continued their global travels—when their passport wasn't held up by the State Department. Linus Pauling's major career disappointment came in this decade, when he failed to be the first to discern the structure of DNA. But he served as president of the American Chemical Society in 1948, continued to lead his Caltech division with distinction, and received the Nobel Prize

Peter, Ava Helen, Linus, Crellin, and Linda, with Linus, Jr., at right, 1946.

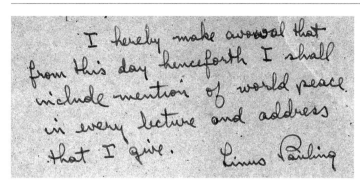

I hereby make avowal that from this day henceforth I shall include mention of world peace in every lecture and address that I give. Linus Pauling

Linus Pauling's peace pledge, June 9, 1957.

for Chemistry in 1954. He was possibly the most innovative and productive chemist in the world.

Nonetheless, conservative trustees at Caltech, enraged by Pauling's increasing role as a vocal opponent of nuclear weaponry, pressured President Lee DuBridge to get rid of their prize-winning chemist. DuBridge, inaugurated in 1946, found that his star scientist was also rapidly becoming the bad boy of the academic universe. The sniping at Pauling came from all directions during the hottest of the Cold War decades: from newly formed California loyalty committees, from the United States State Department, from Joseph McCarthy, from headlines-seeking *Meet the Press* interlocutors, from the Senate Internal Security Subcommittee, and finally, most painfully, from his colleagues at Caltech. Speaking out for disarmament threatened the dominant position of the defense establishment in United States politics and culture.

Ultimately, the Paulings did not pay the staggering price exacted of the Hollywood Ten, Robert Oppenheimer, Paul Robeson, and other notable critics of United States diplomatic and military policy. Later, Linus would say he had been "lucky": lucky not to be fired; lucky not to be jailed for contempt of Congress; lucky not to be cut off from all research funding. Linus and Ava Helen refused to walk through the minefield of American politics with their heads bowed, despite the hazards to life, career, and comfort. The more the Cold Warriors reviled them, the more determined the Paulings became. The best defense, in their eyes, was a stubborn offense. It can't have hurt to lead with a Nobel, as Ava Helen acknowledged in 1960, after Linus had won a major round against the Senate Internal Security Subcommittee. "What of the people who do not have a Nobel prize? Our Constitution and our laws should work for everyone."[4]

Further, largely because of Ava Helen's tireless networking in greater Los Angeles, in cities across the United States, and in countries around the world, the Paulings had not just allies, but friends all over the world to affirm their stand for peace, health, and international cooperation. In the First Unitarian Church of Los Angeles, under Reverend Stephen Fritchman, they had a community of like-minded citizens and wellwishers.[5] After fifteen years of intensive committee work and correspondence, in the late fifties, at the end of this decade of strife, Ava Helen stepped forward from Linus's side and began to speak on her own behalf and in her own words. "I feel such responsibility for the women with whom I have talked everywhere," she wrote in 1960. "I do really believe that women could play a great role if only they would step forward with courage."[6]

Women of Ava Helen's time and class worked on committees, joined clubs, and made sure groups and communities ran smoothly. They put meals on the table for large and small groups, kept churches and schools functioning behind the scenes, and continued their own education and entertainment on an informal level when college and career were trumped by marriage, childrearing, and housekeeping. Ava Helen's early connection with Union Now, and her wartime work with the American Civil Liberties Union against Japanese internment, laid the groundwork for committee work that went beyond school and church and university wife commitments. By 1956 Ava Helen Pauling was spending at least one day a week on local organizing with the Society of Friends, and had also joined the Pasadena chapter of the Women's International League for Peace and Freedom (WILPF). That same year her efforts for the American Civil Liberties Union were recognized with her election to the board of the Southern California branch.[7]

Ava Helen's emergence as a full-time peace organizer with an international profile grew organically from her marital partnership with Linus. Her outrage at the redbaiting attacks on her husband—attacks that ignored Pauling's message in favor of provoking a populist response to his liberal political connections—accelerated Ava Helen's involvement in women's peace groups. In addition, her reputation as a lively speaker and her sparkling presence fused with the celebrity power of her name to expand her invitations. She and Linus traveled together whenever possible. Linus was lonely and a bit aimless without Ava Helen. In 1958 he wrote to her from Quebec, where he was attending the second Pugwash Conference: "Let's make a rigid rule that I go no place without you."[8]

Ava Helen challenged Linus in 1945 to stop talking publicly about atomic weapons until he was just as convincing on war and peace as he was on the science of that horrific weaponry. Certainly Linus was not a political naïf; because of his scientific stature and his extensive wartime work, he found himself in the thick of postwar politics, trading ideas and rumors with his scientific colleagues and his contacts in Washington. "I'm going to a NDRC [National Defense Research Committee] meeting," he wrote to Ava Helen during a flying visit to the capital, "and then shall try to see the Army, the Navy (a part, at least), and Tolman."[9] Nor was Pauling alone among scientists in fretting about the global changes, many horrific, forced by the bomb. His own political bent was clear. He believed that the only way to control atomic information was not to hoard it, but to share it with the Soviet Union. "I think that Union Now with Russia is the only hope for the world."[10] This approach, widely shared in the early days after the war, would soon brand its holder a Communist sympathizer.

Linus had a gift for popularizing science, and he excelled at explaining the bomb's science to lay audiences. He found himself in demand around Los Angeles as an expert speaker on atomic weaponry. But Ava Helen, accompanying Linus to these talks, told him that while he sounded persuasive on technical matters, he came across as much less knowledgeable about the bomb's political ramifications. Linus took on her challenge, pledging to himself and to her that from then on he would devote half his time to the study of "international relations, international law, ... the peace movement, and other subjects relating to the whole question of how to abolish war from the world."[11]

Throughout the 1950s, the Paulings worked as a team, editing each other's speeches and traveling together whenever possible; their interdependence grew, particularly as their roles shifted with the children's adulthood. Linus loved to travel with Ava Helen. He had become accustomed to her constant care during the 1940s, when she was his nurse and dietician as he battled nephritis. For a time, travel for work was riddled with the pitfalls of unpredictable diet, strange beds, and potential exhaustion. Ava Helen too preferred to travel with her husband whenever possible.

Ava Helen, 1946.

Her own travels took on a jaunty cast when Linus gave her a green MG sports roadster in 1950. With the rare exception of road trips with Linus — to Stillwater, Oklahoma, for a chemists meeting, for example — Ava Helen was the only driver. She became a noteworthy figure on the road when she traveled from Pasadena to Los Angeles to attend ACLU Board meetings in the 1950s. Linus remembered Ava Helen's heroics during a trip to Cambridge, England, to visit Peter. A fellow observer at the Oxford-Cambridge boat race couldn't get his MG started after the race. "She discovered by trial that the starter was stuck, looked in his toolbox, got out a wrench, twisted a bolt in the counter-clockwise direction, put the car in gear, and rocked it back and forth until the starter was unstuck, while the young man stood there with his jaw dropped."[12]

Politically as well as automotively, Ava Helen was a quick and adaptive learner. In 1940 she had kept a scrapbook of the activities and press reports on Union Now. Ten years later she and Linus were so busy, so experienced as political agitators, and so focused on their goals, that the original scrapbook bloomed into today's Pauling archive, sprawling and inclusive, a monument to the struggles and celebrities of American science and politics in the twentieth century.

Cold War politics in the academy

Linus's decision to question the ethics of nuclear development at every opportunity commanded immediate attention. California was one of the first states to investigate the political sympathies of individual citizens. In the late 1930s Sam Yorty, a repentant New Dealer, set up a committee to investigate California's State Relief Administration and ferret out its rumored Communist employees.[13] In 1941 the Yorty Committee became the Joint Fact-Finding Committee on Un-American Activities, chaired by the politician and songwriter Jack Tenney. Not surprisingly, the film and music industries, and academic professionals at colleges and universities, became prime targets for Tenney's committee as it navigated from wartime inquests to Communist control activities.[14]

As Pauling spoke out for atomic restraint and international cooperation in the year after Hiroshima and Nagasaki, Tenney and his colleagues took note. As early as December 1946 Pauling was quoted in a newspaper squib on Tenney's investigation of a Hollywood radio station that the state senator joked should take the initials KRED. Grandstanding before the FCC, Tenney argued that the proposed Hollywood Community Radio Group's station would be led by individuals linked to Communist-front organizations.

As a member of the station's advisory council, Pauling naively advocated programs to educate the public on atomic energy. "It is my opinion, and that of every reputable atomic scientist, that a satisfactory defense against the atomic bomb cannot be developed. That type of advice could be given [on the radio shows]."[15] Along with plans to offer a "large amount" of swing and jazz music, which struck conservative FCC members as unlikely to "uplift the youth of this city," Pauling's musings doubtless cooled their sentiments toward the proposed station.

Moreover, the "Communist-front" station was linked to a southern California political lobbying group that had pulled the Paulings into its orbit in 1945, as Americans struggled with the implications of the bomb. The Hollywood Independent Citizens Committee of the Arts, Sciences and Professions, formed in 1945 in the wake of the war's dramatic end, embraced many of Hollywood's left-leaning celebrities as well as others with liberal sympathies and ties to southern California artistic and intellectual communities. The executive council was a roll call of motion picture and literary celebrities; Humphrey Bogart, Charles Boyer, George Burns, Joan Fontaine, Danny Kaye, Jerome Kern, Edwin Knopf, Jesse Lasky, Edward G. Robinson, and Artie Shaw were among those on the star-studded list. Like Pauling, they believed that their prominence conferred responsibility to speak out on contemporary issues. Executive Secretary George Pepper first contacted Pauling to consult with him about the May-Johnson Bill, which would maintain military control over atomic research and establish draconian penalties for security violations by technicians on government projects.[16] In November 1945, Pauling organized a meeting of university professors in Pasadena to explain ICCASP's objectives.[17] "Now is the time when scientists need to be citizens, to work for the good of the Nation and the world in a political way as well as in a scientific way." While he admitted that it would be inappropriate for a professional organization like the American Chemical Society to dabble in political matters, he believed that the ICCASP was just like the National Association of Manufacturers in lobbying for political outcomes that served their interests: in this case, the public good.[18]

Perhaps because it was local, perhaps because Ava Helen so enjoyed the associations with artists, actors, and writers, for a year and a half Linus Pauling put a great deal more time into activities with ICCASP than with the elite Emergency Committee of Atomic Scientists, chaired by Albert Einstein. An informant recalled to Pauling biographer Thomas Hager that Ava Helen shone at one patio party, circulating among the Hollywood attendees with her signature smile.[19] Peter Pauling, then a teenager, later recalled sitting beside Katharine Hepburn at an ICCASP rally.[20] Linus served as vice chairman of the ICCASP—one of the only scientists to give time and energy to the group. After the first few meetings, and after the May-Johnson Bill was rejected by Congress in favor of civilian control of atomic research, few academics seem to have stayed with the group. The Hollywood film community faced its own rifts, particularly after the group attracted the attention of Henry Luce and *Time* Magazine, which published an alarmist article about Hollywood liberals' influence on American culture via ICCASP.[21] the HUAC hearings in 1947—the infamous hearings that produced the so-called "Hollywood Ten" (bold non-cooperators with HUAC's interrogators) and the cruel blacklist—Hollywood ICCASP was severely weakened.[22] Nonetheless, a core membership persisted into the early 1950s, while Pauling and others moved on.[23]

For Ava Helen and Linus Pauling, human health and safety trumped abstract political allegiances and fears about retaliation for imputed Communist sympathies. They saw the loyalty probes as nonsense at best, vicious grandstanding at worst. Like many Americans often described as liberals, they rejected the idea that their right to speak out against clear and present dangers should be abridged by loyalty tests at home in the United States. Pauling aimed a rhetorical cannon at the Communist hunters in an ICCASP meeting in January 1946. Highlighting the Tenney Committee's bullying of the UCLA faculty, he stated: "We cannot permit this treatment of our great state University. We know that the members of the Faculty of the University are thoughtful, able, patriotic men and women, working for the welfare of the people of the Nation and the world, without regard to race, creed, or color."[24]

Though Pauling's affiliation with a private university offered a shield from the state's intrusions on public higher education, he asserted that the state universities must have just as much right to academic freedom as Harvard and Oxford. Flaunting his disgust at the committee's tactics, he suggested that all attacks on academic freedom were staged by "the selfish, the overly ambitious, the misguided, the unscrupulous, who seek to oppress the great body of mankind in order that they themselves may profit."[25] No wonder the Tenney Committee joined forces with some of the Caltech trustees to make things uncomfortable for Professor Pauling, who persisted in raising an alarm not only about atomic policy, but also about those who would abridge his free speech. Interestingly, though, they did not interrogate Pauling until 1950;[26] meanwhile, his scientific career entered overdrive. The publication of *General Chemistry* in 1947; the Presidential Medal for Merit for his scientific war work; the Eastman Professorship at

Oxford in 1948; the presidency of the American Chemical Society in 1949 — all lay ahead as he thundered against the Tenney Committee and other loyalty interrogators in 1946 and 1947.

For many reasons, including their willingness to speak out on national atomic policy as if their expertise gave them special insight, academics were prime targets for state and federal loyalty panels. Naïve, idealistic, outspoken, making their living from exploring competing and controversial ideas, professors and graduate students proved easy to pry away from weak institutional supports and defenses. In some cases those institutions were the academics' worst enemies. The Regents of the University of California system chose to stay a step ahead of the Tenney Committee by initiating a loyalty oath for UC system teachers in the spring of 1949. There was no prior consultation with faculty leadership. The oath was slipped into every instructor's contract for the following academic year.[27] Besides wishing to bar Communists and Communist-influenced academics from employment in the university system, the regents may have noticed the loyalty oath's useful precedent in removing faculty employment from faculty control.[28] The University of Washington had beaten California to the punch, and the regents may also have felt state legislators breathing down their necks. Thirty-one members of UC faculties were fired for refusing to sign the loyalty oath. Though virtually all of them found academic employment in other states, distinguished McCarthy-era historian Ellen Schrecker argues that, contrary to some later claims, the faculty's capitulation did lasting damage to morale and collegial trust.[29] In the following academic year, the Levering oath, more rigorous than the original 1949 loyalty oath, found only one diehard opponent in the UC system and seven stubborn holdouts at San Francisco State College. All eight were fired and their dismissals were upheld by the California Supreme Court.[30]

Pauling was appalled by this escalation of war on professors' legal and contractual right to free speech. In 1949 he defended the principle and prerogatives of academic tenure in a formal debate with a Claremont professor at a Los Angeles town hall meeting. "A politician may well place expediency above principles, but the Nation must not, or the Universities, or we are lost. I am speaking today because of my firm conviction that we are in danger not of communism but of losing our basic principles."[31]

Oxford and early interrogations

The Paulings spent the first half of 1948 at Oxford, where Linus was appointed George Eastman Professor at Balliol College. That year he followed up his honorary Cambridge doctorate with honorary degrees from Oxford and the University of London. For all the Paulings—except for Linus, Jr., who had just married Anita Oser and was headed to Harvard Medical School—England was a great and happy adventure. Linus was a star of science; Ava Helen was in her element, making friends easily and getting her fill of British music, theater, and art. Linda fit right into her girls' school, Crellin amazed his family with his performance in the classics, and Peter found his life's home. The Paulings celebrated their twenty-fifth wedding

Portrait of Ava Helen and Linus Pauling, 1951. Peter Pan Photo.

anniversary at Balliol. From across the Atlantic, Linus, Jr., and Anita sent their parents a check to buy a new Hotpoint dishwasher—presumably back home in Pasadena rather than in their rented flat in England. On their way home from Oxford to California, the family staged a typical Pauling grand tour, stopping in Amsterdam, Switzerland, Paris, Washington, D.C., St. Louis, and Portland, Oregon.

Ultimately, rather than have his point obscured by escalating concern about his own beliefs, he accepted the strategy of writing a letter to Caltech President Lee DuBridge repudiating any Communist affiliation in the context of asserting his stance on academic freedom. "I am not a Communist. I have never been a Communist. I have never been involved with the Communist Party. I am a Rooseveltian Democrat. I believe that it is of the greatest importance that citizens take political action, in order that our Nation not deteriorate." The public university loyalty oath had done "far more harm than good," requiring people of conscience to refuse to sign on principle, while giving true Communists not a moment's hesitation in lying to further their aims. In an outcome repeated in various ways over the next decade, the committee dismissed Pauling after the members read his letter to DuBridge. "Are the statements in this letter true?" the committee asked Pauling. "Yes, of course," Pauling remembered answering. "I wouldn't write statements that aren't true."[33]

Unlike many Americans, the Paulings risked their comfort to continue speaking out. For Linus Pauling, the price was potentially high, since the main weapon the U.S. government mustered against him was abridging his right to travel abroad. A scientist's right to confer with his international colleagues is vital to his disciplinary standing and indeed his ability to carry out his work. Pauling's international standing was second to none in his field. Through all the turmoil over Pauling's politics, he had continued his path-breaking scientific work. In September 1951, the World Chemical Conclave in New York offered Pauling a stage from which to explain his alpha helix theory and its vast implications. Mainstream media covered the event and Pauling's fame was given another boost, this time for his contributions to science, rather than his suspect associations.[34] Nonetheless, Pauling had a bad shock when—by mistake—Caltech put Pauling up for federal security clearance, and he was denied on the basis of his Communist associations. After it became clear that, at the peak of his career, his science would be jeopardized by these continued baseless accusations, he and Ava Helen agreed that he would pull back. He resigned from a number of organizations that had come under scrutiny.[35] For the first time, he blinked.

Ironically, Pauling's withdrawal from the front lines of political conflict had no apparent effect on his official status. That horse had left the barn. In 1952 he was scheduled to fly to London as the first speaker at a Royal Society symposium on the alpha helix. Ava Helen would accompany him. In February he received a letter from the Passport Division denying his application to renew his passport as "not in the best interests of the United States." He had already known that there could be trouble with the division, headed by Ruth Shipley, an anti-Communist bulldog and a stickler on international travel regulations, which had been expanded as part of the Internal Security Act of 1950.[36] Instead of formally refusing his application, the division's favored strategy was to "simply [delay] action," rather than go on record as taking a stand.[37] In this way the Paulings had already missed a much-anticipated trip to India. By the time this decision was reversed, on Pauling's fourth try, it was too late to go to the meeting. He and Ava Helen did travel to England and France over the summer, however, in part to see Peter and Linda, and so Linus could attend several international meetings.

Parenting young adults

Like many American parents, the Paulings discovered that shepherding their children into adulthood was a bigger job than they had anticipated. An informal photograph taken in Stockholm in December 1954 captures the younger Paulings as they gathered to celebrate their father's Nobel Prize triumph. Only twenty-two-year-old Linda gazes full face at the photographer, flashing a brilliant smile at once glamorous and guileless, reminiscent of her mother's charismatic charm. Tall, handsome, teenaged

Ava Helen and Linus Pauling visiting Princeton two days after news of Linus's 1954 Nobel Prize.

Crellin stands near her, behind a couch on which lounge Linus, Jr., and Peter. The children beam: all dressed up, and all grown up. The family formed a "joyous crowd," as Ava Helen noted in a diary of that trip.[38]

By 1948 the Paulings were grandparents, with the birth to Linie and Anita of Linus Fowler Pauling; two more boys and then later two girls followed in that family. In the next decade his brothers and sister followed on his heels with their own marriages and babies. Linus, Jr., had established his independence early and efficiently; he was the child of least worry to the older Paulings in the mid-1950s. Crellin, born in 1937, was still a schoolchild at the beginning of the decade. The middle two, Peter and Linda, seemed to demand the most sorting out. While Ava Helen continued her accustomed role as the hub of family communication and planning into the 1950s, Linus took on more of a parenting role than he had when the children were young and at home. Now, with the children scattered, though held by a leash of financial dependence, he had his fullest realization of fatherhood.

After the family's sojourn in Oxford in 1948, Linda Pauling had graduated from Westridge School in Pasadena. As a high school senior she played the lead in a play at Caltech and had her first experience being surrounded by young men. She then attended Reed College in Portland, Oregon. Reed was a small liberal arts college with a serious intellectual mission. Already in the 1950s, Linda recalled later, Reed was reputed to nurture "atheism, Communism, and free love." While Pauling was being grilled by Senate subcommittees and repeatedly denied his passport in the early 1950s,

Linda, Ava Helen, Linus, and Peter aboard ship, 1948.

Linda may have been shielded from blowback by Reed's latitudinarian political culture. Reed personnel officially protested Pauling's passport denial, and Reed professors, as well as the president's office, prevailed upon her father to visit campus whenever he came through Portland. Linus Pauling gave the Reed commencement address when Linda graduated in 1954.[39] Immediately upon graduation she followed her brother Peter, just a year older, to England, where she planned to work, and where Peter had promised to look after her.

Peter was the real puzzle in the family. Part black sheep, part best hope for another research scientist who might truly collaborate with his brilliant father, Peter chose to pursue his graduate work at the famed Cavendish Laboratory in Cambridge, England. He arrived in Cambridge in the fall of 1952 and began sending home a stream of sparkling, somewhat telegraphic letters, asking for more money and detailing his intricate social life. Cold, damp England suited the volatile Peter just fine, with its parties, theater, and bookshops. He could follow in his father's scientific footsteps and still entertain himself far from parental oversight. When Linda arrived two years into Peter's stay, she fit right into his new life. To his parents he played the concerned older brother. "I think Linda is all right … She is a little batty, but not nearly as much so as I," he admitted. "A year here will do her good[;] I am as yet uncertain whether she should work or play. A year's reading would help her more than a year's English secretarial job." Peter was amused and appalled that upon Linda's arrival she promised to bring them some "good American coffee" from Paris. "Good American coffee my eye. One year is probably not enough," he huffed to his parents.[40] The middle Pauling children set up housekeeping together in a Cambridge flat. Linda worked part of the time as a mother's helper. She shopped and probably cooked for the pair.

Peter was well connected at the Cavendish Laboratory at Cambridge, friends with Jim Watson and Francis Crick, among others. In fact when Linda reached Cambridge, Peter was staying temporarily at the Crick household, and his sister's arrival prompted him to step up his search for a new flat for the two Paulings. His letters home continued to reflect patronizingly on Linda's activities. Hers offered the mirror image: Peter dependent on her not just to cook, but even to open a can of sardines and set the table for him.[41] Ultimately Ava Helen wrote to summon Linda home. Linus sent a ticket and reiterated that Linda should return home. Rather than comply, Linda cashed in the ticket, secured a position as a mother's helper with Odile Crick and stayed on.

Peter's charm and bonhomie were equal to his father's, though his mental focus was less. He did experience mood swings and was prone to reckless decisions. His intellectual interests were as wide ranging as his parents'. He was a book buyer, like his older brother Linus. His parents' hopes for him shine through the correspondence; it was not just Peter's imagination that placed the weight of family pride on his shoulders.

Yet the other children were always aware that following in his father's footsteps posed stark hazards for Peter. "I've been trying to convince [Peter]," wrote Linus, Jr., to his mother in 1956, "that he doesn't have to stay stuck in the illustrious ruts impressed into the earth by his Pop, but may branch off into any and all kinds of endeavor, but I don't know whether it will have any effect."[42] Peter floundered at Cambridge, looking for his topic. He could hardly have had better lab companions, having fallen in with Watson and Crick from his arrival. Yet he did not gallop toward the doctorate. He did serve as a vital link between the Cavendish and Pauling's lab at Caltech, and Linus's correspondence with Peter was full of technical speculation and experimentation. Ava Helen tried to maintain her closeness to Peter through letters as her concern about him escalated.

In February 1956, Linus extended a formal offer to Peter to take up a postdoctoral position in chemistry at Caltech, so that Peter could join his father's effort to discern the structure of crystalline globular proteins through x-ray crystallography.[43] But life intervened. His lover became pregnant. He and Julia married in the spring of 1956.[44]

Cambridge police allowed Linda to stay for her brother's wedding even though her visa had expired. During the winter her father had written resignedly that they hoped to catch up with her either in Pasadena or in England that spring. He also used an entire paragraph at the end of this letter to remark upon a visit to his office of Barclay Ray Kamb, a graduate student in geology who had just been offered an assistant professorship. "He has done unusually well as a graduate student," her father enthused, "otherwise he would not be offered an assistant professorship immediately upon getting his doctor's degree. He seems to me to have developed in a fine manner." [45] In fact Linus had had his eye on Kamb for a few years, commenting on his high undergraduate class standing to Peter, his lower-ranking classmate.[46] It was not just Ava Helen who pressured the children to achieve academically.

By fall Linda was home. She had suffered a respiratory infection compounded by bad diet while she was traveling in Italy, and her parents brought her back to Pasadena. Once recovered, Linda accepted work in a Caltech lab, like all the Pauling children at various times. She also started seeing the graduate student Barclay Kamb, whom her father had pushed on her so pointedly. (He even took Linda and Barclay on a long car journey to view the Paulings' new property in Big Sur.)[47]

Kamb had been Walter Barclay Ray when he enrolled at Caltech. As a boy he had taken the surname of his stepfather, Martin Ray, the notable California vintner, whose friends included Charlie Chaplin, Dashiell Hammett, and John Steinbeck.[48] Barclay Ray had entered Caltech as a sixteen-year-old freshman and enrolled in one of Pauling's chemistry classes. In a furious letter to the HUAC chair in June 1957, Martin Ray, despite his impeccable leftist associations, denounced Linus Pauling as an academic Svengali who sought out impressionable youngsters in order to school them in left-wing politics and persuade them to do his scientific work for him. "During his Freshman year," Ray wrote, "[Barclay] had taken a course in Freshman Chemistry taught by Dr. Linus Pauling, and there and then fell under his spell. With apprehension we have watched, over the years, the development of what has become a complete domination of our son by Dr. Pauling, whose followers … worship him as sort of a God who can do no wrong. It is this group of brilliant young men who do their research for him." Ray cited the close relationship of Pauling and Robert Oppenheimer as further proof of Pauling's political treachery, and demanded that HUAC haul Pauling before the committee to be "brought to his knees as an enemy of our country."

Ray's letter moved to what was probably the heart of the matter: Barclay's engagement to Linda Pauling and his estrangement from his twin brother, a scientist at Harvard, cast here in the role of the good son. He concluded this pained letter by pointing out what he took to be an indictment of Pauling's scientific methodology offered by Barclay Kamb "before his domination [by Pauling] was entirely complete." Indignantly Martin Ray reported that his son testified that the work for which Pauling had earned the 1954 Nobel Prize in Chemistry was due to a *good guess*, rather than "deduction or trial and error."[49]

Despite Martin Ray's opposition, the Pasadena wedding at the Pauling home seemed magical to some of the friends and colleagues who attended. "It was as if we were under a spell," wrote one friend, "which no one wanted to break. The atmosphere was thoughtful yet fully joyous; I feel somehow a better person for the shared experience."[50] Unlike her brothers' first marriages, Linda's marriage to Barclay Kamb lasted until Kamb's death in 2011, and the Kambs' and Paulings' lives became intertwined over the next few decades.

In 1950 Linus Pauling, Jr., turned twenty-five. He continued to pursue his credentialing as a physician while completing his obligations to the Air Force, which he had joined to satisfy his military obligation during the war. "I perhaps might better have been a writer, my brother Peter an architect," Linus, Jr., recalled in adulthood, but the family message was clear.[51] After the war he spent a couple of years at Pomona College, then entered Harvard Medical School and specialized in psychiatry.

While believing that he could never live up to family expectations, Linus, Jr., often served as the voice of reason among his much younger siblings, and sometimes as a buffer between them and their parents. He and Anita and their two-year-old, Linus Fowler, migrated from the Boston area to Honolulu, where Linus, Jr., crafted his career. Crellin spent several summers in Honolulu with the couple, and Anita became a beloved big sister or second mother to the young man. Linus, Jr.'s professional stability and Anita Oser's inheritance—she was descended from the McCormick and Rockefeller clans—allowed the couple to set up housekeeping free of regular financial appeals to the senior Paulings. In fact for a while the couple made a yearly grant of $50,000 to Pauling's CIT laboratory.[52]

Meanwhile, Peter Pauling gradually found his way professionally. He had taken a job as lecturer at University College, London, where he made himself indispensable as an expert and graduate teacher of x-ray crystallography — the field in which his father had made his first mark. At the same time he was finishing his degree (as he said tersely to Linus, Jr., "I have decided that

1959 looks better than 1960 [as a degree date] and so must work hard for a bit").[53] But there were always mysterious tensions in the marriage of Peter and Julia, and much family correspondence in the late 1950s and early 1960s is taken up with how to help, or scold, the now adult Peter.

In the summer of 1959, he had taken his wife Julia and young son Thomas to join his brother Linus, sister-in-law, and parents in Geneva. In September, pausing in Pasadena en route to their home in Hawaii, Linus, Jr., talked into the night with Ava Helen, who pressed her oldest son for his impressions of Peter and Julia during their stay in Europe. Linus, Jr., admitted that he was worried about Peter's "domestic situation."[54] Particularly sensitized to her second son's travails, but unable to figure out how to help him, Ava Helen worried that Peter had stayed in England to escape his parents' meddling, and that for the same reason, he avoided the truth about his marriage.[55] After a particularly harsh letter from father Linus to Peter about Peter's young son's apparent ill health, Peter wrote to his older brother drily, "I don't know what you told the parents but they sure are full of bright ideas."[56] A handwritten note, perhaps a draft of a letter, suggests that Linus *père* toned down his message several weeks later.[57]

Peter's wife, Julia, is a mystery in these exchanges. In the midst of this September crisis Peter wrote to his older brother that things were getting better, that he believed that Julia "genuinely does not realise very much," but when they communicated—"that is, I tell her what my view of things is," Peter admitted—"then she tried pretty hard to fit in with what I want."[58]

Despite the dramatic tone and critical issues addressed in these exchanges, the transatlantic correspondence went on virtually uninterrupted. Peter and Julia continued to search for a house so that they could leave an unsatisfactory rented flat. Though anxious about Peter's professional stasis and young Thomas's upbringing, the Pauling parents continued to subsidize their second son. In January 1960, Peter wrote somewhat uncharacteristically, "Please do not worry about me. I am feeling close to you. I shall solve my various problems." He mentioned a psychologist he wanted to consult, possibly on these personal matters.[59] He and Julia had a second child, Sarah, in February. A few months later, perhaps in a return of intimacy, Linus, Sr., wrote to ask if Peter thought it might be a worthwhile venture to coauthor a high school chemistry textbook—then took back the offer, not ostensibly because of coauthoring issues, but because Linus, Sr., realized, as he told his son, that he had a "little neurosis" about money, possibly stemming from his youth. "I have decided that the bad three months that I had just after my seventeenth birthday, when I was doing pretty hard physical work but not getting enough to eat because of lack of money still bothers me to some extent."[60] There may have been both accusation and apology in Linus's admission to his son that he himself was perhaps too concerned with money and financial security.

Ava Helen wrote Peter regularly; at one point he thanked her for her "many letters." One of these letters escaped Linus's later censorship and slipped into the archive of Peter's 1960 correspondence.[61] Unlike Linus's tone with Peter, which was generally that of an adult to a younger adult, Ava Helen wrote like a mother to a schoolboy. She responded point by point to Peter's news of family travel and a visit to Julia's parents in Nottingham. She recalled Julia's father's vegetable garden. "He seems to enjoy working with vegetables about as much as I do." She encouraged Peter to keep Thomas in school and reminisced about meeting baby Sarah, born in May 1958. "It is really uncanny how much she looks like you, especially when she laughs. I could almost believe that I was holding you again when I held her." After joking sharply that Peter was more ornery and less pretty than his baby daughter, she drilled down to her core message. "You always used to be full of ideas and always managed to get about twice as much done as anyone else in any project and it has been hard to understand these years when you seemed unable or unwilling to think or do anything." Now Peter was compared unfavorably not only to his putative future self but also to his successful past self. She speculated that Peter somehow lost his way when he felt it necessary to rebel against what he saw as his parents' "interference" in his life. Like many parents, she was unable to refrain from both questioning and defending her own parenting. "It is a pity that this is so, because I think that we have been better than the usual parent in allowing our children to select their own way and have shown too somewhat more sympathy with them."[62]

Ava Helen seems to have believed throughout her life that she was a doting mother, and in some respects it is difficult to question that self-perception. It is impossible to know what internal reflections she experienced about her four interesting, active, and gifted children, or her relationship to them throughout their lives. That Ava Helen's primary allegiance was to her marriage to Linus we have seen in her frequent travels away from home—travels that not only left her teenaged children to have a good time alone, but also left little Crellin at the mercy of his siblings and occasional caretakers. As she wrote to Peter, Ava Helen believed that she and Linus had encouraged the children by word and example to follow their own directions. But the children received, at best, a mixed message. Linus, Jr., chose medicine partly as a way to stay close to science without having to live up to his father's example or expectations, and we know that Peter's road into chemistry and X-ray crystallography, which included various scientific collaborations with his father, was studded with ruts and pitfalls. Despite Crellin's later brilliance as a university teacher of microbiology, his closest family members agree that he would have been much happier as an electrician or a pilot.[63]

Crellin

In 1950 the last child at home was Crellin. After the family returned from England in the summer of 1948, this bright boy zipped through middle school. As a thirteen-year-old ninth grader he was sent off to Chadwick School, a new venture with ancient-looking crested stationery, about forty miles away in Palos Verdes. This tiny boarding school might have suited Crellin's unusual upbringing and precocious mind, and it certainly suited his parents' work and travel priorities. But Crellin did not want to be there, and he begged to come home — a petition his parents finally accepted in the last portion of his senior year. Crellin followed his sister to Reed College after he graduated from high school in 1954. In the first term, he flirted with various majors, including philosophy and pre-medical studies. Like Peter, he chose science, settling on biology with a focus on genetics. He stuck to this plan throughout undergraduate and graduate school, working as a geneticist at Riverside and then as chair of San Francisco State University's biology department until his untimely death from cancer at age sixty.

His parents worried about Crellin's independence even as they had fostered it. "We do not want Crellin to have a car in Portland," Linus wrote to Linus, Jr., as Crellin graduated from high school. "He has spent too much of his time this year running around the countryside, and we have told him that he is not to have a car."[64] That parental resolution may have gone by the board. During his freshman fall term he wrote to his parents about skipping "campus day" at Reed in order to drive with some friends out Columbia Gorge to hike just above Bonneville.[65] Ava Helen expressed concern about his missing campus day during his first term, and he reassured her that nobody would notice.

Trading letters with Ava Helen to arrange the smallest details of passport, plane reservations, and the right clothes for the occasion (a specially made midnight blue tux and a Harris tweed suit), Crellin joined the rest of his family in Sweden to witness his father's Nobel Prize ceremony. Like Linda at Reed a few years before, he was able to enjoy his parents' stature without apparent penalty. In 1955 he wrote to his mother to pass on an invitation to his father to address a "liberal" group he had joined ("However, anarchists

Crellin standing on the deck of the Queen Mary during his father's Oxford professorship, 1948.

and other such beings are not permitted to join, people who advocate violent overthrow of the government, etc.").[66]

Before he was twenty, Crellin followed his brother Peter to the altar. In the winter of 1956, he wrote to his mother about Monte, to whom he found himself getting very close—"not immoral, but you know what I mean. Probably too close." Monte was talking marriage and asking what Crellin thought about the religious education of children. Though Crellin professed to be "pretty fond of her," this college sophomore may ultimately have felt he was in too deep. They stopped seeing each other. Soon Crellin had a new girlfriend, Lucy Mills. "She approaches my ideal quite nicely," he wrote to his mother in May 1956. "However, don't get upset … as far as there being a repeat of Peter's fiasco, I feel strongly that there will be little chance of that. For, even though my brothers have tried to educate me otherwise, I have certain feelings in regards to the morallity [sic] of premarital intercourse, to such an extent that I hope, at any rate, that I can control myself. Sometime I would like to talk with you about my ideas on life," he concluded wistfully, "but I guess that I must wait a while."[67]

When he took a trip with Lucy, Ava Helen had admonished him for traveling alone with a girl. She apparently also implied that Lucy's parents were remiss in letting their daughter join such an adventure. "I feel that you ought to apologize to me for the things that you said about Lucy and her family that are so obviously untrue," Crellin huffed back. "That letter was the most slanderous, biased, untrue epistle that I have read in a good long time … Lucy's family are good, respectable people, who certainly do care about their daughters; in fact, it seems to me that you ought to be flattered that they place such faith and trust in your son to allow her to travel with him."[68]

Lucy's parents and grandmother kindly stepped forward in November 1956 when the youngsters found themselves pregnant, despite Crellin's pledge to Ava Helen. They quickly made up invitations for an evening wedding in Oswego, just outside Portland, hosted by Alden and Patsy Mills. "The wedding was as nice as I could have asked for if we had planned for ten years, instead of a bare week, except for one thing," he wrote to Ava Helen, Linus, and his sister Linda: "that you were not there. I am very happy now. I certainly hope that you will take Lucy into the family, and love her as I do, and above all, do not blame her for what has happened."[69] Since they were not away from Pasadena at the time, it is not clear why Ava Helen and Linus did not attend the wedding. On the day before Thanksgiving, perhaps they could not cancel established plans. Or perhaps they were angry or hurt, and decided to forgo the wedding. Patsy Mills, Lucy's mother, wrote a gracious, almost pleading note to the Pauling parents several weeks later. "May time and your love for Crellin bring you to feel that he has made a fortunate, albeit early, choice in our beloved Lucy."[70] Both Crellin and Lucy continued their programs at Reed. Cheryl was born the following July, and two more children followed, Kirstin a year later and Edward Crellin, Jr., in 1961.

World travel, global connections

Between 1954 and 1961 the Paulings traveled the world. The Paulings' passport problems finally receded with the retirement of Ruth B. Shipley, the sternly anti-Communist Passport Division head. Any damage Linus's reputation may have sustained in the United States seemed contained to conservative circles and the paranoid government agencies of the Cold War. His stature as a citizen of the world had been enhanced by the Nobel Prize as well as by his very outspokenness on the threats posed by nuclear testing and the prospect of nuclear war.[71]

The Paulings also organized two massive petition drives against nuclear testing, presenting long lists of signers to first Eisenhower and then Kennedy, and to the United Nations. They launched the first campaign in May 1957; it culminated in the "Appeal by American Scientists to the Governments and People of the World," presented to Dag Hammarskjöld on January 15, 1958. Pauling's scientist allies, among them Barry Commoner and Edward Condon, helped hatch the plan to demonstrate that fears about nuclear fallout were not isolated to a few kooks but were widespread among scientists. "Each nuclear bomb test spreads an added burden of radioactive elements over every part of the world. Each added amount of radiation causes damage to the health of human beings all over the world and causes damage to the pool of human germ plasm such as to lead to an increase in the number

The Paulings working on their first petition drive, 1957.

of seriously defective children that will be born in future generations," the petition stated.[72] The petition spoke of the scientists' concern as human beings and their feeling of responsibility as scientists to urge an end to nuclear testing as the first step to abolishing nuclear weaponry.

Ava Helen joined Linus, and with the help of several assistants they stuffed envelopes and mailed the petitions from their Pasadena home to laboratories and academic departments around the country. Within a few weeks the Paulings had two thousand signatures, which they released immediately to President Eisenhower—to his consternation—and the United Nations. The petition drive continued into the winter of 1958, as Pauling found his scientific nemesis in the nuclear physicist Edward Teller's frightening vision of a "clean bomb" and the necessity of arming against the Soviets' promise to "bury" the United States.[73] The public seemed fickle, both influenced by and reflected in mainstream media's swings between supporting Pauling's position against nuclear testing and implying that he was an extremist and an alarmist. People were soothed by Teller's calming vision of peaceful uses of atomic energy, and then frightened again by a wave of nuclear testing and its attendant fallout in 1957.[74]

Pauling did not limit his political activity to the petition drive. He seeded the drive with a statement on nuclear testing published by the New York *Herald Tribune* on May 4, 1957. He took pains in his public speaking and writing to lay out the biological and ecological consequences of nuclear fallout. "The rays of high-energy radiation are like little bullets that shoot through the body, damaging some molecules, breaking them in two, tearing away some atoms." His message was clear and urgent: there was no safe amount of radiation. If a person were not killed by radiation, she and her subsequent children could be damaged irreparably. Cancer and birth defects were the most obvious forms of time-bomb-like radiation destruction.

Pauling was disgusted by the irrationality of world leaders who continued to pump huge sums of money into these end-game weapons. In fact, he asserted, bombs were cheap. By 1958 the United States and the Soviet Union had stockpiled enough to destroy the entire world, but both nations continued to produce the weaponry, courting both moral and financial bankruptcy. He was also appalled by arguments based on acceptable risk: that the damage produced by nuclear tests was "negligible." To favorably compare the damage done by nuclear tests to the forty thousand annual deaths through auto accidents, or the risk of drowning while swimming in the sea, implied that any death whatsoever in the cause of nuclear testing was acceptable. Moreover, voluntary risk was quite different from risk over which a person had no control.[75]

During the first petition drive, the Paulings took an extended trip to Europe, as usual for several purposes. Linus attended scientific meetings in Paris and in Ljubljana, and the couple visited the Soviet Union for the first time. Along the way Linus made connections with potential signatories to their petition. Hosted by the women's program of the Ljubljana scientific congress—a sign of the times, of course, built on the correct assumption that the scientists were men—Ava Helen visited markets and galleries. She loved the size and variety of the mushrooms, a local specialty in Ljubljana. She also lunched and chatted with the international scientists she and Linus had met over the years.[76]

In Russia, Ava Helen watched for signs of oppression and unhappiness among the people. During a youth festival she watched the police control the crowds lined up along the street for a parade. The crowds "talked back and were not in the least submissive." The unarmed police gradually pushed the people back from the street's edge. Though the people were dressed simply in "drab" colors, she noted the dancing and music everywhere, the people's friendliness to visitors, and the delicious food. They attended the Bolshoi three times, and Ava Helen visited the Trityakov Gallery and the Kremlin. She received flowers at all the laboratories they visited. She and

Linus took a side trip to Leningrad and then returned to Moscow; from there they traveled to Vienna, Munich, and Oslo, not returning to the United States until the beginning of September.

Their trip to Europe in 1957 seeded the Paulings' peace work for the next five years. The visit to Yugoslavia and the Soviet Union, both outside the NATO block, though not aligned with each other, gave the Paulings street-level connections to life beyond the fictive "Iron Curtain." Their political line continued to reflect their staunch refusal to recognize that efforts for peace must stop at the Soviet border, because Communists could not be trusted. But now they had multiplied their human contacts and bolstered their conviction that, to be effective, the peace movement must embrace all people, including those in the Soviet bloc.[77]

Two years later Ava Helen wrote out these beliefs in a report on the Paulings' latest international trip, this time to Australia to participate in the Australian and New Zealand Congress for International Cooperation and Disarmament and Festival of the Arts. The unwieldy title reflected the organizers' hope to create an inclusive gathering that would bring politicians, scientists, professionals, labor interests, peace activists, and artists together to make a statement against nuclear weaponry. Thrilled to attract J. B. Priestley, the English playwright and antinuclear activist, the organizers were dismayed when at the airport he declared he would leave if "communists" dominated the proceedings. In a post-conference report, Ava Helen wrote that, in her talks afterward, she said that she "saw no use whatsoever in holding a conference to discuss peace unless communists were present; we have communists in this world and it is with them that we must come to some agreement about the world in general."[78]

Ava Helen and Linus were both invited to the Australian conference, Linus as a scientist activist and Ava Helen as a representative of U.S. women's peace groups (she had just started serving on the WILPF board). This trip represented Ava Helen's true emergence as an international figure with a following and

Linus and Ava Helen standing outside Dr. Schweitzer's mission hospital in Lambaréné, 1959.

agenda of her own. The 1959 Australian trip was part of an exhausting year of global travel, which coincided with their extended intervention in Peter's complicated life; they traveled to Europe, Africa, Japan, Australia, and New Zealand. The African trip was a longed-for visit to Albert Schweitzer's clinic in Lambaréné, French Equatorial Africa (now the Republic of Gabon). Pauling and Schweitzer had been corresponding for a couple of years, since Pauling persuaded Schweitzer to sign his "Appeal" in 1957. On his invitation, the Paulings flew into Duala, then took flights to Bitan, Libreville, and finally Lambaréné.

Schweitzer had been practicing medicine with the Africans since 1913. A highly educated polymath, with expertise in philosophy and music, he pursued medicine in order to make himself useful as a missionary to Africa, a religiously based quest. Forty years later, a Nobel laureate and aging world celebrity, he continued his "jungle doctor" work in the same international outpost in equatorial Africa. The Paulings were inspired and shaken by their visit. In the politics of international peace, they found complete agreement with Schweitzer. The racial arrangements and attitudes in the hospital compound troubled them a bit. While the entire mission was intended to serve the Africans and follow a theology and ethics of "reverence for life," there seemed to be a clear separation between the Europeans and the Africans. On the other hand, the doctors and nurses worked their hearts out, and were sleepy in the evenings. The work took a toll over time. Ava Helen noted that the British chief medical officer, Frank Catchpool, was about their own Linie's age but looked ten years older: "His hair already quite grey and his face, which is beautiful in a classic way, quite lined with the care and anxiety which he feels for these patients. What inner compulsion moves him!"[79]

As in Italy thirty years before, Ava Helen was drawn to the beauties of the place and its essential strangeness to her, even as she held back a bit. "It is beautiful here, and chaotic—goats, chickens, ducks, pigeons everywhere." She was riveted by the "beautifully tended" garden's variety of vegetables as well as the animals in the compound. "Eggplant, beans, peppers, tomatoes, carrots, beets, lettuce, cabbage, Chinese cabbage, turnips, kohlrabi. Caged pelican, antelope, tame parrots, toucans, wild pigs, sheep looking about like goats except tails hang down, goats' stick up." She illustrated with childlike drawings—not a skill she had cultivated. The place was noisy and it took a few days to begin to understand the sounds and the rhythm of day and night. "We had a restless night with babies crying and baby kids too. It is hard to tell which sometimes." She noted that the nurses often took animal babies, and human babies, into their rooms overnight to calm or nurse them. "This makes sleep rather uncertain as the walls are quite thin." Ava Helen did not specify whether it was the nurses' sleep or her own that was compromised.

The Paulings were struck by Schweitzer's self-sacrifice and the international staff's dedication. They reveled in the strange beauty of the place. People came in and out: press, photographers, fellow philanthropists, and missionary types. They learned that one photographer on site was Olga Detering, the owner of the Shell corporation. "She is a sallow-skinned, tall Englishwoman. Not much oomph, I think, but much, much money!!"

There were Protestant services every day, and Bible reading by Schweitzer in the evening. Though Ava Helen wrote down the hymns that were sung, and admired the harmonies, she would not have resonated with the religious inspiration of Schweitzer's medical outreach work. The Paulings had brought olives from Yakima, Washington, to share with the Lambaréné staff. The staff showered them with gifts on their departure, after a longer visit than most Westerners managed. Ava Helen resolved to send nuts back to the compound; she saw how the staff loved the roasted peanuts they had one night and she feared they risked a protein deficiency in their diet.

From Africa the Paulings flew to Stockholm, Sweden, for WILPF's fourteenth International Congress. As a United States board member, Ava Helen would be intensely involved with planning the next international meeting three years later in the San Francisco area. In this instance, Linus was invited to deliver the opening address, and titled his talk "Our Choice: World Peace or Nuclear Annihilation." His notes are terse, comprising an opening statement and then numbers, to remind himself and his audience of the deadly power of nuclear weapons and the absurd overbuilding of nuclear stockpiles—absurd both in human terms and for the economies of the world. He created a list of priorities: to halt bomb tests, then to impede accidental outbreaks of nuclear war, and finally to cut down the armaments themselves. He appealed to reason by quoting his heroes of present and past: C. Wright Mills and Benjamin Franklin. He ended his speech with the declaration that he was happy to live in this "unique epoch."[80]

From Stockholm the Paulings traveled to Copenhagen and then on to Tokyo for the annual commemoration of the dropping of the atomic bomb. This was not their first visit to Japan. In 1954 they had spent two weeks in the country on a largely academic visit, with plenty of time for sightseeing and shopping. They visited Osaka, Kyoto, and Tokyo. In 1959 the purpose of the visit was very different; they attended the Fifth World Conference Against Atomic and Hydrogen Bombs. Both Paulings took active parts in the proceedings, and both made speeches while they were in Japan,

Ava Helen and Linus in Tokyo, 1959.

Linus sits with a Buddhist monk in Hiroshima, August 6, 1959

Ava Helen at a special women's meeting on August 7. Linus played a major role in drafting the Hiroshima Statement issued by the conference, urging demilitarization of both Germanys as well as Japan, and support of the Geneva conference working toward a cessation of nuclear testing. Throughout the conference Ava Helen kept excruciatingly detailed notes, as she did whenever she found a speech or a meeting particularly compelling. As at the annual Pugwash conferences, which both Paulings regularly attended, science and politics mingled in the delegates' discussions. Here, there was also the painful testimony from survivors of the bomb, who reported on difficulties in getting medical treatment, and the differentiation they perceived between the better treatment accorded the rich and the less afflicted, and the inferior treatment accorded the poor and seriously wounded.

The Paulings loved Japan and kept in touch with a number of Japanese friends and colleagues over the years. They hosted a Japanese exchange student in 1963-1964, that busiest of Pauling years. For both Ava Helen and Linus, Japan seems to have mattered to them—and they to the Japanese—because of their deep sorrow at the aftermath of the war, and because at home, with the internment of the Japanese Americans, and abroad, with the dropping of the atomic bombs on Hiroshima and Nagasaki, the fates of Japan and its people started the Paulings down the road to global activism.

Deer Flat Ranch

After Linus won the Nobel Prize for Chemistry in 1954, the Paulings could afford to realize a dream.[81] They staked out a place along the rugged central California coast where they could get away from the constant demands of colleagues, children, and friends. In the 1950s Big Sur was a wild, grassy, weather-beaten area of ranches, ranger stations, and primitive living conditions, not unlike the coast of Scotland in some patches. Artists and writers had been drawn to its isolated beauty for decades.[82] The Paulings seem to have chosen the site for its remoteness and natural beauty. Linus recalled that by 1950 they had been thinking about "a place in the country" where they could escape the clamor of their everyday lives. Five years later, on a trip up the northern California coast, they decided on a whim to drop

Ava Helen and Linda Pauling on the porch of the Deer Flat ranch cabin, 1956.

over to Route 1, a narrow, winding coastal road of breathtaking landscapes. Linus's attention wandered to a piece of land — "a point of land projecting into the ocean, with a cabin and barn, and with cows grazing on the grass there." In hindsight, it was one of the magical affirmations of their good fortune as a couple. "I said to your mother 'There's the sort of place that we ought to have,' and she replied 'Yes, and there is a sign saying that it is for sale.'"[83]

Some days later, having tracked down the owner's whereabouts and gotten a key to the gate, the Paulings wandered the property. They took a sleeping bag and made camp on one of the cliffs. The 160-acre property was called Salmon Creek, after the adjoining creek and national forest area; the Paulings renamed it Deer Flat Ranch. The next year they bought another five-acre parcel at Piedros Blancos, complete with a Chevron station and store, which they rented out for some years, fixing the monthly rent at the amount of gas sold at the station times 2 cents per gallon. Their property was scattered over a long stretch of Highway 1, with the station twelve miles north of the ranch. The gate to the ranch, which they kept locked when they weren't there, was about a quarter mile from the Salmon Creek ranger station.

The Paulings started visiting and developing the ranch right away, though Big Sur was a three-hundred-mile drive from Pasadena. Ava Helen loved gardening and always maintained a flower and vegetable garden at home, but a ranch was a new enterprise for the couple. They dove into the project. By January 1957 they had arranged to graze cattle on the land and had begun the licensing procedures for that enterprise. The numbers were small: in 1960 Linus wrote to Peter that they now had thirteen head on the land.[84] The windy oceanside perspective offered a chance to hike and observe wildlife. In 1958 Linus wrote to a biologist about the sea otters he and Ava Helen had spotted along the Big Sur coast.[85]

When the Paulings weren't there, the ranch and cattle were overseen by a series of caretakers and caretaking arrangements, with varying satisfaction on both sides. The first was their Pasadena handyman, who mysteriously disappeared back east to his home state of Tennessee within a few months.[86] Caretaking the caretakers generally fell to Ava Helen, who managed the long-distance relations with a combination of intimacy and matter-of-fact command that sometimes ruffled the employees' feathers. Writing a check to the Paulings for the monthly phone bill, probably for the cabin, to settle up accounts, caretaker Michael Hall commented, "I think your charge of $4.00 for cleaning the cattle truck bed is one of your lower grade things I've seen you do."[87] In the mid-1960s the Paulings had a caretaker with a drinking problem whose friends regularly plied him with liquor and pilfered his money on payday. "Things were getting so bad that we had told him we would absolutely not allow him to stay on the property if he continued to have these people come. He says that he does not even know their names, but we are not quite sure about this." Wishing to protect her employee, she nonetheless lost patience with his willingness to put up with his "low life," "derelict" acquaintances.[88]

The Paulings initially used the original cabin on the property; it was simple, with a large central room and a rear bedroom, as well as an indoor bathroom. There was running water to the main room and the bathroom, and a refrigerator. There were two single beds in the big room, and a collapsible double bed that could be maneuvered into the small rear bedroom.[89] Larger groups could pitch tents outside the house. By the late 1950s, spending a few days each month at Deer Flat Ranch, they already viewed the ranch as a healing escape, a breathing space from their increasingly busy lives.[90] Linus remembered his wife saying, "Do you know, we have been here for one week, you and I, without seeing a single other person. This is the first time in our 40-odd years of marriage that this has happened."[91] Ava Helen wrote to an associate in 1960, relative to the breathless pace of their lives in peace work, "We get a great deal of pleasure from our ranch and have now stocked it with wonderful animals so that we feel not only a very close connection with the world and its people, but with the earth itself. This is a good feeling and does a great deal to restore us both spiritually and physically." Continuing a wistful theme of those busy years, she wrote: "We hope that we shall be able soon to spend much more of our time there."[92]

The ranch proved an anchor in their lives together, but they did not use it solely as a retreat. Over the years friends and family visited, and from early on, trusted friends were invited to borrow the ranch when the Paulings weren't in residence. During the summer of 1957, when Ava Helen and Linus were traveling in Europe, they loaned the house to several of Linus's colleagues.[93] The service station manager—Luther Williams, initially—agreed to hold the keys to the ranch house and tool shed for visitors.[94]

When they could stay for longer periods, they made improvements on the original cabin. In 1960 Linus became engrossed with building bookshelves from birch boards and brass rods in both the bedroom and the main room. He stocked them with that intellectuals' favorite, the ninth edition of the Encyclopedia Britannica, though the scientist in him was understandably bothered by the archaic factoids (Los Angeles with a population of six thousand, for example).[95]

But a few years later the Paulings had outgrown the old cabin and had enough money to dream larger. In 1965 they built a new house at Deer Flat Ranch and gave the cabin over to the caretaker. In 1970 part of the ranch burned in a grass fire that swept through Salmon Creek. Undiscouraged, but feeling besieged by family, the Paulings decided to build a bunkhouse on their property, "so children and grandchildren can come there without interfering too much with us," Ava Helen wrote frankly to a friend in New York.[96] The bunkhouse also made it possible for the Paulings to host even more friends.[97]

At the end of January 1960, Ava Helen experienced one of the most frightening episodes of her life. She and Linus drove up toward Big Sur on Wednesday, January 27, via Asilomar, where Linus attended a spectroscopy conference. They arrived at the ranch on Friday, probably anticipating much-needed rest from their world tour that fall. On Saturday morning, Linus left on a walk, telling Ava Helen that he would be checking the fence lines, possibly to prepare for an exploratory discussion about exchanging some of their land for land in Los Padres National Forest. When he wasn't back by noon she began to worry; by early evening she was frightened. She left him a note saying that she didn't know where he was and had gone to the ranger's station for help. The ranger quickly organized a search, but halted it at 11:30 p.m. and then sent out a much larger crew in the morning. Ava Helen's diary entry for Saturday, January 30, read tersely: "Paddy lost."

Linus had gotten stuck on a cliff during his walk the previous day. Rightly alarmed when he realized he could move neither forward nor back without risking a rock slide that would propel him far down onto the rocks by the sea, he sat down, sat still, and thought—about Ava Helen, about chemical bonds, about the periodic table—about anything that might keep him awake through the long night. Though his actions to stay safe were quite rational—digging a depression to stay immobilized on the ledge, moving his arms and legs, staying awake, and keeping warm—his retrospective account suggests that he was paralyzed by fear. "It seems to have been beyond my decision; I had got frightened enough so that I was unable to leave the ledge." In the morning a crowd of searchers, and a crowd of reporters, gathered at Big Sur to continue the search. A reporter precipitously called in a story that Pauling was dead. That was the news Linda and Crellin heard.

Just before 10 a.m. Pauling spotted a lone searcher on the beach, and called out to him. The searcher in turn summoned the deputy sheriff, making his way along the cliff above the ledge. The sheriff actually joined Pauling on the ledge; one could get *down* to it or *up* to it, but not, Pauling had believed, down *from* it. While the searcher ran to tell Ava Helen that Linus was all right, the sheriff eased them both down from the treacherous ledge.

After Linus was found and shepherded back to the cabin on Sunday morning, Ava Helen dispatched telegrams to family to let them know that he had been saved. Then they stayed at the cabin to try to recover from the ordeal. "I found that Mama was very much upset by her long wait," Linus later wrote to the children, "and the uncertainty as to what had happened to me." That was putting it mildly. But Linus had little reserve to offer Ava Helen; he himself, without yet knowing it, was in shock. Ultimately he would have to retreat from his university appointments the next week and take to his bed. News of the crisis had gone out over the wires and appeared in newspapers around the world. Perhaps for his children, perhaps for his parents, perhaps to allay his own shock, Crellin had already written a detailed account of his own perspective on his father's accident, including having been told that Linus was dead. Pauling made amends as best he could to his wife and his family. "I am very sorry that I caused you and Mama so much anguish and concern," he closed his long account to his children of the horrific night at Big Sur.[98]

CHAPTER 4

"A Team of Paulings"[1]

I feel such a responsibility for the women with whom I have talked everywhere. I do really believe that women could play a great role if only they would step forward with courage.
—AHP to Annalee [Stewart?], November 1, 1960.[2]

The Paulings don't stand in each other's shadow; they walk in each other's light.
—Mary Clarke, November 12, 1960.[3]

Linus's night on the cliff at Salmon Cove proved a stutter but not an interruption of the Paulings' accelerating peace work from the late 1950s into the early 1960s. Typically, Ava Helen did not pause, at least in writing, over her scare that night and Linus's post-traumatic reactions. By early 1960 she had plunged into her service as a board member of the United States section of the Women's International League for Peace and Freedom. Within WILPF, she had a new cause: the promotion of an international congress of women for peace.

Linda Richards, a student of nuclear politics, has posited that there is a style of activism that might be characterized as "swirling" or circulating: one individual flowing through a number of different networks and organizations, planting seeds of ideas, making connections, circling back to remind people of their promises and possibilities.[4] This is the kind of activist Ava Helen became. Though her name appeared on the masthead of her organizations for limited periods of time, and is not frequently found in the national and international archives of these groups, her correspondence attests to her wide-ranging contacts, her polite yet direct approach to getting things done, and her persistence. In addition, the blunt and sometimes impatient Ava Helen rears her mischievous head.

Ava Helen's service in WILPF and her breathtaking international travel schedule, as she talked with and befriended women around the world, fertilized the feminist thought in her approach to activism. More and more she was called on to be the voice of women acting for peace. Claire Walsh at the United States WILPF headquarters in Philadelphia asked Ava Helen after her appointment to the national board if she would be available to give talks to small groups of WILPF members. "I should be very happy to speak … if you think that I have something of interest to say to them. I suppose that you are suggesting that I tell about such matters as our visit to Dr. Schweitzer and other things of interest which I may have observed on our many travels." She had already given speeches on Russia, particularly conditions for women and children, on conservation, and on the international WILPF meeting in Stockholm.[5] She was mobbed after her speeches, and her skills grew. "I don't know why you should fret over a speech; you couldn't make a bad one, not with that delivery power you sway," a friend assured her.[6] In March 1961, inviting her and Linus to speak to the recently organized Canadian branch of the Voice of Women (VOW), Jan Symons wrote to Ava Helen that, according to the VOW members, she was "becoming as much of a celebrity as your husband."[7]

When the Paulings traveled together, now most of the time, there was little hiatus from demands on their time and energies. "I only regret that we are such dreadful guests," she wrote one hostess on returning from New York in late 1960. "The telephone rings every two minutes and I am sure that our hostesses are always glad to see us leave."[8] The Paulings welcomed the new student movement of the 1960s, and student activists began inviting both Linus and Ava Helen to their events. In May 1960 the Paulings joined the San Francisco Peace March.

On June 18, 1960, Linus was served a subpoena to appear before the Senate Internal Security Subcommittee, chaired by the Democratic Senator from Connecticut, Thomas Dodd. Taking a leaf from Harry Truman's manual on out-Communist-hunting the Republicans, Dodd had become the leader of anti-Soviet Democrats. Eviscerating the anti-bomb movement became his urgent goal. Somewhat ungrammatically he reflected for the press, "[S]ome of the propaganda activities against nuclear testing is Communist-inspired or directed."[9] The subpoena was slipped into Pauling's hands at the end of a Washington, D.C., WILPF meeting at which he had given one of his usual anti-bomb speeches. From the Willard Hotel the Paulings called their lawyer, Abraham Lincoln Wirin, who flew into town for an intensive

Ava Helen with Vally Weigl, a peace movement friend, at the WILPF annual conference in Washingto, D.C., in 1960. Weigl was a German émigré, a musician and composer.

strategy meeting the next day. Ava Helen notified her WILPF contacts, and the Paulings activated the press, first through a press conference and then through a further set of calls when they learned that the SISS had decided to meet with Pauling in a closed (executive) session.[10] Embarrassed by the Washington *Post*'s prominent coverage of this obvious harassment, the committee backed down and held a public hearing, though it was postponed by a day, to the 21st.

In a room packed with Pauling supporters (or Dodd opponents), including Ava Helen and her WILPF colleagues, Dodd and his staff quickly showed their hands, grilling Pauling on how he had gathered the signatures for the United Nations petition two years before. Agreeing to provide the committee with the signatures—obviously a matter of record, since they were signatures—and with lists of people to whom the Paulings had sent copies of the petition—though these were at home in Pasadena—Pauling balked at providing the committee with lists of those who had helped solicit the signatures. "My conscience does not allow me to protect myself by exposing these idealistic people. As a matter of conscience and morality I have decided not to conform to the request."[11] The committee gave him a month to come up with these names.

Ava Helen's correspondents responded with sympathy and outrage. "How shocked we all were," wrote Thea Gould from New Zealand, "to hear that the 'Internal Security Committee' had called up our dear friend. The audacity leaves one speechless—but I suppose after the U2 affair and its follow up one should be surprised at *nothing*." Of course, New Zealanders too, she remarked, were coping with the irrationality of official anti-Communism. "McCarthy walks again not only in your country but in mine!"[12] An expatriate friend from Tokyo remarked that, though she knew the hearing was more serious than it appeared, "it is hard to imagine that it could have any serious reverberations, but then it is even harder to imagine the depth of the stupidity that Professor Linus is up against—probably I am over-optimistic in labeling it 'stupidity.'"[13]

The Paulings continued their exhausting schedule as they waited for the next round with SISS. Ava Helen attended the California Democratic caucus meeting at the Huntingdon Sheraton Hotel in July. Characteristically, she took extensive notes on the speakers angling for the nomination: Kennedy, Johnson, and Symington. A few days later the Paulings flew to Europe for a two-week stay in London, where they saw Peter, and then Switzerland, for quick visits to Linus, Jr., and Anita in Geneva, and to Linda and Barclay in Zurich. They had truncated their plans for a longer trip, waiting on the whim of SISS and knowing that a failure to appear could lead to a costly contempt charge.

They returned to Washington in August. Linus again refused to provide the names. Groups and individual citizens wrote letters to the Committee, protesting their questioning of Pauling.[14] Perhaps he would not be recalled to Washington at all: "We hear rumors that the committee means to vacate the order." The Paulings' plans hung suspended as they waited for the committee's decision. One event that buoyed the Paulings' anxious spirits was the local ACLU's decision to throw a huge party in their honor. Fifteen hundred people attended. Ava Helen hoped that their trial would be justified by the elimination of the subcommittee itself. But she also knew there were precedents for harsh reprisals against Linus. "You must know," she wrote in September to Dorothy Crowfoot Hodgkin, that despite First Amendment protections, "there are a good number of people in prison right now in the United States for the exact reason that they were citing Linus, namely, the refusal to produce names." The subcommittee's actions were obviously "an attack against the peace movement in the United States."[15]

One of the persons imprisoned for refusing to name names was Dr. Willard Uphaus, a Methodist lay minister whose lifelong peace advocacy cost him professional positions and his place in the Methodist Church. In early 1960 he was serving a year's prison sentence in New Hampshire for refusing to hand over lists of members of the World Fellowship of Faiths, which maintained a summer headquarters in Conway, New Hampshire. The conviction dated from 1956; after the United States Supreme Court refused to overturn the New Hampshire Superior Court decision in 1959, Uphaus began serving his year for contempt of the state legislature. He was very much on Ava Helen's mind in early 1960, and she wrote him a letter of support. "Knowing your concern and that of Dr. Pauling," Uphaus responded, "I have never felt alone."[16] Later that year, upon his release from prison, Uphaus was honored along with Pauling at a banquet at New York's Hotel Commodore. "[T]here has been such a demand for tickets," Ava Helen wrote to an associate, "that they had more reservations than the Waldorf could accommodate, so they have had to move to a dining room which holds 400 more people."[17]

In early October, another subpoena brought forth another refusal from a bold but worried Pauling. With plenty of support outside the halls of the Senate, he still risked imprisonment for contempt of Congress. As had happened several times before, when the stakes were only a bit lower, Pauling faced down his accusers once again. "I am unwilling to subject these people to reprisals by the committee," he insisted. "I could protect myself by agreeing, but I am fighting for other persons who could not make a fight themselves."[18] He was let go without a citation and without having relinquished the names, but not before the committee had fired questions at him for another five hours about his associations with Communist and Communist-front groups and individuals.

"The summer has been a very difficult one for us and we are exhausted, both physically and financially," Ava Helen wrote to Lady Jessie May Street, as she turned down an invitation to a women's conference in Warsaw. "I feel that I should not leave my husband at this time."[19] As Thomas Hager points out, despite a surge of support and new public respect for Pauling after his SISS appearance and apparent triumph, Linus had a hard time shaking off his anger and frustration at the unjust and nerve-wracking ordeal.[20] Ava Helen tried to put a more optimistic face on the financial drain of the legal defense, flights, hotels, and general bother of the SISS attack. "You are quite right," she wrote to a friend at the radio station KPFK, "that we have had a great expense in connection with our hearing before the Subcommittee. Of course, the real victim has been the public, which is usual in this case. I hate to think of the amount of money which the taxpayers have had to pay just to have the transcription of this hearing printed."[21] To another friend she professed to have learned a lot from the ordeal, "and so do not really look on it as a completely horrifying experience."[22]

In 1959 she had been excited to learn about an English translation of the heart-wrenching Japanese book Arata Osada's *Children of the A-Bomb*. First published in Japanese in 1951, the book compiled children's first-person accounts of the Hiroshima bomb. She encouraged Norman Cousins, editor of the *Saturday Review* and an ally in the peace movement, to publish a review. When she saw no review, she wrote one herself and submitted it to Cousins in August 1960 with a brief cover note. "One can get a good idea of what happens to a city when a small atomic bomb is dropped on it from this book. But one learns, too, about the love and tenderness of Japanese family life; the affection and respect that children have for their parents, their teachers, and their country. One sees the heroism with which the people of Japan met this disaster, the patience with which they endured their agonies, and the dignity with which they met their death," wrote Ava Helen in the review.[23]

Since the decision to bomb Hiroshima and Nagasaki still provokes storms of controversy in the United States in the twenty-first century, it is perhaps not surprising that the *Saturday Review* deflected Ava Helen's review with the excuse that, because of space limitations, they never reviewed literature published outside the United States.[24] There were additional reasons for the *Review's* editorial decision. Ava Helen's review emphasized the humanity of the Japanese, without reference to their nation's wartime enemy status. Further, Ava Helen was an amateur book reviewer. Her review was crisp, eloquent, and effective, but in the world of magazine publishing, that may not have weighed much next to a lack of literary credentials. Finally and most important, Ava Helen was married to Linus Pauling, currently under attack for purported Communist associations. Norman Cousins, a founder of the Committee for a Sane Nuclear Policy (best known as SANE), found his group under siege as well that summer and fall, by the same group of conservative senators, who raked SANE members over the coals for fellow traveling. "I suppose you know," Ava Helen wrote a friend in September, "that they have called in many people working for SANE in the New York and Boston areas, but always in executive session, so that the public knows nothing about it."[25]

Unlike the Paulings, whose backs stiffened under the onslaught of late-season redbaiting, SANE started an internal purge of radical members — members whom the leadership deemed dangerous because tainted with Communist associations. Toward the organization itself, Ava Helen was sympathetic. "You know that our session with the Subcommittee was a victory for us, but I am afraid a catastrophe for the peace movement," she wrote to a New Hampshire friend in November 1960. "This is what we foresaw last June and which we tried to keep from happening. Perhaps SANE can still be saved, but it surely now is so filled with dissension that it is unable to do very much about working for peace."[26] But toward Cousins, she was increasingly impatient and indignant.

SANE had followed the Hollywood producers' line of fifteen years before. Even in the early days of SANE, in 1957 and 1958, leaders Larry Scott and Norman Cousins had been preoccupied with the perceived challenges of Communist infiltration in certain local branches of SANE. They were sure that SANE would be perceived as a Soviet tool if word got out that there were fellow travelers in the membership. They also believed that SANE would make a compelling target for Communists wishing to control the American peace movement. In 1958 Cousins went as far as to ask the FBI for lists of potential Communist infiltrators! As SANE historian Milton S. Katz points out, even beyond the SANE leadership's self-policing compulsion, the irony of the SISS investigation is that Cousins and Senator Dodd were not only neighbors but also colleagues in the United World Federalists.[27]

The first SANE officer Dodd called was Henry Abrams. Cousins pleaded with Dodd to hold off on investigating SANE until after the huge Madison Square Garden rally scheduled for a week after the first subpoena. He also asked Abrams to resign from SANE after Abrams refused to say point blank whether or not he was a Communist. Dodd made matters even more difficult for Cousins among peace advocates — among them the Paulings — by praising Cousins' eagerness to cooperate with the SISS. Though Cousins protested this characterization of his position, his difficulties were exacerbated by the SANE board's adoption of a kind of "don't ask, do tell" policy on Communist and fellow-traveler identity among leaders in the local chapters: SANE members were expected not to be Communists, and any serious suspicion should be answered in an appearance before the national board. As Katz points out, the fallout from this policy move was the loss of half the New York chapters, fully a quarter of the United States chapters.[28]

SANE offered a two-pronged response to the summer of SISS. On the one hand, the organization defended Pauling, a prominent SANE member, against committee harassment "outrageous in its contempt for civil liberty and sinister in its implications for peace."[29] On the other hand, the SANE board would not take out a New York *Times* advertisement defending Pauling and other SANE advocates against the Dodd committee, and Cousins forcibly denied that Dodd was just another McCarthy — rather, he said, Dodd was just as dedicated to peace as he himself was.

Ava Helen was confounded by Cousins' performance, particularly after their work as allies in the antinuclear movement. "We … are having a difficult time in understanding Mr. Cousins and what his objectives are," she wrote to Catherine [Cory?] in November 1960.[30] Among her SANE associates in the Los Angeles area, she had felt that Peter Charlton treated the Paulings differently after SANE headquarters issued the new guidelines for strict anti-Communist vigilance. "We do not yet see how the dissension within SANE can be resolved, or perhaps I should say ironed out, but certainly everyone must do his best to do it."[31] To yet another friend she was even blunter about Cousins. "I agree with you that he is a moral coward."[32] Cousins further muddied the waters, as far as Ava Helen was concerned, by holding a secret confabulation with a group of Soviet visitors to the United States in Dartmouth, New Hampshire. "We do not know what will come of this, but we think it rather strange that one so sensitive to suspected communism in New York, should be shut up with people who are no doubt avowed Communists. Perhaps he has more confidence in his strength of character than in the strength of character of other people. His actions, however, lead me to doubt that he has much character at all."[33] Linus resigned from his position as a sponsor of SANE because the Paulings could not reconcile Cousins' capitulation to the Communist-hunting juggernaut with their own priority of working for peace, no matter what their allies' affiliations might be. Ava Helen cancelled their subscription to the *Saturday Review*.[34]

There were advantages to allowing her woman-and-wife status to keep Ava Helen under the radar. Linus was the family bellwether, but Ava Helen had always been the ideological radical. At the very moment that Linus was being grilled as a fellow traveler, Ava Helen was corresponding with her friends in the Soviet Union, offering a report to the magazine *Soviet Woman* on the April 1960 Los Angeles gathering, "Your Family's Stake in Disarmament—A Woman's Conference." Sponsored by the American Friends Service Committee, a group Ava Helen had worked with for years, the event brought together five hundred women from a wide variety of peace, women's, church, and social justice organizations in a daylong workshop offering information on the risks of nuclear war and brainstorming local and global actions for disarmament. Ava Helen co-chaired the event with Catherine Cory, manager of KPFK radio, a liberal Los Angeles station. She introduced the main speaker, Sucheta Kripalani of the Indian Parliament, general secretary of the Congress Party and former Indian representative to the United Nations.[35]

Ava Helen talking with two women in a classroom, in the 1950s.

WILPF

Ava Helen carried her hostility to ideological labels into her tenure on the national board of the Women's International League for Peace and Freedom. As soon as she began her service as a WILPF national board member, she recognized splits in that organization that resonated with the issues wracking other peace organizations—splits of a decade's standing about how to deal with internal differences over members' perceived political leanings. From 1915 to the mid-1930s, WILPF had held to an integrated perspective on peace and social justice. Peace was not merely the absence of war. Peace was impossible in the face of persistent and pervasive racism and economic injustice. Founded in wartime in 1915, WILPF faced predictable enemies in the United States from 1917 on, and an aggravated assault on its American members' patriotism from the time of the Red Scare through the 1920s. Nonetheless, worldwide the group persisted in taking a place at the diplomatic table and attracted many powerful women, from housewives to professors to diplomats and politicians. Buoyed by a noble history of recognition by world leaders and world bodies, including consultative status at the United Nations, the Women's International League for Peace and Freedom had in 1931 been honored when WILPF founder and settlement house pioneer Jane Addams shared the Nobel Peace Prize. Again in 1946 WILPF received a boost when the Nobel Peace Prize was conferred on Emily Greene Balch, another WILPF founder, social activist, and reformer.[36] WILPF needed this kind of headline. Its European sections had been devastated by World War II, and in the United States, the organization was often perceived as irrelevant, administratively top-heavy, and skewed toward older women, with limited appeal to the new activist generation.[27]

The Cold War brought special challenges to the United States section of WILPF. Some local branches seemed sufficiently effective to merit FBI surveillance, and as historian Harriet Hyman Alonso discovered, a number of WILPF members were called up in front of loyalty panels.[38] "The organizers in the 1950s tried to walk a very thin line between defending free speech and denouncing the ideology of 'communism.'"[39] Some local chapters went further. More blatantly than SANE later on, the Metropolitan New York chapter scrutinized new members for their political affiliations. In 1953, even as the executive secretary Mildred Scott Olmsted reported a gratifying absence of external attacks, in contrast to the post-World War I years, several local groups were imploding over differences on how to deal with perceived threats from Communists.[40]

These ideological and strategic conflicts continued into the early 1960s, as Ava Helen learned in her service on the national board between 1959 and 1963. She had connected with the local Pasadena chapter some time between 1953 and 1956. Already her prominence as Mrs. Pauling made her a desirable speaker, and she addressed the Los Angeles chapter on "World Development" in 1956, her talk touching a theme that foreshadowed her major contribution to WILPF over the next decade: the ways in which peace, prosperity, and social justice were globally intertwined.[41] This stance, idealistic, optimistic, and WILPF-like as it might sound, put her in the line of fire from those who felt it imperative to balance the quest for peace with a recognition that the Soviet Union and its allies had different and sometimes murky objectives.

Because WILPF played such a large role in her peace activism in the 1950s and early 1960s, we might ask why she did not join the small but conscientious Pasadena chapter in the 1930s. One good answer is that the chapter was founded in 1932, the year Linda, her third child, was born. One seven-year-old and two babies were a lot to handle at home. In addition, the mid-1930s were the years of Linus's meteoric professional rise because of his work on the chemical bond. Pauling family life — which meant Ava Helen's life — had been very much focused on Linus's career. Another possible explanation was personal. One of the most important local WILPF leaders was Madeline Dickinson, the wife of Roscoe Dickinson, Linus's graduate school mentor and after 1926 his colleague in the chemistry division at Caltech. Ava Helen disliked Madeline Dickinson — found her, in fact, "vicious," "awful," and even "mildly insane." Ava Helen did not mince words when somebody crossed her. (We don't know the nature of the offense.) But this animus perhaps helps explain why she did not join Pasadena WILPF in the 1930s.[42]

Finally, like Linus, Ava Helen had been compelled to action in the late 1930s by global bullies. Her response had been to help those who wanted to fight back. Her political temperament was more easily roused by oppression and injustice, and her instinct was to fight back. WILPF too took the high ground during the war, but the organization had to work through its own historical commitments before being able to make recommendations for action against the Nazis, Mussolini, and Japan.

After her election to the National Board in the spring of 1959, Ava Helen's first official service was to attend the Fourteenth International Congress in Stockholm in 1959. Linus had been invited to give the keynote at the opening session. "Our Choice: World Peace or Nuclear Annihilation," he called it with characteristic urgency. The Paulings stayed in Stockholm for the five days of the WILPF congress, which was only a fraction of their astonishingly energetic world tour that year, discussed in the previous chapter. When the

Paulings returned home, they found themselves in demand as speakers; again, often in tandem. Ava Helen reviewed the Stockholm highlights for the Los Angeles branch of WILPF. Both Paulings spoke at the WILPF California state meeting at the end of September, Ava Helen reporting on the WILPF congress and Linus on the World Peace Conference in Japan.[43]

Linus's night on the cliff, and his ordeal with SISS, sucked a huge amount of the Paulings' energies in 1960. But in addition to their emotional, legal, and political challenges, and in some ways drawing sparks from these, Ava Helen began seeking allies in WILPF to call a general international meeting of women to discuss disarmament. This mission dominated her correspondence for the next year. San Francisco had been chosen as the location of the 1962 triennial international WILPF conference. Ava Helen joined a few other voices pushing for a general call for a universal, open conference of women to follow the WILPF congress. Agnes Meyers, Andrea Andreen, Mary Phillips, Jan Symons, and Lotte Meitner-Graf were among the WILPF activists with whom Ava Helen plotted to leverage the WILPF congress into a larger mobilization adventure to push forward the disarmament process.

Why did Ava Helen and the other activists not see the WILPF triennial as sufficient for the purposes of rallying international women around the disarmament struggle? First, these women believed that WILPF did not truly represent the world's women. It was too small. The members' average age was advanced. It was internally torn by arguments over whether anti-Communist ideology trumped pacifist ideology. Not just in the United States, but globally, women in the western democracies argued about how to work for global peace when their national leadership was preoccupied with Cold War positioning. Andrea Andreen reminded Ava Helen in the summer of 1960 that discussion in WILPF about a "World Congress of Women for Disarmament" had been quietly broached at the 1956 triennial. "That year only a very private discussion after the Congress was allowed — England was mostly against, USA divided, the Scandinavian countries against, France, Switzerland, Finland, West Germany for." Andreen thought that opinion might be more favorable now, at least judging from her fellow Swedish WILPF-ers.[44]

Andreen pinpointed one of the dilemmas underlying international disarmament politics for NGOs (non-governmental organizations) like WILPF. It was difficult to clear the floor of pressing political and military conflicts to simply talk peace. At the recent World Peace Congress, the troubles in the Congo and the revolution in Cuba had pushed unconditional peace to the background of discussion.[45] For Andreen, this underlined the need for a *women's* congress solely devoted to peace. Like many but not all WILPF members, she trusted a gendered approach to organizing for peace.

Other WILPF members wrote to Ava Helen about the disturbingly conditional pacifism of the anti-Communists. For these correspondents, a conference of women discussing disarmament just might bypass the pacifist establishmentarians, who were hampered by their fears of Communist infiltration in the peace movement. "Indeed, why doesn't WILPF issue a general invitation to ALL women, of whatever race, society, creed etc?" wrote Sarah Lampin, a New Zealand associate. "Men meet, and quarrel, and go away again, for the most part, leaving the situation worse." She confided that Auckland's Movement Against Nuclear Weapons had chosen to be unaligned with the older peace societies in order to avoid red-baiting: "We therefore made it plain that anyone who wanted to join us, from either party, was most welcome; but we also made it plain that we could not afford to be affiliated." Ava Helen and Linus's 1959 visit to New Zealand was, she claimed, the happy outcome of that distancing policy. "All the peace-minded organisations joined together for that, without any purpose but to serve the cause of peace." A gathering of women would invoke The Hague gathering of 1915, she added, "only even more important, since the omens are even more menacing, & the whole problem not now confined to Europe, as it then was."[46]

Marjorie Avery of San Francisco, also enthusiastic about a wider meeting of women, cautioned Ava Helen about the apathy she saw among peace advocates. "Due to the late Sen McCarthy and the present Sen Dodd everybody seems to be afraid of being branded a Commie if they live by their spiritual ideals." She too wished to see a connection between the energies of women united and the success of a peace movement—"You are so right Mrs. Pauling, the woman of the world will have to unite and work unceasingly for a peaceful world in which to raise their sons"—but she was skeptical about their willingness to rise above cocktail parties and contract bridge. "Such a small group has to bear the responsibility for such a great number."[47]

Mary Phillips, who signed herself "the peace gardener" after developing a garden dedicated to peace on Chicago's lakeshore, concurred that anti-Communism could derail the peace movement. "The investigating committees set to work on outstanding persons in any peace organization the moment it begins to catch on with the public." Hunting down Communist infiltrators would intimidate and distract adherents. "[M]any WILPF women might so fear having WILPF smeared, split, or even destroyed, they would hesitate to exert effort for a world conference of women which included communist women, as an organization project."[48]

Gertrude Baer, onetime WILPF representative to the United Nations and *éminence grise* in the international organization, mentored Ava Helen as she attempted to reignite enthusiasm for an international meeting of women. Ava Helen had run up against the strong personality and beliefs of Orlie Pell, current president of the United States section of WILPF and one of the staunchest anti-Communist voices in the organization. "Do not get discouraged, Mrs. O.P. cannot alone decide what is to be done about the matter." Baer suggested a meeting of women primarily from the United States and Latin American countries. "The trouble is," she admitted, "under present conditions, no woman from the Peoples Republic of China would be allowed into your country and we wonder, whether you could count on women from Cuba?"[49]

Baer encouraged Ava Helen to ally herself with Mildred Scott Olmsted, the WILPF leader who held in the United States a similar position to Baer's in the international. National Administrative Secretary in 1960, Olmsted was indeed one of Ava Helen's strongest allies; she had been one of the WILPF leaders who urged Ava Helen a few years earlier to reach beyond the California chapters to become more active in the United States section.[50] She also encouraged Ava Helen to follow up on her resolve to contact Eleanor Roosevelt, a quest that finally proved discouraging. "I was astonished to hear her say how such and such a person was a very fine, good man, but friendly to communism and accordingly she could not have her name associated with his," Ava Helen wrote to Olmsted in November 1960.[51] To another friend Ava Helen wrote that, though Mrs. Roosevelt wanted to hear more about Linus's ordeal before SISS, it was difficult to engage her on the topic of an international gathering of women. "I am so afraid that if we were to go ahead with a congress she would make some statement in her column or somewhere about its being Communist-dominated, and then the whole thing would be lost. How can she behave so?" she fretted with her usual candor.[52]

WILPF had worked hard as an organization to avoid the actions of SANE, the ACLU, and other liberal-leaning groups in formulating a statement directly excluding members of Communist sympathies.[53] But the individual branches, both in the United States and abroad, failed to sidestep Communist-infiltration controversy. And the stakes seemed to swell in the early 1960s, as the new generation of American political leadership went toe-to-toe with the Soviet Union.

Thus the same signs of the times that seemed to mandate such an international women's meeting—nuclear testing, hot spots tempting confrontation between the Cold War great powers, and at the same time the agonizingly slow but palpable successes of the anti-testing movement —

seemed also to militate *against* the conference. Women from China, Cuba, and other nations faced travel restrictions imposed by the U.S. State Department or their own governments. Such a gathering might be better situated in Canada or elsewhere, and called under the auspices of the International WILPF rather than the United States section. Another problem, raised by Katherine Arnett from the Philadelphia office of WILPF, was practical. "[E]ven if we were asked to go ahead with the Congress by the International, [we] are not equipped to run such an enormous undertaking on such short notice."

Arnett suggested that the alternative was to make the WILPF triennial in San Francisco "as large and representative as possible." If there were not active WILPF branches in certain countries, "these women can come as visitors."[54] That was not what Ava Helen wanted to hear. Returning in December 1960 from another lecture tour in the Midwest, followed by one to the Northwest, Ava Helen thanked Arnett for her "kind" letter and assured her that there was much enthusiasm for the idea of what she was now calling a "truly international meeting of women everywhere." She conceded that Canada might be a better venue, unless the United States hurried up and recognized China and sponsored her for membership of the United Nations. "We can hope that this will not be too long delayed."[55]

Ava Helen seemed to be carving out a role for herself in the national WILPF leadership by advocating the congress of women—ironically, a congress that would be distinguished by *not* being a WILPF affair. Though she was usually relaxed in exploiting her symbiotic relationship with Linus, in WILPF her stature as the wife of Linus Pauling—so notorious that summer and fall for his stance against the SISS—seems to have made her uncomfortable. After the October national board meeting, she wrote to one or two members that she had felt awkward as the board began its discussion of their official response to SISS and in particular Linus's harassment by the subcommittee. She left partway through the session, and people noticed. Both Katherine Arnett and Mildred Scott Olmsted averred that it would have been completely appropriate for her to stay. "I believe there is no real difference of opinion among the Board members," Olmsted argued, "as to both the House and Senate committees doing outrageous and intolerable things. The difference comes on how it is best to control them or whether we ought to work, as I believe, for their complete disappearance."[56] Here again was the elephant in the room—the caution of some WILPF factions in the face of their association with suspect causes and individuals, including Linus Pauling. Olmsted tackled this topic in relation to the Jane Addams centennial of 1960. "I was much impressed with how many of the governors making proclamations and how many of the magazines and papers carrying articles just omitted our name as being, I suppose, 'too controversial.'"[57]

Andrea Andreen disagreed with the notion that asking Socialist women to attend an international congress might doom the meeting. "It is not new," she wrote from Sweden, "for WIL to invite women from socialist countries to their Congresses." A bit drily she observed, "My experience … is that very nice, prominent and charming women come from the 'Iron curtain' countries to these meetings of women with different views on politics. They are … scientists, physicians, authors, members of parliament, teachers at universities." She argued that the United States was a better venue for an international conference, with a higher profile than Canada, despite its onerous entrance requirements. She urged Ava Helen to go ahead with the conference plans.[58]

At the beginning of 1961 the Paulings launched two related projects: a new petition drive to stop the proliferation of nuclear weapons, and a May meeting in Oslo of world scientists and intellectuals to precede a scheduled NATO ministers' meeting in the same month. The young Kennedy administration seemed willing on the one hand to go forward with test-ban negotiations, and on the other to share nuclear weapons with NATO allies. The Paulings shifted their focus slightly to take on the issue of proliferation. The petition drive of 1957 to 1959 had worked very well. Now they sent the new petitions to two thousand of their previous signers and received seven hundred signatures back, including thirty-eight Nobel Prize winners. These Pauling presented to the United Nations, as before, and immediately broadened the appeal. The Pauling home again became command central for a mailing drive of international proportions. The response was positive, though there was a bit of confusion about a simultaneous petition circulated by SANE calling for an end to testing. Ava Helen had to explain to at least one correspondent that both petitions were "worthwhile," but that theirs focused on nonproliferation.[59]

Simultaneously, the Paulings started rounding up support for the proposed meeting in Oslo to bring together scientists from Soviet satellites as well as western countries, to contest the NATO stance that it was impossible to cooperate with Soviet-dominated governments. Underlining that this project was theirs alone, they had stationery made up under the title "Conference Against the Spread of Nuclear Weapons, Oslo, Norway, 2 to 7 May 1961," under their names and home address in Pasadena. Individuals listed as sponsors included Karl Barth, Max Born, Mrs. Cyrus Eaton, Erich Fromm, Lewis Mumford, Gunnar Myrdal, Alan Paton, Bertrand Russell, Albert Schweitzer, and Hideki Yukawa.[60] The Paulings had emphasized to

The participants at the Oslo conference in 1961.

prospective attendees — only about seventy-five were invited — that there were no organizational sponsors except a Norwegian group handling local arrangements. The Paulings also offered to pay the travel costs of participants.

Ava Helen used her network of connections to push the petition and raise money for the conference. Her friend Jan Symons, a recent migrant from New Zealand to Canada, warned her that some of her new acquaintances in Quebec shied away from the Paulings' petition for several reasons, chief among them the Communist bugaboo. Their new Canadian organization, the Voice of Women, was feeling the anti-Communist heat, and the Paulings were perceived as leftwing and untrustworthy (Linus's warnings about smoking apparently representing a medical fringe element). Within VOW, Symons claimed, Ava Helen was declared to be "as much of a celebrity as your husband," but outside the group, both VOW and WILPF were suspect. "One nice Quaker woman psychiatrist told me that it undoubtedly had a bad name in U.S. as Communist." Like Ava Helen, Jan Symons was exasperated. "We are told we are peace-loving, that it is the Russians, the Communists who want war ... I notice that when people get Russian scientists to sign petitions against war, however, they are dismissed as only another Communist front."[61]

Despite some peace workers' reluctance to sign the petition, the Oslo conference was a heartening success for the Paulings. On the way they visited France, where Linus received a prestigious award from the city of Paris[62]; they arrived in Oslo on May 4. Sixty scientists, intellectuals, and peace activists attended from around the world, including the Soviet Union. Else Zeuthen, international chair of WILPF, joined nine or ten other WILPF leaders at the conference.[63] Without agendas in hand at the beginning of the meeting, the participants shifted into high gear almost immediately to draft, collectively, a statement for post-conference circulation among the citizens of the world. The group included members of the test-ban negotiating teams of both the United States and the Soviet Union; the collective level of expertise at the conference was high, attesting to the Paulings' global credibility. The statement the group hammered out called for a ban on the spread of nuclear weapons to any more nations or groups of nations; universal disarmament to prevent a "cataclysmic nuclear war"; and international controls and inspection of nuclear weapons "such as to insure to the greatest possible extent the safety of all nations and all people." Linus Pauling and Ava Helen Pauling were the first signatories—and the only ones directly under the statement text (other original signers were listed on the back of the copies circulated throughout the world for additional signatures).[64]

Ava Helen opened the conference on the first night, and Linus gave a speech. In the mornings and evenings the Paulings circulated around the tables, checking in with people. Their friend from Berkeley, Dr. Frances Herring, remarked in a diary of the conference that Ava Helen looked "tragically tired." Herring discovered that few of the attendees realized that the Paulings had underwritten the conference financially as well as morally. "There is to be a torch parade, winding from the Nobel Institute to the Grand Hotel (about a mile) tomorrow night, to honor the Paulings. That should make them feel good!"[65]

In fact, despite their exhaustion, both Paulings were delighted with the conference. "Everything has gone along almost perfectly," Linus wrote. "The Aula meeting was grand. The Vice-Rector gave a speech thanking us. Friday night there was a great torchlight procession in our honor—quite a sight!"[66] Else Zeuthen offered a longer reflection on the evening in her report to the WILPF membership. "A most striking moment of those eventful days was one evening after sunset, when the Paulings received the homage of a torchlight procession, standing on the balcony of their room on an upper floor of the Grand Hotel. Many members of our Norwegian Section were among the procession, whereas Inga Beskow and I enjoyed the wonderful show from the vantage point of a neighboring balcony of the Hotel. The torches flared beautifully in the soft spring night and filled the whole of Karl Johan, the impressive main thoroughfare of Oslo, as far as the eye could see. Numerous cries of 'Thank you, Pauling' sounded from the procession. The Paulings were much moved by this beautiful display of confidence;

and how they deserved it for their brave and indefatigable work! Marie Lous Mohr [a Norwegian WILPF leader] at the festive dinner given to the Conference made a speech expressing a hope that Oslo might once more welcome Professor Pauling, and then as Nobel Peace Prize-Winner."[67]

They stayed on in Oslo for several days. Linus gave a radio address and both Paulings spoke at the university as well as holding a press conference. They attended a cocktail party at the Russian Embassy. As always, every meal was an event. To Peter, Ava Helen admitted that they were exhausted, but "fairly contented" with the outcome. She too was impressed with the ceremony called out by international meetings: in this case, the NATO ministers meeting that directly followed their own. "The 50 star USA flag did, I must say, look beautiful waving in the spring winds. All the flags looked fine. I see why there must be a flag."[68]

The day after landing in New York, the Paulings addressed an overflow meeting at Carnegie Hall to report on the Oslo Conference. The next night they had dinner with friends, and both Linus and Ava Helen addressed a seventy-five-person WILPF audience in Bergen, New Jersey.[69] Landing in California on May 14, Ava Helen caught up with her mail for a day. Then three nights of dinner engagements preceded a blessed four-day retreat to Deer Flat Ranch. Their return to Pasadena plunged them back into the social-political whirl, with cocktail parties, teas, and lunches. Nonetheless they managed by October to distribute fifty thousand copies of the Oslo Statement, through the Unitarian and Methodist churches, the American Friends Service Committee, the Society for Social Responsibility in Science, and at their public talks.[70]

The pace of the Paulings' lives is hard to fathom. If there was any rhythm to their itineraries, it is reflected in the bursts of correspondence that Ava Helen managed between trips, and their regular visits to the ranch. The drive itself may have been a time when Ava Helen and Linus could take a breath and be alone with each other, as they loved to be. But surviving family calendars tell the story of a couple always on the go in these years. Their days in Pasadena were frequently filled with family as well as academic and organizational duties. Linda and Barclay would come for dinner, or Ava Helen would watch their children. In 1961 all the children, including Peter from London and Linus, Jr., from Honolulu, flew in to Pasadena in late February to celebrate their father's sixtieth birthday.

But then, abruptly, Linus and Ava Helen would be off on another speaking trip, often combined with a ceremony in which Linus received one of his hundreds of lifetime honors, or a conference with WILPF or, later, Women Strike for Peace (WSP), or Pugwash, or another one of Linus's

Ava Helen and Linus at his sixtieth birthday celebration, 1961.

scientific organizations. When they traveled, they kept up an even more frenetic schedule that must have been increasingly challenging even for this vital couple as they moved into their sixties. It was punctuated, rarely, by sick days—in April, Ava Helen stayed in bed in New York with a cold the day before they flew to Paris. A letter copied to Ava Helen by a friend who thought she would not be offended reveals that the Paulings could be difficult guests, charismatic and pleasant, yes, but also somewhat headstrong and impulsive in their movements, which could disrupt their hosts' carefully laid plans. "[M]any tensions apparently arose last year with the Friends Service Committee and the Paulings because the Service Committee made certain arrangements for them and then they decided they would rather do other things, changed dates, and things like that. Estelle has just been through some of this sort of thing with Pete Seeger and does not think she could take it again."[71] Many individuals on the celebrity circuit undoubtedly found the same salvation as Seeger and the Paulings, surviving the grueling pace and relentless encounters with new people by sidestepping carefully laid plans to do what they'd rather.

Occasionally they traveled separately—less frequently than one would guess given their different professional commitments. From the tenth Pugwash Conference in London in September 1962 Linus wrote to Ava Helen in Montreal, as she attended a joint Voice of Women and Women Strike for Peace conference. "How soon can you come to Philadelphia?" he asked poignantly. "If you go immediately after the Toronto meeting, I'll come the same day, and stay with you in the Benj. Franklin. Did you reserve a room? Can we meet there on Tuesday the 18th? I want to see you. Perhaps we could have a day or two of holidays— just fun."[72]

After the Oslo conference, the Paulings found themselves in demand at home as well as beyond California. In June Ava Helen Pauling was the third seminar leader in a three-week series, "A Course for Survival," sponsored by the Los Angeles chapter of WILPF. The first speaker was Dr. Albert Baez, physics professor at Claremont College, who addressed human survival (and whose daughters, Joan and Mimi, were poised to achieve international fame as folk singers); the second was Dr. Frances Herring, professor of governmental studies at Berkeley and an Oslo attendee. She discussed economic survival in a nuclear age. Ava Helen's topic was "our responsibility for survival in a nuclear age." Coming directly from Oslo, she carried the themes of the conference to a larger audience. Her audience asked questions about the Oslo Conference for two hours. In October she connected with sympathetic WILPF members in San Jose when that chapter honored her and Linus with a tea. Ava Helen gave a talk on "Women and World Progress toward Peace."[73]

One of Ava Helen's subsidiary aims in offering talks on peace topics in these years was to help WILPF chapters revitalize their membership. It was a tacitly understood problem that the WILPF membership was aging, and new members were needed to push the organization forward. Ladies' hats could still be spotted at WILPF conferences. Lenore Job, the San Jose leader who organized the Pauling tea, wrote with delight after the event that "there was great enthusiasm expressed about your talk … I do feel that your presence marked a turning point in our fortunes." Job also expressed satisfaction when a younger woman, Barbara Ulmer, was elected to the state presidency. She believed Ulmer would bring needed change to the organization. "It will be interesting to see what happens to 'State' in the next year."[74] Nancy Reeves of the Los Angeles chapter wrote to Ava Helen that they had a shortage of "working members." Though they were a large branch on paper, there were "only a very few women who do anything beyond attending meetings. Many are elderly." Others saw WILPF as a "token" membership and worked mainly for their other organizations.[75]

From the Oslo Conference excitement, Ava Helen turned immediately to the upcoming 1962 triennial WILPF Congress, originally planned for San Francisco. As a California WILPF member, Ava Helen would have been called upon to pay special attention to the triennial; as a national board member and a peace movement celebrity, she might influence the planning and agenda for the meeting. She had allies both in California and beyond. They brought their pleas to the annual conference at St. Paul, Minnesota, in

Left: Ava Helen on lawn with two women at a WILPF meeting. Inscribed on back by Vally Weigl.
Right: Ava Helen at a breakfast table with three women, at a WILPF meeting in St. Paul (both photographs probably 1961).

June. The Northern California regional meeting had drafted a proposal for observers from "communist and undeveloped countries," and asserted that Los Angeles and Atlanta were ready to join them. They proposed that the observers be invited to participate in a range of activities, including a post-conference two-day program in San Francisco, around themes of educating children for peace and nonviolence. Olive Mayer of Palo Alto, a passionate and complicated advocate of U.S.-Soviet friendship, spearheaded this proposal and sent Ava Helen a stream of letters in mid-1961 explaining her ideas and her disappointment with WILPF leadership on these issues.

Ava Helen understood these disappointments. At the WILPF annual meeting in St. Paul she had a good time with her friends at the opening supper, until President Orlie Pell neglected to announce her talk on the Oslo outcomes, a last-minute addition to the program, at 8:30 the next morning. "What is the matter with her?" she scribbled to herself in annoyance.[76]

Ava Helen communicated with the international leadership in August. If they were cool on the additional conference, Mayer was set to volunteer her own Palo Alto chapter to organize it. She hoped to find additional California women (obviously including Ava Helen) to join the project. She also offered short lists of women she would like to work with and women she intended to avoid. "Ostrander is *wildly* opposed to the project and Shamleffer has little or no enthusiasm for it."[77] Mayer argued that the ideal leaders were Ava Helen or Ruth Gage Colby, another longtime and sympathetic WILPF-er. She wrote an additional letter to Dorothy Hutchinson of the U.S. Section, explaining the urgency of a peace discussion that included women from

Latin America, the Middle East, Africa and Asia, as well as "those nations aligned with the eastern bloc of the East-West conflict."[78] She confided to Ava Helen that several WILPF leaders, including Laurie Sisson, Erna Harris, and, as expected, Wilma Ostrander had raised a "great protest" against the post-conference proposal, arguing that the Palo Alto women were "wrecking" the congress.[79]

Gertrude Baer, the feisty international leader, longtime WILPF consultant first to the League of Nations, and then to the United Nations, also urged Ava Helen to attend the International Executive Conference in London in August in order to help her exhume the underlying issues dividing these WILPF factions. In a letter marked "STRICTLY CONFIDENTIAL," she offered anecdotes illustrating the deep fears in various European WILPF sections, including being associated with "leftist" groups. Baer told Ava Helen that the only reason many WILPF members were willing to sign the Oslo Statement, despite the Paulings' left-leaning reputation, was because of Linus's Nobel Prize of 1954. Baer was loath to give up on WILPF quite yet. Her life's work was sunk into that venerable organization. She advised Ava Helen to discourage Anne (Mrs. Cyrus) Eaton, a prominent peace advocate, from launching a Women's Peace Party until after the California WILPF triennial. She hoped that by then there would be enough movement back toward WILPF's founding impetus to make alternative peace organizations redundant. "I have done quite a bit of thinking … & am pretty sure that the conditions in the WILPF are such that we who are obsessed by the situation & obsessed by the things we MUST do, cannot be satisfied with making a tea club of an organization which was established to FIGHT for peace."[80]

Ava Helen wrote back to Baer broaching Olive Mayer's idea of a post-conference conference. Baer was enthusiastic, but she urged Ava Helen to get the Palo Alto women to shift their focus away from peace education for children and back to the core mission of WILPF. Children were important, yes; but "World Disarmament and World Construction is the very urgent, the imperative work women MUST do at present. We are on the brink of war and can't afford *NOT to demand total* and *universal* disarmament which is our specific work." She strongly recommended that the post-conference conference be considered a high-level selective meeting, not a mass meeting; she pointed out that such a conference would attract the most intellectually powerful of women, who would be offended to think that the westerners considered them only interested in folk dancing and games. She suggested that the organizers would duplicate the work of UNICEF if they focused exclusively on issues of childhood.[81]

Else Leuthen also corresponded with Ava Helen about the Palo Alto plan, in the context of discussing the distribution of the Oslo appeal. She hedged,

Ava Helen speaking at "No More Hiroshimas" march, sponsored by Women Strike for Peace, San Francisco, August 1961.

observing that the United States executive had turned down the idea, and said that she would be happy to entertain it at International, though she did not know how they could manage it if the U.S. section was hostile to it.[82] Ava Helen wrote urgently to Mildred Olmsted: "I feel so strongly about the critical situation in the world and a meeting between the women of the various countries that I ask you once more, dear Mrs. Olmsted, to use your great influence to bring about this Meeting of Women under the auspices of the WILPF." She begged Olmsted to pass the request to the other international leaders assembled, including, of course, "dear Gertrud Baer." "Let us make this a memorable International Congress in the best tradition of Jane Addams and the courageous women who stood with her."[83]

Ultimately the International Executive settled on a compromise: inviting a number of women from non-WILPF nations to attend the triennial the next year. Olive Mayer, after all her work, seemed satisfied with the outcome (and perhaps relieved not to have to organize the huge undertaking she had proposed). The other project that had gained in popularity in the United States section, even among leaders who shuddered at inviting Soviet bloc women to form their own WILPF sections, was international visits of delegations of women who would penetrate the Iron Curtain and enhance their understanding of the other side's point of view. This was a project that for some reason appealed to leaders such as Orlie Pell, who was part of an initiative to invite a handful of Soviet women to a kind of summit in Princeton in November 1961. She invited Ava Helen, perhaps as an appeasement gesture. Ava Helen had planned to attend, but then begged off because, ironically, she and Linus had decided to travel to the Soviet Union to attend the two hundred fiftieth celebration of the birth of Mikail Lomonosov, a celebrated Russian scientist.[84]

The WILFP conference location had been settled as Asilomar, on the Monterey Peninsula south of San Francisco, rather than in the city. Founded in Pacific Grove in 1913, Asilomar had evolved from a YWCA summer camp to a conference center managed by a nonprofit company on behalf of the California State Parks system. Asilomar had just entered a period of planned development and modernization, and in many ways it made sense for WILPF to streamline the conference by holding it in one unified and accessible venue.

The conference went forward in July 1962. Ava Helen found it under-whelming: dull, unchallenging, trivial, and irrelevant. "No one seems willing to transcend the personal rivalries and jealousies and idiosyncrasies in order to have a look at the real problems which menace the world today," she complained to her friend Virginia Foster Durr, another WILPF-er and a bold white voice in the civil rights movement in the South. Ava Helen suggested that the one thing Durr had most missed in skipping the conference was the setting itself: "Asilomar is such a beautiful place ... the pines growing right down to the sea, and this beautiful white sand and the lovely dunes make it really a wonderful place." Ava Helen and a few other "adventuresome" souls got up early enough to swim in the fifty-degree waters. The conference facilities mandated roommates, and for Ava Helen that was a high point of the conference. She roomed with her friend Lucila De La Verde, a peace activist from Bogota, Colombia, and Jan Symons, who in 1962 was living in Australia. Symons and De La Verde were both full of life: the woman from Colombia "warm, friendly, lovable," and Symons difficult, funny, and "volatile." The three of them had parties in their room where they connected with some of the younger women at the conference, one of whom expressed Ava Helen's opinion of the conference even more bluntly. Apologizing to Durr for the language, Ava Helen quoted the New Yorker as dismissing the conference in disgust as "nothing but shit."[85]

To Ava Helen, the current leaders seemed fossilized and inbred. They allowed only certain voices to be heard—among them Pell and her allies—while silencing others, including the venerable Gertrude Baer. "Baer is difficult," Ava Helen wrote, "but her integrity is absolute, and

122

she certainly knows more than anyone else—not only about the WIL but about international relations and what is needed." Nonetheless, Ava Helen witnessed a "vicious effort" to get Baer off the International Executive. "I couldn't really believe that the top brass preferred having a flop rather than include people who knew something about international gatherings and the world. But they did prefer to have it a failure and spent all of their time in the most shocking underhanded intrigue and skullduggery which disgusted everyone who knew of it even including the foreigners who tried to be polite and grateful but were having a hard time when they thought of all the time & money and the small, small return."[86]

One of the initiatives pursued by the triennial organizers was to invite and "integrate" African American women into the organization. This too met with mixed success. On the one hand, leaders like Vera Foster, Bess Walcott, and Flemmie Kittrell did attend; on the other hand, Ava Helen felt that they were either silenced or silenced themselves, a reality that made Ava Helen impatient, though she tried to be compassionate and empathetic. "I only wish that they would be more vocal in their protest at meetings such as this one. The WIL feels that just having them there proves that everything is getting much better, and Mildred Olmsted even talked about how much had been accomplished by the non-violent methods in the South. Can you really believe that things have been non-violent in the South?"[87] She had to stifle herself so that she was not always the only voice heard; apparently Ava Helen was not put in the same category as the others, whom she felt were actively discouraged from talking. She told Durr she wanted to laugh at one leader's admonition that WILPF should only talk to people who could talk to their governments. "I wanted to say that perhaps we talk to our government, here in the United States, but we had never had the slightest inkling as to whether or not we are ever heard." She took her angry cynicism one step further: "At the next Board meeting I am going to ask straight out for concrete examples of when, if ever, the government has paid the slightest attention to what the WIL has ever said."[88]

Virginia Foster Durr

Ava Helen Pauling's correspondence with Virginia Foster Durr from 1960 through the end of Ava Helen's life in 1981 is singularly full (particularly in the early 1960s), frank, and affectionate. These two active, opinionated women were both married to successful and often embattled men (Virginia Foster was married to Clifford Durr, onetime federal official and subsequently a major civil rights attorney in Alabama). Their relationship began through

WILPF meetings in the late 1950s, where each offered her unique insights on movements of the day: Ava Helen on the test ban movement, of course, and Virginia Foster Durr on her hazardous front-row perspective on the African American civil rights struggle in the South.[89] They drew close through their letters in 1961, agreeing on crucial points where each had felt alone and isolated, but also daring to disagree. They fell into a lively correspondence. Recovering from a foot surgery, Durr wrote to Ava Helen in the summer of 1962, "I too wish we could be together and do foot exercises and have time to discuss all of our acquaintances and ideas. It seems hard to discover someone like you and then to be so terribly far away." Virginia Durr joined wholeheartedly in Ava Helen's fatigued disgust with the anti-Communist campaigns that distracted from pressing issues and silenced willing voices. Both women condemned the liberals who kowtowed to the pressure of the red-baiters and "swallow[ed] the big lie." "[A]ll of these rights are being taken away as they were in Germany and in Italy and in Spain and in Japan on account of the terrible danger of the 'Communist Conspiracy' and so we go closer and closer to fascism on the basis of a big lie," wrote Durr. [90]

For her as for Ava Helen, the consequences of resisting that "big lie" were palpable. In 1948 Clifford Durr had turned down Truman's offer of reappointment to the Federal Communications Commission because he refused to administer Truman's loyalty program in his agency. The FBI had been keeping tabs on Durr since the war because of his civil liberties stances, akin to Linus Pauling's.[91] In fact the Paulings and the Durrs may have had their first significant, though impersonal, encounter in the early 1950s. After Durr bounced himself out of federal service, he went to Denver to take up a private position as attorney to the Farmers Union Insurance Company. He lost that position when his wife, Virginia, signed a petition circulated by Linus Pauling against bombing north of the Yalu River during the Korean War.[92]

For Virginia Durr, who like Ava Helen had spent several decades with a high-profile spouse constantly under scrutiny or under fire, the fundamental importance of civil liberties was clear. "I look at things from the standpoint of the Law as that is what I live in and among as you do among science and I feel that the struggle for Civil Liberties (not Civil Rights) is the most important struggle of all, for if that is lost, then no one can do anything constructive at all for we will not be allowed to speak, meet, write, or even think."[93] Clifford Durr had bailed Rosa Parks out of jail in 1955. The Durrs were close to Anne and Carl Braden, journalists who survived persecution and danger when they helped a black family purchase a house in a white neighborhood in Shively, Kentucky. The house was bombed. Carl Braden was afterward imprisoned on trumped-up sedition charges connected to the bombing and served eight months before the Supreme Court invalidated state sedition laws. Anne Braden was a WILPF member, though too distracted by her civil rights work to be particularly active in the peace movement in the 1950s. (Ava Helen sent a check to Virginia Foster Durr in 1962 to help Anne Braden get to the triennial—"She'll be good for WIL"— but she was unable to come.)

Agreeing about the maddening foolishness of potential allies who gave in to red-baiting, Virginia Durr and Ava Helen both regretted what had happened to SANE in its attempt to avoid government condemnation. "I have a real fear of that Homer Jack," Durr wrote of one of the SANE leaders, echoing Ava Helen's opinion. "I know him and think he is very dangerous as in spite of what they _say_ they talk in terms of waging a 'Holy War' against Communism and while they say they are for 'Peace' they contribute all the time to the very premise that makes for War." [94]

Likewise, they both worried about the WILPF leadership faction that seemed to condone and even foster anti-leftist divisiveness. "I agree completely on the awful Orlie," Durr wrote early in their friendship, "and there is nothing I hate so much as the kind of Peace People who spread hate and fear by protecting themselves by red baiting." [95] Two months later, on receiving Ava Helen's apologetically jaded report on the triennial, Virginia wrote back satirizing the position of anti-Soviet peace advocates: "Although you are a son of a bitch, and my position is plain that I think you are one and I will not associate with you, still I want 'PEACE.'" [96]

On the other hand, Durr cautioned Ava Helen Pauling to see the good in an often-frustrating organization, largely because she had witnessed WILPF heroines in the Southern struggles putting their principles on the line. "What they have done in the South has been unique—they were the first National women's group that came South and did not segregate. All of the others, no matter what pious profession they make in Convention, come South and segregate themselves but the WILPF did not. Thus they won the confidence of the Negro Women and through them the idea of the necessity to have Peace in order to get any Civil Rights is slowly leaking into the rising Negro movement here." [97] To the Durrs, who risked their lives and livelihoods for civil rights, the "Negro movement," as Virginia called it in 1962, "is the one, new, rising and shining movement in the country." [98]

Durr also pleaded with Ava Helen not to resign in disgust. The "genteel (or as you say not so genteel)" red baiting was everywhere, she asserted, and not just in WILPF or the peace movement more broadly. "I think it is dangerous and evil and is going to bring about our ruin unless it is stopped

Clifford Durr, Ava Helen, and Linus Pauling standing outside Robert and Decca Treuhaft's house during the Durrs' California trip, 1963. Decca Treuhaft was the married name of Jessica Mitford, the author of The American Way of Death, *which Ava Helen admired and cited. The Durrs and the Treuhafts were close friends.*

but I do not see how you can simply withdraw from every organization that does it. I think the thing to do is to stay in and fight it. Let them throw you out on a principle and NEVER resign until they do … [N]ever leave a vacuum or the evil forces will certainly fill it up."[99]

As a witness to and sparkplug in the civil rights movement, vilified by family and peers in the white professional communities of the South, Durr knew evil intimately. Yet she believed that ignorant and frightened people outnumbered evil ones even in the dark places of human interaction. "They [the ignorant and frightened] may turn on you but still the only chance they have to escape death, destruction, war and all horrors is to stick with them."[100]

Ava Helen in turn urged Virginia to run for the WILPF board. "I was once elected to the Board," Virginia admitted, "and had to resign as I could never go." Now, she said, she might be able to go, but couldn't afford to unless WILPF could subsidize board members to attend meetings. Civil rights attorneys in the South did not make a pile of money in the early 1960s. Virginia worked in Clifford's office to consolidate family finances. Durr suggested that part of WILPF's current problems might be alleviated by a rotating board attendance scheme whereby younger women could be brought in to the inner circles of leadership.[101]

Ava Helen found the civil rights movement deeply compelling. In 1960 she wrote to the president of the Greyhound Corporation protesting the arrest of several black youngsters attempting to ride on an interstate bus. They were the children of the Reverend Fred Shuttlesworth, a Birmingham minister and a colleague of Martin Luther King, Jr., in the Southern Christian Leadership Conference. By 1961 Shuttlesworth was a leader in the dangerous Freedom Riders actions, crossing state lines on Greyhound buses to challenge segregation. For Ava Helen as for Virginia Durr, the civil rights cause was at base a civil liberties issue. On that same September day in 1960 she wrote to the governor of Florida protesting the imprisonment of two men for refusing to name names by giving up the membership list of the NAACP. "I speak with more feeling and knowledge than the usual person, because I have, in the last few months, experienced what it means to be called before the Security Subcommittee of the United States and ordered to give lists of names to them," she asserted. "It is ridiculous for us to be sending protests to Africa for the same things which happen here at home. I hope that you will see to it that the First Amendment to the Constitution of the United States is put back in its rightful place in Florida" by releasing the two ministers penalized by this "witch hunt."[102]

These letters, however futile, offer a window into Ava Helen's political and moral world at this time.[103] The civil rights movement to her represented social justice as outlined and supposedly guaranteed by United States law. She did not escape the well-meaning condescension many liberal whites expressed toward the African American liberation movement. "I have been interested for many years in the progress the Negroes have been making and have tried to be helpful. I have realized that until they themselves made vigorous efforts to change their condition, not much could be done. I rejoice that at last they know that they themselves must break their chains," she wrote to a friend in 1963—eight years after the Montgomery bus boycott and the rise of the Southern Christian Leadership Conference to the forefront of an invigorated direct action campaign in the South. "I believe that the most intelligent Negroes are beginning to realize that more is involved than just the right to enter a restaurant, and I am afraid that we shall have many difficulties before we solve this problem."[104]

For a white woman from Pasadena, Los Angeles was still a few years away from being a hot spot of racial confrontation, and we may put Ava Helen's archaic talk about the "most intelligent Negroes" in that context of social privilege and distance. She certainly saw clearly the enormity of white resistance. "Our Negro people are making great progress," she wrote to a friend in New Zealand, "but they are being abused in a terrible way.

It is almost of revolutionary magnitude. Perhaps you saw in your papers how our police used cattle prods, high pressure water hoses, vicious dogs against these people who were only making a non-violent protest against the injustices which they have endured ever since the formation of our country. Our Emancipation Proclamation was not really of much significance to the Negro people."[105]

Ava Helen Pauling and Virginia Foster Durr were not the only women in WILPF who worried about the crosscutting currents of civil rights and peace work. African American women spoke in the women's peace movement from the founding years of WILPF, as Melinda Plastas has written. Addie Hunton and Mary Church Terrell were among a handful of black leaders who "brought together the threads of race and gender and war and demanded a place for black women in the international movements emerging from the war."[106] Evelyn Alloy, Pauling's correspondent in this instance, was a Philadelphia WILPF member who may have been aware of her own city's pioneering effort in cross-racial peace work embodied in the Interracial Extension Committee.[107] These women may have been reinventing a wheel whose previous copies were, like the entire history of race relations in the United States, simply unfit for the road.

It may also have been the very vigor of the postwar civil rights movement that cast previous efforts at interracial cooperation, not to mention previous phases of African American-led protest, into the shadows. It was a new world, with new movements that addressed the same old problems. As Joyce Blackwell points out about WILPF during the difficult civil rights/ McCarthy years, a cautious WILPF national board did stutter for a moment before endorsing 1954's *Brown v. Board of Education* decision, to the shock of the African American women on WILPF's Civil Rights Committee, but the board finally agreed to help enforce the school desegregation ruling through their official pronouncements as well as members' participation in demonstrations and other direct actions.[108]

Conflicting loyalties complicated Virginia Durr's job as diplomat and activist, trying to inject the civil rights movement with peace ideals. Having helped arrange the African American women's attendance at the WILPF triennial, she began feeling the backfire almost immediately. Bess Walcott, a friend of Durr's from the Tuskegee Institute who had attended the triennial with funds donated by Ava Helen, began to chill toward Durr upon returning to Alabama. "I feel almost sure she has been propagandized and is now scared of you, and of me. This of course is the kind of insidious smearing that we hate so and that is so hateful and so hard to combat." Durr pointed out that the African American civil rights activists were as prone to credulity about rumors of Communist conspiracy as white people, and that, further, they were vulnerable in ways she and Ava Helen could only imagine. The Tuskegee Institute was chronically under scrutiny and had been for seventy years. The institution was "dependent both on Northern millionaires and the Alabama Legislature" (a daunting one-two punch, to be sure). No wonder there was a chill in the air toward the Paulings and their allies.[109] Further, as Virginia Durr understood, at least as far as a person privileged by color could understand, no friendship could be complete when one party was socially forbidden to host the other party in her house. "[W]e are struggling all the time to make conditions in which it would be possible to have a normal friendship here and as it is, any social contact of that kind is fraught with so much danger of arrest and newspaper exposure and attach, that it hardly seems worth it … It is such an unequal friendship."[110]

It was gratifying for Ava Helen to find a kindred spirit in Virginia Durr, a woman she could both admire and understand, in these years of intense pressures and public demands. "I think," she confided to Virginia in the midst of planning an upcoming tour, "this is one of the difficulties with the world that we live in that there is never a time when people are not under pressure and this becomes very wearing."[111] As the friendship bloomed, stimulating and comforting both of them, they started to plan mutual working visits. The Paulings were happy to consider coming South, but again, the politics of peace, and the difficulty of championing any liberal causes in the segregated South, stood in the way. Ann Braden offered to help Ava Helen arrange a series of appearances at the traditionally Negro colleges, but Vera Foster, the African American leader, said no—at least not at Tuskegee. As Virginia quoted her, "Race is all we can fight right now, Peace on top of Race is too much."[112]

Finding California audiences for Clifford and Virginia Durr was a different story. The Durrs' tales of the dawning of public television, of civil rights struggles, even of peace, were all welcome in the liberal churches and community forums there. Ava Helen had just taken on the chair of the forum at the First Unitarian Church in Los Angeles. The Durrs had old friends from Washington days in both Los Angeles and San Francisco. The journalist Jessica Mitford (known to friends as Decca Treuhaft) and her husband, Bob Treuhaft, were in Oakland, and had lots of ideas for the Durrs' appearances, including the Lawyers' Guild there. As is often the case, money trailed behind eagerness in making the tour come together. Ava Helen finally took matters into her own hands, a welcome development as far as Virginia was concerned, considering that both families were now red flags for liberal as well as conservative bulls. "[I]f we come and it all can be arranged, please understand that both of us are coming on your invitation, as your guests and on account of you and your husband, whose integrity as well as whose wisdom we have absolute trust in."[113]

As the time for their visit drew near, the women celebrated the limited nuclear test ban treaty successfully negotiated by Kennedy, Macmillan, and Khrushchev and signed on August 5. "You will be happy to know," Ava Helen confided, "that we have been receiving congratulations from everywhere about the bomb-test agreement as if it were Linus's own doing, as indeed it is, to a large extent, and one of the gifts that we like best is a bottle of champagne, which perhaps we will save until you come, providing we can control the baseness in our natures."[114] The Durrs sent biographies and pictures, as well as previews of their proposed talks. Virginia wrote that she always gave the same talk, beginning with the "race issue" she knew so well, and then expanding that to suggest that the larger struggle was the one to "make the country the kind of country we promised it would be." If we fail, she averred, "we simply fail as citizens and the country fails and we are in danger of slipping down the slippery slope into violence, police terror and a form of the corporate state."[115]

Characteristically, the Paulings stood between celebrity and outsider status, balanced somehow on the thin edge of respectability. They illustrated this accustomed but uncomfortable position once again when Linus received an invitation to the White House in the spring of 1962. "A most exciting invitation has arrived!!" Ava Helen wrote to Eleanor Fowler. "Dinner at the White House on the 29th in honor of the Nobel Laureates!"[116] Though a dinner alone could not persuade her to "approve of JFK," Ava Helen as well as Linus experienced the occasion as a life event; she preserved the menu as well as the list of guests at her table. The couple played it both ways, using the occasion, perhaps relishing the occasion, to make their political point. On the 28th and 29th of April the Paulings joined anti-testing demonstrators at the White House gates, carrying a sign that declared, "Mr. President, We have no right to test!" On the evening of April 29, they entered the White House as honored guests. Both faced explicit challenges of their decision to protest on one side of the fence and dine as celebrities on the other. Jacqueline Kennedy, according to Linus's notes, asked him whether he thought it was right for him to "walk back and forth" where little Caroline could see him and ask her mother, "What has Daddy done wrong now?"[117]

Ava Helen too faced an insider's wrath. Her dinner companions included Arthur Schlesinger, Jr., the Harvard historian turned White House assistant and biographer of John Kennedy. Ava Helen found Schlesinger so annoying and unpleasant that much of her personal record of the occasion is taken up with a detailed account of her conversation with the historian, perhaps for the relief of itemizing his offenses. First, he pulled his chair leg over her chiffon skirt. Secondly, he asked if she shared Linus's opinions about politics. When she assented, he challenged Linus's decision to demonstrate against Kennedy and then accept an invitation to "break bread" with a man he had criticized. Schlesinger then pulled the Harvard trump card—perhaps, he said, she thought he asked such questions because he was a professor at Harvard. She retorted that Linus had been offered a Harvard professorship some years earlier and had turned it down! Finally, Schlesinger made the most damning *faux pas* in Ava Helen's eyes by surreptitiously gathering up all the White House matchbooks (a strange action, it is true, for a man presumably privy to the innermost circles). Ava Helen caught him and pointedly asked *where all the matchbooks had gone*—so that he had to give them back, one to her and one to the wife of Van Wyck Brooks, also seated at their table. Disturbed beyond her normally fine command of English, she wrote that Schlesinger was "a clout and a boor."[118]

The encounter between Ava Helen Pauling and Arthur Schlesinger, Jr., so comical in hindsight, was fraught with the painful tensions of those Cold War years, and the splits among liberals that created such lasting resentments. The Paulings not only challenged the young president Schlesinger revered, whose coattails he enjoyed grasping, but also typified the foolish dangers posed by fellow travelers who refused to understand the Soviet danger. To Ava Helen he criticized his Harvard colleague H. Stuart Hughes, running for Congress in Massachusetts on a liberal ticket that counseled coexistence with Communists. Soviets couldn't even get news from the West, Schlesinger insisted. Apparently anxious to establish his own liberal *bona fides*, he told Ava Helen that the American Legion always picketed him when he appeared in Columbus, Ohio (his home town).

"You cannot imagine how much we are looking forward to the visit. It is like a golden apple to be plucked," wrote Virginia to Ava Helen in early August. The South was hot, and would continue hot well into autumn. She wondered what she should wear, as pictures of southern California always showed women in shorts and bathing suits, and she wondered what "nice, respectable, middle aged ladies do wear in October."[119] The South was also volatile, and the Durrs needed a break. Life became even darker after the Sixteenth Street Baptist Church was bombed Sunday morning, September 15, killing four children. Standing "in shame" and grieving the "horrible and dastardly" murder of the children, Virginia blamed Governor Wallace and reflected that the majority of the "White South" was in a "very dangerous frame of mind."[120]

The visit was crowded and delightful.[121] The Durrs' visit confirmed the couples' regard for each other. After the bustle of Los Angeles area appearances and dinners, the couples meandered up the coast toward San Francisco by way of the Paulings' Big Sur ranch. They argued and joked and had a wonderful time. "I don't know when I have laughed so much or felt so young," Virginia wrote afterward.[122] On the morning of October 10 the Paulings and the Durrs were eating breakfast in the simple house so beloved by Linus and Ava Helen when the ranger arrived from the station and asked Pauling to come with him to take a call from their daughter, Linda. The day the test ban treaty took effect, the Nobel committee had announced its intention to give the Nobel Peace Prize for 1962 to Linus Pauling.

While the peace prize committee grabbed the historic moment with wild success, the members missed, of course, another opportunity. "Today's wonderful news," wrote Janet Stevenson to Ava Helen, "is only slightly clouded for me — and I must confess, my feminist mother — by the failure of the Nobel Institute to recognize that it is a team of Paulings which deserved the prize (Mother says the judges must be men). I know — and I'm sure most of those who have walked 'behind' the team's leadership know — that your contribution has been an indispensable complement to Linus's. I'm very proud to have been for a little while a cog in the human machine the two of you set in motion years ago — the machine which I hope will produce perpetual motion for peace. One of the most important lessons of my later years has been the one that the pair of you have taught me of how a team should and can work — with creative differences and fundamental unity. It's more than a lesson. It's an inspiration. So I congratulate you *both,* with grateful affection."[123] Stevenson had captured the Paulings' style, the dynamic collaboration of intimates that created their contribution to world dialogue.

CHAPTER 5

"The Second X Chromosome"

We think that the situation in the world is somewhat better now although there is still very much to be done. The Peace Movement in the United States as you know, is badly fragmented and we still many of us spend most of our time proving how anti-communist we are.
— AHP to John N. Dragoumis, November 27, 1963[1]

You know, of course, that if the WIL and the AFSC were to do really effective peace work, they would become subversive too. The appellation of organizations as subversive is one of the most wicked and cruel unjust things that has ever happened in this country and it should be resisted by everyone who believes in human dignity. This is one of the criticisms that I have of the WIL who are themselves guilty of going around in their whisper campaign against people and organizations.
— AHP to Vally Weigl, October 25, 1963[2]

No woman wants to be up on a pedestal (substitute shelf for pedestal) where she can be easily ignored and neglected. She wants to be taking and doing her part in the affairs of the world with her feet on the ground and sharing in and contributing to the life around her.
— Ava Helen Pauling, "The Second X Chromosome"

"A modern feminist," Ava Helen called herself in 1963, in an interview with *The Advertiser.* She was well launched on two projects: promoting Women Strike for Peace, the new organization that had already made its mark in Washington, D.C., and articulating a platform for women's improved status.

The celebration of Linus's second Nobel was bittersweet for both Paulings. Friends wrote from all over the world to congratulate him. Several

Linus and Ava Helen Pauling at CIT Biology Department tea in honor of his second Nobel prize, December 1963.

echocd Janet Stevenson's plaint: this should have been an award for both Paulings. Ava Helen was appropriately modest and generous. To Blanche Murphy she admitted that many people had said the prize should have been for both of them, but "I am afraid I cannot concur in that. Of course, any man who has lived or shared his life with his wife the number of years my husband and I have been together, must surely share his honors with her. We feel that this is a prize to the Peace Workers of the world and as such we are happy to represent them at this ceremony."[3] However, in less guarded moments her comments acknowledged some feeling of personal entitlement. As she wrote to Stanislawa Zawadecka in response to her letter of congratulations: "We think that this Nobel Prize is a vindication of the rightness of our position over many years." But she went on to credit Linus: "My husband's great courage and knowledge and his almost sublime faith in truth seems now to have some vindication."[4] She used the term "vindication" not once, but twice in that letter—a choice that underlines long years of struggle against their opponents. And indeed, along with the reporters and television cameras came whispers and grumbles of dissent. "Not everyone seems to be as happy as you," wrote Ava Helen wryly to Stuart Innerst of Pasadena.[5]

By November the Paulings were in full planning mode for their trip to Oslo, and additional implications of the prize had sunk in. "I was going to give a talk about women in which I was to say that Madame Curie had been the only person to win two Nobel prizes," she wrote to her friend Catherine Colburn. "Now my husband has interfered with my speech." She went on proudly and pedantically, "Of course, Madame Curie shared the first prize so that in a sense, Linus is unique. No one else has received two full prizes in different fields."[6]

The bitter part of bittersweet was generated close to home. The California Institute of Technology was unenthusiastic about the global honor bestowed on its most famous chemist. In the end, in fact, it was the biology faculty rather than his chemistry faculty that celebrated Pauling with a formal tea. By then it was too late to do anything except pretend to smile; the die had been cast in October, when President DuBridge responded to news of the Nobel Peace Prize by saying publicly that the prize was a "spectacular recognition" of Pauling's "long and strenuous efforts to bring before the people of the world the dangers of nuclear war"; but he could not refrain from adding that "many people have disapproved of some of his methods and activities." The long years of conflict seem to have made it just too hard for DuBridge to lead with institutional pleasure at the singular honor of a second Nobel. Further, tensions had mounted in the chemistry division as the new head, Jack Roberts, essentially pushed Pauling out of the lab space, where he had been doing innovative cross-disciplinary work on the role of chemicals in mental illness.[7] For the Paulings, DuBridge's lukewarm reaction was the final straw. Pauling immediately ended his long career at Caltech and moved his lab and activities to the Center for the Study of Democratic Institutions in Santa Barbara. By mid-November Linus was laying plans for the grants he would apply for in his new institutional home.[8] And Ava Helen was preparing to leave the house she loved so much, where she had raised her children and entertained so many cohorts of Linus's graduate students, at 3500 Fairpoint Street in Pasadena. As usual, her public face smiled: she wrote to friends that moving to Santa Barbara would put them closer to their ranch at Big Sur, where "we can really do good, creative work."[9] Linus, too, could not shake off decades of loyalty to Caltech. His own press announcement stated that having won the Nobel Peace Prize, he felt an obligation to work for peace, and he might do that more effectively in the context of the Santa Barbara institute.[10]

Women Strike for Peace

Long before what would have been the beginning of her second term as a national vice president, Ava Helen had decided that the WILPF board was not for her. The Asilomar triennial confirmed her decision. She would not break with WILPF, but she would withdraw from leadership. The hardest part for her was telling her Pasadena friends. "Our Pasadena group is a good, shy, earnest small one, and I disliked telling them I didn't want to serve on the board any longer. I mean to keep my membership and I want to be useful but I mean to do what I believe is necessary if we are to make and keep a decent world."[11] To Otto Nathan, her much-admired friend in WILPF, she confessed, "I felt that I was not contributing anything and it was always a most depressing experience for me." She took satisfaction, still, in noting that the board election results had put her ahead of her nearest rival by a hundred votes.[12] Her invective against the leadership had grown increasingly sharp and sometimes nasty; it was time to leave.

Discouraged by what she experienced as the lumbering pace, stubborn institutionalism, and anti-Communist divisiveness of WILPF, Ava Helen found her silver lining in a new group, Women Strike for Peace, bursting upon the peace activist scene at the end of 1961. From the beginning Ava Helen was part of both the West Coast and the international network thrown over sympathetic souls in the first few years of the group.

Women Strike for Peace was the brainchild of women activists oppressed by the lead weight of political inertia in WILPF and SANE—not to mention the Congress and President of the United States. At the end of 1961 a group of Washington, D.C. women met at the home of Dagmar Wilson, a successful illustrator who identified more as a stay-at-home mother than a professional. From this initial meeting came the call for a new kind of organization—an "un-organization"—that would include anyone, in particular any woman, who wanted to mount an action for peace and disarmament at any time, in any place. "We don't want any 'organization,'" claimed the first typewritten manifesto and call to action. "We don't want chairmen, boards, committees, long series of meetings. We just want to speak out, loudly, to tell our elected representatives that they are not properly representing US by continuing the arms race and increasing the threat of total destruction." The first uprising would occur on November 1, 1961, when women would "go on strike" from "domestic and business duties." Women would march in the streets and call on their elected officials. "That's all. We're not asking anyone to sign anything, join anything. Details in your town are up to you. You may want to hold a city-wide meeting sometime on November 1—or you may not."[13]

Amy Swerdlow did incisive work on the history of Women Strike for Peace, beginning with her own pioneer participation and extending into scholarly analysis after her peace career led her back to graduate school and a PhD in history. Her article, "Ladies' Day at the Capitol," first published in 1982 and later incorporated into her monograph, *Women Strike for Peace: Traditional Motherhood and Radical Politics in the 1960s* (1993), offers a lively rendition of the WSP women's appearance under subpoena before the House Un-American Activities Committee in December 1962. The narrative confirms that the "un-organization" organization of WSP brilliantly addressed the vulnerabilities of individuals and organizations called up to answer for their questionable affiliations. If there were no organization, there were no membership lists. If there were no membership lists, there could hardly be leaders. If there were no leaders (a fiction, of course), there were fewer opportunities for investigative bodies to divide and conquer the rank and file by challenging their loyalty to the organization. "Even in Phila.," wrote Evelyn Alloy, "where we have had a remarkable amount of WILPF direct action projects (at least one a month ranging from protest walks to petitions, etc) I am finding that women who temperamentally are like myself are finding WSFP [sic] more congenial. I keep wondering whether the way the top echelon of WILPF maintains close control has something to do with it?"[14] Further and most important, as Swerdlow points out, "WSP had, even before the HUAC hearings, decided to reject political screening of its members, deeming it a manifestation of outdated cold war thinking."[15]

Though there was no organization *per se*, a large committee of New York and Washington WSPers got together as the subpoenas began rolling out, to hire defense lawyers and plan a response. True to their founding principle, they decided that all women called before the committee, regardless of their political affiliations, would be entitled to the same level of defense. On the day of the hearings, WSP members packed the room with babies and toddlers in their laps or in the aisles. Members spontaneously rose as each witness was called to the stand. They handed bouquets of flowers to those about to testify. They applauded each member's statements. The witnesses for the most part kept their cool sufficiently to launch wisecracks and lead the committee through Alice in Wonderland rhetorical contortions. Some invoked the First Amendment, and some the Fifth. Some called it as they saw it. As Virginia Foster Durr reflected, "I think Dagmar Wilson got to the heart of the matter in her testimony, when she said of course she would accept the support of Communists in any movement for Peace and of Fascists too if they would only support a Peace movement."[16]

Perhaps most importantly, the WSP women won the amused sympathy of the national press. Though Swerdlow points out that press coverage of WSP was condescending, jokey, and dismissive, she also captures the admiring irreverence of the great political cartoonist who had one committee member say to another, "I came in late, which was it that was un-American—women or peace?"[17] If WSP had one resounding victory, it was helping to bury HUAC under its own irrelevance.

Ava Helen was thrilled by the idea of WSP when she heard about it in mid-October 1961, and spread the news among her WILPF friends and associates. "I have had several copies of the women's Strike for Peace and I think it is a splendid idea. I am hoping we can do something about it in this area, although our Los Angeles WIL is quite reactionary and we do not believe that they will help very much."[18] The WSP women recognized the Paulings from the start as inspiring allies. In April 1962, shortly after the Kennedy administration announced the resumption of atmospheric nuclear testing, the Paulings joined three thousand United States WSP members picketing the White House. The line of marchers snaked around the White House several times. Linus accepted a placard from one of the women demonstrators, and it was the picture of him carrying that sign that hit the newspapers. That evening, Linus and Ava Helen joined the receiving line for their Nobel recognition dinner inside.[19]

The Janice Holland Award, presented to Ava Helen and Linus Pauling by the Pennsylvania chapter of Woman Strike for Peace, September 1962.

Not only did Linus's predicament before the SISS in 1961 help inspire WSP's strategy before HUAC a year later, but in August 1962, well before the HUAC meetings, the Washington, D.C., WSP invited the Paulings to attend their one-year birthday celebration in order to receive, jointly, the Janice Holland Peace Award. Holland had been both a WILPF member and a WSP founder.[20] The Paulings flew from New York to Washington on October 21 to accept the award. The next year the Paulings sent greetings to the second birthday celebration, where they were warmly remembered.[21]

Turning the HUAC hearings into a circus, and catching Kennedy's attention in front of the White House, were not WSP's only victories. Over the next few years these indefatigable women took their collective organizing experience, as well as several new techniques, into the international field. Amy Swerdlow suggests that enthusiasm from peace workers in a number of nations precipitated what she believes would never have otherwise been undertaken at that time: a truly international organization—or at least an organization with an international label. Ruth Gage Colby, the most internationally minded of the WSP-ers, unilaterally renamed the organization "WISP," for Women's International Strike for Peace. As was appropriate to their founding philosophy, not all members followed suit.[22]

Gage Colby was typical of WILPF members eager to try a new approach to multilateral cooperation, and atypical in that she was deeply experienced in United Nations politics, as well as a bit of a loose cannon.[23] She and Ava Helen corresponded periodically. Gage Colby skillfully organized WSP's first big internationally coordinated action, a simultaneous multi-nation demonstration for disarmament in January 1962. The next international operation, involving fewer women, was in some ways far more ambitious. New York WSP members decided to take a delegation of women to the scene of international negotiations to end nuclear testing, in Geneva, Switzerland. The Paulings' schedule was chock full of travel in March 1962; in addition Ava Helen was in the midst of helping to plan the WILPF Asilomar meeting. She heard accounts later of the astonishing WSP feat of getting fifty Americans to Geneva, figuring out how to get foreign delegations, including the chief U.S. and Soviet negotiators, to talk with them, and taking all important decisions by consensus, so as not to fall victim to the divisions that had wracked WILPF and SANE. And finally, they coordinated with European and Soviet women to stage a march and vigil at the Palais des Nations.[24]

Compared to this spectacular achievement of political activism, which gained admirers within the international peace movement and among diplomats and journalists, the Asilomar meeting must have seemed — as previously narrated — flat and disappointing. Ava Helen forged ahead with her new non-WILPF peace activities. In early August 1962 San Francisco's Women for Peace, another name for the WSPers, sponsored a "Hiroshima Walk" to commemorate the bombing by walking nine miles, symbolizing the area that would have been destroyed had the same atomic bomb fallen on San Francisco. Ava Helen Pauling and Mildred Simon were the featured speakers. In October Ava Helen took part in an international conference of women sponsored by the new Voice of Women (VOW) in Canada. In the progressive New York *National Guardian* article about the conference, she was singled out with a head shot and identified as "Mrs. Linus Pauling." Even before the Nobel Peace Prize, the Pauling name was notorious among progressives.[25] The VOW conference had been set to coincide with International Cooperation Year. Helen Tucker and other Canadian women had worked hard to put together a responsive, active women's peace organization, and had reached out to Ava Helen and a handful of other Americans to set up a credible meeting. A trusted friend, Frances Herring, a professor of governmental studies at Berkeley and an expert in nuclear, environmental, and urban planning issues, was also a key American involved in VOW planning.

At the successful meeting the women believed they had created a structure for continued collaboration. In fact their initiative to launch an International Co-operation Year, as exemplified in the title of their meeting, was picked up by Nehru of India and adopted by the United Nations in 1963, to take

139

place in 1965.[26] But after the attendees went home the fireworks began, with a multilateral correspondence flying between Canada and the United States that painfully illustrated the difficulties of bringing many groups, of many philosophies, under one roof. Ava Helen had decided during the meeting that with her multiple commitments, she would choose to hand off the job of U.S. liaison coordinator to Herring, and she believed she had informed all relevant parties. Helen Tucker, the Canadian coordinator, wrote to her apologetically that Catherine Menninger among others had created a large fuss over the way that Herring had taken over without agreement and was asking for consent to measures the group had not yet discussed.

Ava Helen wrote back in exasperation, once again blindsided by the internal politics of the peace movement. She pointed out that Menninger had not been at the Montreal meeting at which Ava Helen believed most of these personnel details had been ironed out. In a four-page letter rare for its length among her correspondence, she tried to offer Tucker some deep background for what she believed was going on.

> *You know, of course, that the WILPF is an old and honored organization of women who have worked quietly and consistently for peace and world disarmament. It is, contrary to what some of you think in Canada, quite a reactionary organization. Perhaps reactionary is too strong a word, and certainly this does not apply to all of the members, but I think on the whole it is a reasonable word. Perhaps I should say conservative. You must know that it has only some 5,500 members, although it has been in existence for nearly 50 years. I think it is only reasonable for the WIL to look on these new vigorous organizations with some suspicion and perhaps a little envy. The tradition of Jane Addams and the wonderful women from all over the world who worked with her should be an example for all of us.[27]*

Here we see the contrary impulses pulling at Ava Helen, who was in fact still part of the national board of WILPF. On the one hand, she understood the pride of position that many WILPF members felt at their seniority and longevity in the peace movement, and their "quiet and consistent" presence through two world wars and now the nuclear age. On the other hand, Ava Helen herself was fed up with sectors of reactionary recalcitrance in WILPF's leadership, and she clearly welcomed the new breeze blown in by WSP—which in turn seized upon Ava Helen's passionate directness.

To return to Linda Richards' activism model, described in the previous chapter, Ava Helen was not only a "swirler," whose forte was making connections among sympathetic actors in order to accomplish political goals. She had also become somewhat entitled, to put it bluntly. The success of the Oslo conference in the winter of 1962 confirmed to the Paulings that they could parlay Linus's fame into real accomplishment, and they could do this without legitimation by an external organization, but simply by seizing the bull by the horns. If they declared their intention to do something, and invited others to join them, they could often succeed. This truth allowed Ava Helen to step away from the frustrating politics of WILPF to pursue the much more satisfying role of speaker, cheerleader, and correspondent: a movement gadfly, in some sense. In 1961 she had taken pardonable pride in making a lecture tour to help the California WILPF chapters add members. "I gave a small talk at the [state] meeting and talked down in San Jose to a large audience. I had meant to keep account of the number of people who joined because of my lectures, but have already gotten so far behind that I no longer know the number, but I think it is an impressive one."[28]

In January 1963 Ava Helen and Linus traveled to the U.K. to attend the Oxford Peace Conference, a gathering of "non-aligned" peace organizations. Heading the American delegation was Homer Jack, a Unitarian minister and SANE founder with impeccable progressive credentials and cautious Cold War politics, whom Ava Helen had come to despise over the years, as she had Norman Cousins. Other attendees included Martin Luther King, Jr. Ava Helen delivered a greeting from the Los Angeles and Washington, D.C., Women Strike for Peace groups. Their message made it clear that WSP women gazed at the Oxford delegates with apprehension, fearing that they were pushing the same old Cold War politics into the new era. As Ava Helen delivered their message at Somerville College on January 4, 1963, WSP pleaded with the delegates to move their politics away from the playground approach of who started it and toward what we could do about it. "The only constructive course is to have the courage and humility to participate wherever any group of people are sincerely working for peace … That is the role of the true peace movement—not the divisive one of criticizing others who are as eager to live as we are, and who may be presumed to have the same motives we have for seeking to avert a nuclear disaster."[29]

Later in the year the Paulings faced challenges and disasters. News of the Nobel Peace Prize transformed their lives in October. On November 22 John F. Kennedy was murdered, an event that staggered the Paulings as much as it did most Americans. They felt an ambivalent connection to him as they had both struggled to stay in dialogue with his administration about foreign policy. The Paulings continued to prepare for their Nobel trip, answering their mail and absorbing the often hostile press reaction. In addition, they were laying plans for their new lives in Santa Barbara. Ava Helen wrote ironically to a friend that they were now getting calls from people in

Pasadena saying that they must not leave. An underlying pain emerges in her light (and somewhat disjointed) comment, "I suppose everyone thought that we were an evil which said, has to be endured but that we, like all evils, are missed when we are gone."[30] And in the midst of this flurry of change, on December 1, 1963, a week after Kennedy's assassination and a week before they embarked once again for Oslo, Ava Helen delivered for the first time her major statement on women and feminism, at the Los Angeles First Unitarian Church.

"The Second X Chromosome"

Like her letters to her global correspondents, Ava Helen's paper on women, "The Second X Chromosome," used simple language to deliver a confident and impassioned assertion that it was time for all women to receive the equal standing and opportunities to which, in many places, their legal status already entitled them. Following her initial drafts through her final typed presentation for distribution, it is evident that she wrote easily when she was excited, in many cases framing the ultimate argument in her first handwritten draft. Linus too contributed to the paper, although his surviving notes addressed not rhetoric, but background research that he or Ava Helen thought would be helpful: information about Jane Addams, Bertha von Suttner, and other figures she introduced in the body of the paper.

She indicted American hypocrisy. "While her legal and social status under law are now more or less secure in most parts of the world, discrimination against women is still very real and nowhere more than in the United States which lags woefully behind the more advanced Western Nations and indeed in many respects behind the socialist countries in equality for women." Whereas women were admitted to Soviet medical schools strictly on the basis of "scholastic ability," she said, "in the United States ... the ratio of women to men in medical schools is smaller than in 1900." Perhaps in a nod to her more conventional audience, she joked that while Japanese women were often cited as the "ideal of complete subjection to men," at least a woman walking behind her husband could keep an eye on him.

Ava Helen's use of genetic imagery ("the second X chromosome") to frame her argument exemplifies not so much an essentialist position on women's special nature—although she could never quite separate herself from that possibility—as a Jane Addams-like strategy of promoting a "both-and" philosophy of equal opportunity. Like Addams fifty years earlier, Ava Helen skirted essentialism (the "nature" of women) by discussing women's social and cultural roles throughout history—even prehistory.

She argued that, because of their role in carrying the embryo, the earliest women were undoubtedly "observant, wary, cautious, and persevering": the first scientists, as they figured out how to feed and warm their families. Some anthropologists saw women as the stabilizing force in society, as they established agriculture, fire, and private property under primitive matriarchies. Ava Helen argued that historically, as her indispensable skills were recognized, woman fell victim to male efforts to keep her "under subjection." Ten thousand years ago, matriarchy gave way to patriarchy "and women returned to the status of chattels."

Only in the last two hundred years, she argued, had patriarchy faced new challenges. Women had written two of the nineteenth-century novels that successfully changed social perceptions of great injustices: Harriet Beecher Stowe's *Uncle Tom's Cabin* and Bertha von Suttner's *Die Waffen Nieder* [*Lay Down Your Arms,* or as Pauling translated it, *Down with the Weapons of War*]. In the twentieth century, Rachel Carson's *Silent Spring* and Jessica Mitford's *The American Way of Death* likewise analyzed the social and environmental infrastructure: "In each of these four books the author, a woman, is attacking and exposing a well entrenched economic asset of society in areas controlled completely by men, eg. slavery, war, poisonous chemicals, and the funeral industry."[31]

Ava Helen brought her no-nonsense brand of political argument, fronted by her stance against interventionist warfare, to her position on modern feminism. She was not a fan of Betty Friedan's recent *Feminine Mystique,* which, she wrote to a friend, "has some very foolish ideas in it."[32] She indicted Friedan for blaming the inability of American POWs in Korea to withstand their imprisonment on their permissive, smothering mothers.[33] Pauling had no patience for an analysis predicated on the legitimacy of America's military engagement in Korea. "I won't agree," she asserted, "that a woman's highest role is to teach her sons to fight nobly the kind of war that was fought in Korea." One can imagine the L. A. Unitarians nodding at this point.

Coupled with her disdain for Friedan's tacit acceptance of the normality of the Korean War, Pauling resisted the invidious distinction between housewife-mothers and women who worked outside the home. "[W]ere the brave, napalm bomb throwing heroes of the Korean War the sons of career women? This would make an interesting study." She went on: "A way to verify the *Feminine Mystique* would be to conduct a survey among women who work outside the home and compare them to women who work within the home with regard to happiness, contentment, joy of life, and adjustment to family and friends. I believe such a survey would show that work outside the home is not the answer to the American woman's dissatisfaction and unhappiness. It is an oversimplification of the problem. Many women who work outside the home are just as unhappy as women who don't." The answer: equal access to college education; equal weighting of professional and household labor; public nurseries to allow mothers as well as fathers to go to school or work outside the home; and women's active participation in politics.

Ava Helen's feminist reform philosophy reflected her immersion in the Women Strike for Peace movement, whose primary *image* was that of active mothers protesting on behalf of the generation they were carrying in their wombs and raising, but whose most powerful spirits were women in their thirties, forties, and fifties, veterans of other peace movements, some of whom still had children at home and others of whom were primarily professionals.[34] Pauling's evolving philosophy also offered her a way to resolve her own existential dilemmas. She had put her college education aside to marry and bear four children. Her identity for twenty years was the wife who protected her husband's creative and intellectual life from family demands. Yet she had also excelled in chemistry as well as language and social science at Oregon Agricultural College. She had left her first toddler and a brief manual on modern child rearing in her mother's hands in order to tour Europe with her husband unencumbered by maternal responsibilities. She had tutored her husband in social justice issues during the Depression of the 1930s. She had plunged into political work as Europe collapsed again into bloody war, and then as the United States imprisoned American citizens on suspicion of hostile loyalties. She had inspired Linus's activism after the war to help fellow Americans understand the dire implications of United States' development of nuclear weapons, and over the following decade had stayed by his side as he risked his career against panels of accusers and political adversaries. And from the mid-1950s on, she had accepted her own career as a peace activist, her skills as a strategist, networker, and speaker enhanced by her notoriety as Linus's wife and his partner in the petition drives that ultimately earned him the peace prize.

Her friend Corda Bauer picked up on Ava Helen's ambivalence as part of a snapshot Ava Helen sent her along with the manuscript of her "Second X Chromosome" paper. The photograph shows the Paulings at their ranch, with Linus in the foreground leaning on a fence, and Ava Helen slightly behind him. Bauer requested permission to ask an "impertinent" question:

> *Was it design or chance that kept you in the background of the photo? As an advocate of women's rights I would have liked to have seen you leaning on the fence too, in an attitude of secure accomplishment. Linus deserves the place*

between the gateposts, where he can come and go as he pleases. Had you sat on top of the fence, it would have symbolized that women have to overcome many hurdles, but by golly no mere fence is going to stop them.[35]

She was Linus's equal, yet a step behind him, like the Japanese women Ava Helen had joked about. Linus Pauling, Jr., remembers that by the 1970s — and perhaps earlier — Ava Helen had started aiming sharp comments at Linus as they went about their daily routine. He remembers hearing her mutter that she too might have won a Nobel prize had she not been busy keeping the house and raising the children.[36] This memory probably does not detract from the other things we think we know about the Paulings' marriage: that the couple shared an unusual intimacy; that they preferred being together to being apart; that within the walls they were colleagues in their peace activism; that Linus always credited Ava Helen for her inspiration and companionship during the years of peace work; that he was most likely not a tyrant behind closed doors. From the year of courtship through his distracted grief after her death in 1981, Linus held Ava Helen as the most precious force in his life. "When asked to name someone else in the United States who might merit recognition for his efforts towards peace," said Wallace Thompson during a Nobel celebratory dinner, "Dr. Pauling unhesitatingly said: 'My wife.'"[37] Nonetheless, in the early years of marriage she suffered the decentered isolation of virtually all stay-at-home parents. This was exacerbated by Linus's early and persistent fame, and his multiple scientific commitments. After the first few years of their marriage, she could not keep up intellectually with his work, and that must have added another dimension to any resentment she felt at her position in their life together. Did she encourage their peace work in order to climb to an equal footing with him in their marriage, and in the world's eyes? If she harbored that motivation, it really seems to have been obscured by her genuine passion for political change, coupled with her anxiety for Linus to be as effective as possible in his advocacy work. Yet by the early sixties, as she received multiple invitations to speak to progressive groups and women's groups, and as she established a position as a key consultant among peace advocates, as she was for the WSP founders and Canada's VOW activists, she also articulated her feminist vision of the equal value of all kinds of labor, professional or domestic, paid or unpaid, as well as the power of women to move the world politically. Rosa Parks, Rachel Carson, Harriet Beecher Stowe, Bertha von Suttner — all applied their personal and intellectual power to identify and redress social wrongs. Corda Bauer understood Ava Helen's core message when she compared her friend's talk to Camilla Anderson's assertion in *Saints, Sinners and Psychiatry*: "Once women have tested their strength and overcome their rebellion, they are then free to return to homemaking and bringing up children with love and understanding by *choice* rather than being forced into it."[38]

In 1964, as Linus gradually transferred his office and his projects from Pasadena to Santa Barbara, Ava Helen stepped up her peace activities with WSP. She threw herself into helping to plan a May 1964 action at The Hague, to coincide with a NATO ministers' meeting at which a new multilateral nuclear force was supposed to be launched. Two aspects of the plan disturbed WSP members: the proliferation of control over nuclear devices, and the participation of West Germany as a NATO partner in nuclear exercises. WSP sponsored a well-researched and well-received pamphlet, *The German Problem: Roadblock to Disarmament,* analyzing Nazi resurgence in postwar Germany.[39] In March Lorraine Gordon wrote to Ava Helen, pleading with her to join the action in The Hague. "I just spoke to Dagmar in Washington and she, Amy Swerdlow and every other woman in New York and elsewhere including me, want you to come to the Hague May 11th for two weeks and help us make this a resounding success."[40] Anne (Mrs. Cyrus) Eaton likewise lobbied Ava Helen to join them in May. She reported working on Benjamin Spock to join the peace endorsers. "I'm going early, the 7th, with three others to try to do some preliminary on-the-spot work for press, etc. Could you come then? … I wouldn't miss the Hague, and there's nothing I'd rather do than picket the generals in tulip time with you." Eaton offered Ava Helen a bed for the night at their farms in Ohio on the way back as well as a seat at the Eatons' cattle sale on May 16th![41]

Ava Helen planned to attend the meeting (sandwiching it in after a visit to Mexico with Linus). She also served as one of the internationally respected members to solicit endorsements from a range of celebrities and Nobel Prize winners.[42] It must have been initially to her shock, and later her delight, that upon landing at Schiphol Airport on May 11, she and Katharine MacPherson of VOW were denied entrance to the Netherlands, with no reason given.

Amy Swerdlow, one of the advance guard from WSP delegated to set up the protest, later offered her version of the story. The Dutch police, with the silent acquiescence of the American embassy, had decided to block the women they suspected were entering Holland with the intention of demonstrating. The police had learned to fear sit-down demonstrations, especially from British pacifists, who they believed always sat down at the slightest provocation. The WSP leaders negotiated with the Dutch minister of justice for hours, and finally gave in and agreed to sign a pledge to obey all Dutch police orders. They relayed this agreement back to the WSP women waiting to board a plane for The Hague from New York. Those women were upset, but finally agreed to sign.[43]

After she was detained, Ava Helen had contacted Linus, who called the Dutch embassy in Washington, which had been bombarded by calls from stateside WSP members apprised of the border action. The embassy first told Linus that the meeting had been cancelled, then called back later to tell him the demonstration would be permitted. Meanwhile, undaunted, Ava Helen managed to enter Holland from Copenhagen while, as one newspaper reported, the "Dutch frontier guards watched newly-arriving tourist groups for members of the 'Women's International Strike for Peace,' the organizing group." If found, the women were required to sign the no-demonstration pledge before they were admitted.[44]

Ava Helen's part in the story is not easily parsed. Though she did contact Linus, who in turn contacted the Dutch embassy from California, she maintained and believed that she had not used his name to "bribe" her way into the country, and she took much pride in that stance of "honor and integrity."[45] Certainly after her initial refusal at the border, her connection to Linus Pauling was discovered and had an impact on the reporting of the event. The Associated Press picked up the story, and two articles covering WSP's demonstration at The Hague appeared in the San Francisco *Chronicle*

Ava Helen marching in the Marathon to Athens peace march, May 1964

in mid-May. The first featured Ava Helen's refusal at the border, and the second reported the dispersal of hundreds of women demonstrators from The Hague back to their home countries to carry forward the protests against the multilateral nuclear force. Linus in turn took up the matter with the New York *Times*, which had reported Ava Helen's initial refusal at the border – referring to her as "Mrs. Linus C. Pauling, wife of the Nobel Prize-winning scientist" – and then neglected to report the admission of the WSP women and their subsequent demonstration.[46] It seems that for one brief shining moment, Ava Helen handled the incident as an anonymous participant; it is telling to what extent she believed in the importance of that anonymity – even stating to Linus that had she used his identity at the border, the entire meeting would have been scuttled. "Had I bribed the officials by revealing myself this meeting in the Hague would not have taken place."[47] It is not clear why she held this seemingly grandiose belief. Of course, once her identity had been established, she earned additional press coverage. After the Hague demonstration, she flew to Greece, where she joined Greek women on a march from Marathon to Athens.[48] She wrote to Linus that the march was "one of the most inspiring and dramatic affairs that I have ever seen." She spoke at the Athens meeting, where she estimated the crowd to be between three and five hundred thousand.[49]

For Ava Helen, it was a stimulating if exhausting adventure—Linus recalled that she refused to sit down during the three hours that the Dutch immigration officials initially detained her—and she wrote a short article about it for *The Minority of One* on her return to the United States. "In all of my interviews," she recalled, "I was asked whether or not the officials knew that my husband was a Nobel Laureate. I said that I was certain that they did not and as a matter of principle I did not tell them. This seemed completely irrelevant to the issue at hand. The right of free speech and free assembly should not depend on whether or not one has a Nobel Prize."[50] This had become one of Ava Helen's mantras during the 1950s, after the Nobel Prize for Chemistry seemed to throw a protective cloak over Linus's political offenses, as the inquisitors saw them.

Ava Helen was also featured in the West German magazine *Frau und Frieden (Woman and Peace)*, which carried an illustrated article about the Hague demonstration complete with dramatic photographs of the women from all nations—fourteen hundred, according to the reporter—carrying paper flowers as they marched in the rain outside the conference. Dagmar Wilson led the column of women walking obediently on the sidewalk. Ava Helen smiles mischievously at the photographer in another shot. She is identified not as "Mrs. Linus Pauling" but as "Ava Helen Pauling."[51]

In her post-Hague article, Ava Helen surmised that the WSP action, and the Dutch government's capitulation, had most likely sowed the seeds of success for the fiftieth anniversary WILPF meeting coming up in 1965. "People in Holland said to me that this successful confrontation with the Dutch government over the refusal to allow people to assemble peacefully is of importance for the holding of the meeting of the WIL next year." The meeting also successfully highlighted the opposition in West Germany and around the world to the proliferation of nuclear arms to NATO.[52]

Ava Helen enjoyed the trip to The Hague. She found it exciting to join an international body of women, many of whom had never demonstrated *as women* in a collective. But a new cause commanded her attention. Like many others, she felt a special urgency to stop the American war in Vietnam. "In a sense," she wrote to Olive Mayer before she embarked for The Hague,

> *I think it is shutting our eyes to reality for the women to be doing almost nothing about the situation in Viet Nam at the same time they are making a big fuss about the probability of a war if nuclear weapons are given to NATO. Here we have this terrible war going on right now, which is beyond all description in brutality and evil, and yet we avoid it and avoid doing anything about it because, of course, it is easier to struggle against a hypothetical future war than to struggle against one that is going on right now.*[53]

Just a week earlier, on Good Friday (March 27), her WSP coworker Ruth Gage Colby wrote an impassioned letter to the Paulings, thanking them for being among the men and women willing to be "crucified" for their political beliefs. "Fulbright is being censored for speaking out on the need to re-think policies on Vietnam," she wrote in disgust, "and Mansfield has all but re-canted." While she hoped Ava Helen would be going to The Hague, Gage Colby concluded, "But quite honestly I put stopping the war in Vietnam first. It is an evil ghastly thing to kill people because they are (or we say they are) Communists! I'll work hard to get WSP to give this top priority."[54] While Ava Helen may have received this letter before she wrote to Olive Mayer, she and Linus had been active since the mid-1950s in tracking and protesting American policy in Vietnam. Linus had used one of his talks at the Unitarian Church in Los Angeles to call for the impeachment of Lyndon Johnson.[55] In addition, WSP played a major role in coordinating protest against the war in Vietnam from the inception of the group. For WSP as for Ava Helen, Vietnam and the continuing civil rights struggles came to the forefront in the years 1963-1965.

After Ava Helen returned home from Europe she resumed her extraordinary daily duties. In 1963 she had agreed to chair the Forum Committee at the First Unitarian Church of Los Angeles. As she admitted, this turned out to be a far larger job than she had anticipated, requiring not only many letters and calls to line up speakers, but also many hours of organizing and hosting their appearances, generally on the first Friday of each month in 1964. The Paulings finally bought a house in Santa Barbara over the summer, at 794 Hot Springs Road. In addition, and surely the project that gave them more joy, they had begun building a larger house at the Big Sur ranch.

In August, as the Paulings were surrounded by boxes and still running back and forth to Pasadena, while Linda, Barclay, and their children were moving into the old house at 3500 Fairpoint Street, a reporter from the Santa Barbara *News-Press* caught Ava Helen for a long interview. Though Linus was by any measure the bigger Pauling star moving to town, at this moment the reporter foregrounded Ava Helen, in particular her views on women and feminism. In the friendly interview, she was able to carry forward her message of "The Second X Chromosome." She underlined her conviction that all work done by women was of equal value: that in fact "any work done happily is a contribution to the whole world." Like Betty Friedan, she believed that, to be happy, women needed a "sustained intellectual interest" as well as social recognition, but she did not agree that women's work needed to be paid labor in order to be worthwhile. Did she and Linus ever disagree? "Well, of course we do," she answered her own rhetorical question. "We have the very hottest of arguments at times. To live with someone with whom one always agreed would be unbearable. Surely one would have to be a nincompoop and the other a tyrant. Or possibly both could be liars?"

With her signature humor, directness, and a bit of flirtatiousness, Ava Helen wooed her audience. The reporter described the domestic chaos as one generation moved out of the Pasadena home and the other moved in, and Ava Helen's bustle to get the new Santa Barbara house decorated. "I spend time here doing things like scraping wallpaper covered with powder puffs off one bathroom wall and having rooms painted with colors a tiny bit cooler than those in Mexico, and then I go to Pasadena to visit the grandchildren and put together more boxes. Paddy stays here and measures walls to see where we can possibly put all our books." We catch a glimpse of the Paulings' taste for modern color and Mexican art as the reporter describes the objects they have moved first:

a scrubbed looking Norwegian peasant table and chairs in the kitchen, a modern black easy chair and hassock in the living room, Japanese prints for the entry way, art books such as one on the muralists after the Mexican revolutionary period, a watercolor of a white frame house in a typical American small town given Mrs. Pauling when she addressed a women's organization in the East; a clay trio of figures done by Julie Koontz, a secretary at the Center for the Study of Democratic Institutions; a modern version of an ancient Aztec by Doris DeLario; and a very impish and very pink cupid which they keep because a friend maintains it is a character study of Mrs. Pauling.

Still not moved from Pasadena was a signed original print of Charles Schultz's Linus, with his blanket.[56]

CHAPTER 6

The Prime of Life

The impact you've had on my life, and surely many, many others, is very great and I'd like to communicate to you how much you've helped me. Even tho I was much younger than yourself and full of doubts and undirected, your friendship, strength of personality and convictions and commitment to bettering human life (even all life) in the world, has given me a role model – and understanding of how woman can be compassionate, discriminating and effective.
—Sharon Reddin Iverson to AHP, December 7, 1981

Someone has said that the greatest handicap that a woman has who wants a career is that she hasn't a good wife. I think there is some truth to this.
—Ava Helen Pauling, "More about Women," April 11, 1965.[1]

On September 23, 1964, the day the Paulings returned to their new home in Santa Barbara, a terrible brush fire forced them to evacuate. "There were twelve of us working," she wrote to a friend, "and in two hours we had completely emptied the house—completely is not quite right as we left behind our beds, desks and other large pieces of furniture. We were able to remove our treasures."[2] Staying in a nearby motel, they expected to hear that their Hot Springs Road house had burned, but miraculously, the fire spared it, though some of Pauling's new colleagues were not as fortunate. (Robert Hutchins, the center's founder, lost his house and everything in it.[3]) Two days later the Paulings were able to start moving their precious objects back into the house. The next week they departed for a long lecture tour in Australia.

The Paulings' move to Santa Barbara did not bring a slowing in their activities. Instead, their work broadened. After a long trip to Australia in

153

1965, Ava Helen begged off their usual hosting of a pancake breakfast for the WILPF chapter in Pasadena (in what was now Linda's and Barclay's house). "We have such a heavy schedule this spring that we are filled with despair most of the time...There is always the pressure of the uncompleted work and the many tasks which are waiting for us," she moaned, letting down her guard in the face of relentless invitations.[4] For Linus, the transition to the Center for the Study of Democratic Institutions initially promised to allow him to merge his science and his politics, without the tacit disapproval of CIT colleagues and trustees hanging over him. In February he had given an inaugural lecture at the center, "Science and Peace," that recapitulated his Nobel address of December. He reviewed the history of the test ban movement and paid tribute to the recently murdered President Kennedy, from whose death the world was still reeling at the time of the Nobel ceremony. He also characteristically reminded his listeners of the futility of nuclear war by citing the certain casualty counts, both immediate and delayed, that would result from a war using just 1 percent of existing weaponry. "No dispute between nations can justify nuclear war. There is no defense against nuclear weapons that could not be overcome by increasing the scale of the attack."[5]

The Nobel Peace Prize had given Linus Pauling one of the world's most prestigious and influential imprimaturs. Despite his disappointments at Caltech, he was now free to pursue and integrate all of his interests. Yet not surprisingly, the loss of his daily academic and research leadership role hit him hard. Following his SISS appearances in 1959 and 1960, he and Ava Helen

Ava Helen and Linus, and Boris Davydov after Linus received the Lenin Peace Prize, June 15, 1970.

had launched a series of costly and long drawn out libel suits, challenging publications from the tiny *Nevadans on Guard* to William Buckley's popular *National Review* for their editorial portrayals of Pauling as a Communist fellow traveler. Over the next six years, the suits failed one after another. Several papers did settle out of court, but for minuscule amounts: a total of about thirty-five thousand dollars, by Thomas Hager's estimate. Legal history in the making turned against Pauling with the Supreme Court's *New York Times Company v. Sullivan* decision in 1964, which established a different libel standard (the "actual malice" standard) for public figures. (Ironically, this decision that cut the legs out from under Pauling's libel suits also cleared the way for the national press to report fully on the civil rights campaigns in the Southern states without fear of lawsuits from Southern officials.)[6]

While the Paulings fought these lawsuits as a team, Ava Helen continued to build her own peace circuit and list of correspondents. The trip to The Hague had put her in the headlines. In her summary article for *The Minority of One*, she linked Women Strike for Peace with the Women's International League for Peace and Freedom, perhaps positioning the newer group as complementary to the well-established, hard-working, but somewhat stodgy WILPF. As her fame among progressive internationalists continued to rise, Ava Helen dove into her peace and human rights activities. She worked from 1963 on to integrate her passions for peace, social justice, and feminism. She became more radical, using economic motivations as fundamental factors in her social analyses. She found herself in step with students and feminist leaders who launched the new liberation movements and protested the Vietnam War in the name of humanity and for the sake of a humane and rational economy. Though Vietnam had been on her radar since the 1950s, the war's escalation and the converging protest movements in the United States and worldwide provided new opportunities for commentary and action.[7]

In 1965 Ava Helen followed up her talk on "The Second X Chromosome," once again delivering an important position paper on feminism at the First Unitarian Church of Los Angeles, where she had recently spent a year as head of the church's high-profile forum series. The church bulletin declared: "Sunday, April 11 is 'Pauling Day' at First Unitarian!" While Linus would speak in the afternoon about his participation in the Convocation on Pope John's "Pacem in Terris," recently staged in New York by the Center for the Study of Democratic Institutions, Ava Helen would give the morning sermon, simply called "More on Women."

While the earlier speech was well structured and decisive, this one tumbled forth as a torrent of ideas and themes, intertwined, philosophically consistent, expansive, but loosely organized. In her written draft, even paragraphing was thrown to the winds in the middle sections of the talk as Ava Helen seemed to rush to get in all her new thoughts about the retrograde status of women in American society.

While the first talk focused on elevating the status of women who did not enter the workforce, Ava Helen's second venture into feminist policy took a new tack: still honoring the tasks of mothering and homemaking, she criticized opponents of Betty Friedan like the poet Phyllis McGinley, who praised the joys of "remaining at home" while engaged in creative work that had little to do with the drudgery of normal housekeeping. Of McGinley's book, *Sixpence in her Shoe,* Ava Helen said slyly, "Miss McGinley even includes some recipes and very good ones to prove her point that she is really domestic. However in the preface she rather gives herself away by saying, when I speak of housekeeping, I do not of necessity refer to housework [sic]." Fine, said Ava Helen, but if women are restricted to housekeeping, rather than being "given an opportunity to develop themselves and to take a part in the world about them," then they are also going to fail at their home duties. And the other side of the coin, she argued, was that most women's work outside the home was deadly dull, so housework might well shine by comparison. "I think we must never forget that most women work at very uninteresting jobs when they work outside the home and that they do this from necessity and not from choice. When we discuss women and women working, we must consider this entire body of women and not the few who, like Miss McGinley, have a pleasant home and have a very satisfying career in the writing of witty and interesting poetry."

Nettled by the contention of an audience member at her first talk that there was no sex discrimination in the professions, Ava Helen had studied the literature on women in the workforce, and in particular, the workplaces ruled by what people in the 1980s would call "the glass ceiling." She cited the case reported in the New York *Times* of the two women police officers who sued to be allowed to take the sergeant's exam after over twenty years each on the force. Both had degrees from Hunter College; one had written a book; the other had two master's degrees. The police commissioner refused to let them take the sergeant's test because he believed that a sergeant's duties were "physically unsuitable" for a woman. "I should like to know," Ava Helen said indignantly, "how many male police sergeants have this amount of education." Ignoring the commissioner's argument from biology, she homed in on the blatant discrimination against women who were if anything educationally overqualified. "Yes indeed, the feminine revolution is on its way all over the world. Someone has said that the greatest handicap that a woman has who wants a career is that she hasn't a good wife. I think there is some truth to this."

Ava Helen tackled some of the strong antifeminist writing masquerading as social science. As she had earlier criticized Friedan for repeating the argument about "smothering mothers" ruining their sons' characters, she now quoted British anthropologist Eric Dingwall as arguing that American women were "sex hungry, spoiled, self-centered, aggressive, clothes-happy, frustrated, neurotic and … in control of the United States." Against this wildly hostile portrayal she arrayed Lee Grimm and J. B. Priestley, both of whom had observed that American women were more than ever second-class citizens, denied professional opportunities and instead offered "useless fripperies and adornments." Ava Helen also cited studies comparing the academic achievements of girls and boys, highlighting the work that formed the prelude to later observations of girls' declining achievement in math and science during the middle school years.[8] For Ava Helen, the route away from essentialism was to recognize that society's values reinforced girls' and women's tendency to be more conformist than boys and men. While she suggested that women were "by nature conservative or perhaps I should say conservators," she believed that the higher value of encouraging women to cultivate their intellectual abilities mandated a new "system of values" that allowed different paths for different women. "Are the active, striving, independent women attractive to men? Must women be passive and submissive in order to be good mothers? I do not think so."

Ava Helen did not shy away from her growing conviction that American individualism helped maintain the oppression of women. She used Elizabeth Mann Borgese's *The Ascent of Woman* (1963) to ride her own collectivist steed into the feminist fray.[9] The daughter of Thomas Mann and a wide-ranging intellectual in her own right, Borgese had been the Paulings' occasional correspondent since the mid-1950s, when she asked Linus to contribute to an upcoming issue of the new periodical *Common Cause.* "Mrs. Borgese stoutly maintains that woman is a collectivist and that this is born out by the advancement of women and their more equal status with men in the socialist countries."

For Ava Helen, also, the key to women's advancement was collectivism, which also brought cooperation, peace, and the erasure of separation between men and women. "Group maker from the beginning[,] the female thrives on the forces which the group in turn releases." She cited a friend from Europe who asked why Americans were so unhappy — "certainly less happy than the people of the Soviet Union," Ava Helen boldly quoted her friend, "in spite of having so much more." A year and a half after her first salvo in the feminist war against oppression, Ava Helen repeated her main contentions that women deserved equal educational and professional opportunities, and that women who chose domestic roles likewise deserved social and cultural approbation. "It is not surprising that women do not want to work in the home when everyone has said it is a stupid and unrewarding occupation to do so. It is time that we changed our training in this respect also." France offered the example of a union that protected part-time workers, so that women could stay home part-time and also earn a satisfying and dignified wage in the marketplace. She quoted Simone de Beauvoir's assertion that "the road to collectivization is also that which grants to women a human dignity."

Ava Helen's "both-and" approach to feminist change had moved even farther into Jane Addams's philosophy of embedding women's opportunities and obligations in a collectivist imperative. Currently, she said, women were blamed for everything, whether they stayed home or entered the workforce. "The unhappy and unsatisfactory condition of our society generally is laid to the door of women." Taking a leaf as well from the process orientation of Addams and other pragmatic Progressive Era reformers, she argued that, while she did not know what the solution was, she knew that it had to rest with men and women working together, breaking down the differences that kept them apart and uninterested in each other's activities.

Ava Helen could have offered her own marriage to illustrate women and men working together on global change. She and Linus often referred comfortably to their partnership of four decades. In addition, though, one can hear the "could have beens" in Ava Helen's increasingly certain voice: those arguments bursting forth, those note cards scrawled with new discoveries, new ideas. Sixty-two years old in 1965, Ava Helen was fully engaged in social change: not just advocating it, but pushing forward to an imagined future, and along with that, looking backward on a past that had been in some ways very traditional: twenty years of bringing up babies and micro-feeding a famous husband; ten more years of cheering him on, defending him from political enemies and government agencies, listening to his theories and ideas and speeches. Now she had not just her own committees and correspondents, but also her own speeches, her own tours, her own following among her contemporaries and also among younger women who had found their way to the peace and justice groups both old and new. A grandmother many times over, she was just hitting her stride. She was happy. But she could hardly help wondering what life would have been like if she had finished her college degree. She had been the smartest girl in her class. Maybe she could have been a chemist or a writer. Maybe, if she had had a wife instead of being one …

The April 11 talks at the First Unitarian Church represented a homecoming for the Paulings. In moving to Santa Barbara in 1964, they put the church, as well as the other landmarks of their Pasadena life, beyond the radius of a normal Southern California errand. On Fairpoint Street, they had lived about half an hour from the Los Angeles Unitarian church on 8th Street; their Santa Barbara home was more like two hours away. Even when they lived in Pasadena, with their frenetic travel schedule, they were hardly weekly congregants; but in moving out of the Los Angeles basin they said

Stephen H. Fritchman and Linus Pauling, 1969.

goodbye to the expectation that they would participate actively in the church's affairs.

Under the longtime leadership of Stephen Hole Fritchman, the First Unitarian Church of Los Angeles had been a staging ground for progressive, civil rights, internationalist, and peace activities. Fritchman had landed in Los Angeles in 1947 after a bitter controversy at the ancient heart of Unitarianism, Boston, had lost him the editorship of the denominational magazine, the *Christian Register*. An unquenchable partisan of radical causes, he embroiled himself in the the early Cold War as an advocate of cooperation with the Soviet Union, among other sharply controversial stances. Under Fritchman the First Unitarian Church of Los Angeles, as a congregation, refused to sign the loyalty oath that California had imposed on nonprofit institutions as the price they paid to stay tax-exempt. The U.S. Supreme Court threw out the California law four years later, which restored the church's tax-exempt status.[10]

Stephen Fritchman and Linus Pauling were tailor-made friends. They probably met for the first time when the Dean of Canterbury visited the United States on a peace advocacy mission. Characteristically, Fritchman had cooperated with the American Russian Institute, an organization tainted with Soviet associations in the postwar years, to organize and fund the dean's visit. Shortly after their first formal exchange, Fritchman sent Pauling a note asking if he had an opinion about the most important scientific achievement of 1948, anywhere in the world, which the minister would include in his sermon that Sunday. Fritchman also leaned his ear toward Pauling's insights into the medical and biological hazards of atomic fallout, but he did not need medical data to thunder against the hydrogen bomb. In a sermon in March 1950, he declared that the user of a hydrogen bomb was an "arch-fascist, the ultimate enemy of civilization itself," and he compared pro-bomb congressmen and newspaper publishers unfavorably to bloodthirsty Roman emperors and Genghis Khan.[11]

In the early 1950s the men exchanged notes of understanding and sympathy on their shared tangles with the federal government. Fritchman had been hauled before the House Un-American Activities Committee in

1946, as the crusading editor of the *Christian Register,* and then again in 1951. The same committee evoked Fritchman as a dangerous Communist in the course of their inquisition of Methodist bishop Bromley Oxnam in 1952.[12] Fritchman served as a vice president of the Hollywood Council of the Arts, Sciences and Professions several years after Pauling had held a similar post. And Fritchman had his passport denied as he was making plans to attend a Unitarian conference in Australia in November 1952, six months after Pauling had been denied his passport. Pauling wrote a high-toned letter of protest to Dean Acheson, defending Fritchman as "one of the most honest, forthright, straight-forward and high-principled man [sic] that I have ever known." It would be a shame if the United States were to "interfere with religion in the way that it has interfered with the progress of science."[13]

At a deep level, Pauling and Fritchman connected in their philosophical approach to the world. Humanism was the bedrock of Linus Pauling's moral and ethical universe. Fritchman exemplified—in some ways helped create—the modern humanist philosophy that characterized Unitarianism in the mid-twentieth century.[14] Pauling's argument for the urgency of a test ban treaty—that even one birth defect resulting from fallout was reprehensible—captured the valuing of individual human life embedded in the Unitarian principles. "[E]very single human being is important," he had stated in his Nobel speech, "and ... we should be concerned about every additional child that is caused by our actions to be born to live a life of suffering and misery."[15] It is not surprising that Linus won the Humanist of the Year Award in 1961. Just as Linus and Ava Helen were unified by their fundamental moral principles, so the Paulings and Fritchman never had to justify their worldviews to each other. Humanism rested on respect for individual lives and choices. It also required and presupposed rationalism— the kind of rationalism that could lead to anger and frustration when not all parties agreed to abide by its methods.[16] Along with a belief in rationalism often came a skepticism about the role of emotion and other *irrational* factors in human actions and decisions that may sometimes seem akin to denial. Linus, Jr., a psychiatrist, was sometimes frustrated and befuddled by his parents' refusal to accept any notion of the unconscious or the possibility that one might not always be in perfect command of one's mental life.[17]

It is not clear when or whether the Paulings began attending the Los Angeles church regularly. Linus responded to a number of invitations to speak at the church, until finally in the late 1950s he begged off several times, suggesting that time constraints dictated that he save his speaking engagements for larger audiences farther from home. Nonetheless, the Paulings formally joined the church in 1962, and the next year Ava Helen began serving on the forum committee. She offered her first rendition of "The Second X Chromosome" at the church—though she gave Fritchman an out, telling him that if he had changed his mind about her giving the talk about women, it would be quite all right. It is surprising that she would worry that this man, who had broached all of the most untouchable political topics in the previous twenty years, would be put off by the proposed title or subject of her talk.

Stephen Fritchman, his wife Frances (Franny), and the Paulings grew closer through the early 1960s. When the Durrs visited California in 1963, the three couples spent a convivial evening eating out in Chinatown. Fritchman did not hesitate to consult Pauling on politically delicate matters, once asking him to support a student socialist group in the making, and another time requesting his aid in counseling a young man away from a military career. By 1966 they were all deeply involved with the protests against the Vietnam War and Fritchman urged Pauling to be a part of the church's Christmas Day Meeting of Protest against the war. "I am so angry at the billions of dollars spent on gifts by affluent America this year as we blacken the land and slaughter the people of Vietnam that I planned this protest for the day when we mouth words about the Prince of Peace." Though Pauling begged off the meeting, citing his and Ava Helen's impending Indian trip, he wrote, "You are great in your continued work for sanity and morality in the world," and reported to Fritchman that he had drawn a crowd of five

The Paulings with hosts in Madras, India, 1967.

thousand in Corvallis and a thousand at both Gonzaga and the University of Washington as he toured the university circuit speaking against the war.[18]

Ava Helen too found herself oppressed by world news, and sometimes deeply pessimistic about the negligible outcome of all their work. "The world is surely in a terrible situation," she wrote to friends in March 1965, "and it is hard to see how we can restore our Country to some sensible way of acting."[19] President Johnson disgusted her, and even more the Senate's "carte blanche" offered through the Tonkin Gulf Resolution. "It is quite unconstitutional, however," she commented to a friend, falling back as usual on her reliance on law and reason to produce social justice. Despite her pessimism, she threw herself into the war protests. In October 1965 she acted as teach-in moderator for the International Days of Protest at the University of California at Santa Barbara. Her host sent her $7 of the proceeds to be donated to the peace organization of her choice! At least there *were* proceeds. "You were really splendid, kept things moving nicely, talked just enough, and managed to bring in one or two good critical points."[20] As her participation deepened over the next months, she struggled to develop an analysis of the war that carried the military-industrial complex into Americans' startled rediscovery of persistent mass poverty in the 1960s. She also understood that the Vietnam bombing constituted one more attack, akin to nuclear testing, on the earth itself. "Sometimes I am quite depressed, chiefly by this assault on this earth. How can anyone wantonly destroy any part of this small planet?"[21]

Her despair was deepened by the shocking suicide of Alice Herz, who had fled the Nazis in the 1930s and settled in Detroit. Herz had chosen to protest the Vietnam War by immolating herself, not quite dying after setting herself alight, but lingering in the hospital for a week with terrible burns before succumbing. Ava Helen had known Herz and corresponded with her. "This sacrifice is useless I think but, nevertheless, a most moving one and certainly was done with the intent of drawing attention to just what is happening in the world."[22]

She turned to philosophers and political scientists. She explored the value science of Robert S. Hartman, Linus's correspondent and a prominent ethicist. She gathered clippings and took extensive, though cryptic, notes, trying to puzzle out the best way to persuade people to turn away from military confrontation and its ancillary industries. In notes for a speech on world peace in 1966, she protested that, among peace groups in the United States, none pursued the idea that social and economic change must underlie the quest for peace. "Nearly every one denies the connection between war and the social structure." Seventy million languished in poverty in the United States; rich nations grew richer and poor nations poorer; rich people grew richer and poor people poorer. In 1967 Ava Helen moderated a Santa Barbara forum on discrimination against women—a topic still so threatening that one speaker from the clinic at UCSB withdrew at the last minute, fearing reprisals if she revealed the conditions there for women patients.[23] That same year she held an All Day Peace Workshop for Women in the garden at the Paulings' new house at 794 Hot Springs Road in Santa Barbara. She was joined by Donna Allen, her friend and colleague in the peace movement, another crossover leader of WILPF and WSP, and now the D.C. member of the Committee to Abolish HUAC. Malvina Reynolds, the political musician most famous for her song "Little Boxes," offered the entertainment.

Ava Helen also joined Linus in trying to educate the public in the hazards of radiation. In a speech to a women's group drafted sometime in the 1960s, she painstakingly reviewed the history and science of high-energy radiation. Linus's pen left light touches throughout the manuscript, attesting to the couple's practice of vetting each other's work, and in particular Ava Helen's dependence on Linus to interpret science to her and to the public.[24]

From 1964 to 1965, the Paulings finally built the permanent house at Deer Flat Ranch that they had been dreaming of for ten years. Perhaps this felt like the right time because they had given up their longtime base in Pasadena, and perhaps the second Nobel Prize along with Pauling's textbook royalties made the project economically feasible. "We have been building a house at our ranch where we intend to retire if Linus ever comes to that point. And with all of the other things we have tried to do, it makes a heavy schedule for us."[25] Built largely of the native stone of the region, the house stood on a knoll near the eucalyptus grove on the property, a short distance from the original primitive cabin, which would be used by the caretaker and by visitors to the ranch.[26] Floor to ceiling windows overlooked the breakers washing against the cliffs. The year after they completed the house, they unexpectedly spent most of the summer there after Linus broke his leg at the end of June. "He was restricted in his movements," Ava Helen wrote to friends, "but has been able to do his work quite well, and it is so beautiful here that one cannot feel really regretful of having been forced to stay here."[27] As usual, the delay was only temporary, and the Paulings were off to Canada, England, and France in September.

By the later 1970s the ranch house interior had taken on a simple elegance: Eames chairs, driftwood, a grand piano in the living room.[28] The ranch proved a refuge and respite not only from their frenetic world travel, but also for Ava Helen from repeated moves as Linus continued to develop his post-

Ava Helen and Linus with Peter, Linda, Linus, Jr., and Crellin, on the deck at Deer Flat Ranch celebrating Ava Helen and Linus's fifty-second wedding anniversary, June 17, 1973.

Pasadena career. In 1967 the couple moved to La Jolla when Linus accepted an appointment at the University of California at San Diego. Then in 1969, restless and unhappy with the situation there, Linus arranged to move his scientific activities to Stanford. The Paulings relocated to what would prove to be their last house, aside from the ranch, on Golden Hills Road in Portola Valley, just outside Palo Alto. This proved a satisfying base of operations and Ava Helen made new friends. A granddaughter remembers a group of women who got together occasionally to go skinny-dipping in the pool.

Pauling's broken leg in 1966 was the first of the health crises that punctuated the next fifteen years. More alarming was a small stroke that Ava Helen suffered a few days before her sixty-fourth birthday in 1967. The Paulings had returned from dinner with several of Linus's colleagues. It had been a good meal, preceded by a cocktail and accompanied by a glass of wine. There was nothing upsetting or unpleasant about the occasion, in Linus's memory; it was one of the Paulings' accustomed "quiet evenings" with casual friends, good food, and good conversation. As she sat in bed near midnight on December 2, chatting with Linus and doing a crossword puzzle, Ava Helen suddenly complained of being dizzy, and then lost consciousness. "I got out of bed and got in bed with her, putting my arm around her. I spoke to her two or three times, and she did not answer. I then turned on the light, spoke to her and shook her, without getting an answer. Her eyes were half open, but did not follow me and did not respond to motion of my hand in front of them." He checked Ava Helen's pulse and heartbeat and found them strong. Typically, Linus's dispassionate retrospective account contrasts sharply with the panic we must guess he experienced in the moment, as he tried to call the family doctor and was rerouted by the answering service to the Physicians' Emergency Service, which dispatched an ambulance. Miraculously, there was no permanent

Ava Helen and Linus with Linda and her children in La Jolla, Thanksgiving, 1968.

damage from what the emergency physician concluded was a blood clot. Fifteen hours after the incident Ava Helen was talking and showing strong vital signs.[29]

In 1970 and again in 1972 Ava Helen underwent cataract surgery, at the time a process with a long and disorienting recovery time. For months after each surgery Ava Helen saw the world through one eye. By then all her correspondence was done by dictation, so she did not fall out of touch with her friends around the world. Typically, her letters were written in bunches, as she and Linus caught up on correspondence between trips abroad or to the ranch.

In the late 1960s Ava Helen's peace work found a new audience among college students. She strove to understand the worldwide student movements, and was inclined from the outset to like them, seeing the students as fellow progressives and protesters. The rhetoric of unified causes that emerged from the student movement resonated with her. Characteristically, for a talk in 1968, she gathered information on student rebellions in far-flung places: Pakistan, England, Quebec, Mexico, Italy, Germany, France, and Holland. Her approach was sympathetic and analytical. She tried to tease out the students' alliances, their demands, and the movements' potential outcomes. Did they represent a student revolution, or a general revolution? Where had the students found allies among the workers? What were their causes? What actions did they pursue? She concluded tentatively that the students were anti-authoritarian but "not anarchist," and she saved her most potent quote for last: from the Students for a Democratic Society she culled the adage, "No class today[,] no ruling class tomorrow."[30]

In 1969 she and Linus spent two weeks in residence at Wilson College in Chambersburg, Pennsylvania. One of the nation's first women's colleges, Wilson's invitation to Linus Pauling as First Centennial Visiting Scholar turned into a "twofer," with Ava Helen visiting political science and sociology classes while Linus lectured in science and biology classes. Together the Paulings had informal discussion sessions with groups of students and faculty on world peace.

Ava Helen merged idealism with a realistic and often dark assessment of human motives. She was comfortable with the student rebels because she herself had been speaking directly and irreverently for twenty years. At San Diego City College in 1970, she might have been mistaken for an SDS speaker if her gray hair and matronly voice hadn't given her away.

"Say NO to the war in Cambodia.

"NO to the war in Vietnam.

"NO to War!

"NO to the draft.

"No to economic exploitation all over the world.

"NO to imperialism.

"NO to Pentagonism!

"Let us fight the real enemies of mankind.

"Hunger, disease, poverty, illiteracy, discrimination, and exploitation.

"Let us recognize that economic power is the real force behind our military actions abroad and that the huge profits in armaments are the basis of all our military adventures."[31]

Ava Helen had been invited to San Diego to give two talks on the status of women. Instead, ten days after the murder of the Kent State University students by National Guard soldiers, following the revelation of the U.S. bombing of Cambodia, she offered an impassioned speech condemning the entrenched military-industrial complex, the profiteering of companies contracting with the Pentagon, the naked economic motivations driving U.S. actions in Nicaragua, Korea, and Southeast Asia. In the middle of her speech, she asked the student audience's indulgence while she tried to give some historical background to the peace movement by delivering part of her original speech, the story of Bertha von Suttner, who increasingly commanded Ava Helen's imagination. Von Suttner, she told the students, wrote *Die Waffen Nieder* and "devoted her life to the abolition of war." Ava Helen then returned to her call to action. "The war is being fought by the poor and paid for by the poor." She advocated support for Senators McGovern, Hatfield, Church, Goodell, and Hughes, and rallied the students to send even a dollar to peace candidates. "Resist all the evils in our culture but protect the good. Be non-violent in your protests, and in your resistance to militarism and injustice." The cadence of the last few lines of her speech recalls the rhythms of "Desiderata," one of Ava Helen's favorite pieces.[32] The San Diego students may have had quite a surprise. Ava Helen Pauling did not look like a student leader, nor did she look like most of the radical professors from whom they had heard similar rhetoric.[33]

In 1970 Linus once again became a household name with his popular publication, *Vitamin C and the Common Cold*. Pauling had first been alerted to the therapeutic potential of Vitamin C in the mid-1960s by the biochemist Irwin Stone. Intrigued by Stone's personal experiences with the vitamin, Linus and Ava Helen started taking large doses of Vitamin C and found that indeed their colds vanished and they felt better overall. As was his scientific *modus operandi*, Linus turned his personal observations into clinical and laboratory projects. The Vitamin C project became a subset of the work of Pauling's Orthomolecular Medicine Laboratory, which moved off campus and into its own Menlo Park building in 1972. The next year the laboratory became an institute, under Pauling's and Arthur Robinson's direction.[34] The

The Paulings visiting a hospital in Shanghai, China, 1973.

Ava Helen and Linus holding an award in the shape of a molecular model, 1974.

Linus, Ava Helen, Linus, Jr., Linda, Crellin, and three of Linda's children, 1976.

work on Vitamin C and the common cold expanded into explorations of the uses of ascorbic acid in cancer treatment.

The Paulings undertook vigorous tours abroad between 1972 and 1975, including a journey to China in 1973 and return trips to Australia and Japan. In Sydney, Australia, in the spring of 1973, Ava Helen spoke of the defense budget recently proposed by Richard Nixon to "maintain the military strength we will need to support our negotiations and diplomacy," as she quoted the president. Outraged by a budget dominated by corporate interests, the second largest military budget in U.S. history (topped only by the 1969 budget, at the height of the Vietnam War), Ava Helen again asserted that women bore a responsibility to defend the world's resources for the uses of all humanity.[35]

The Paulings returned to Japan in September 1975 to celebrate the centennial of Albert Schweitzer's birth. Addressing the symposium, Ava Helen remembered the Paulings' trip to Lambaréné in 1959. She combined a tribute to Schweitzer's devotion to health and social justice with a statement on the increasing lethality of weapons of war. "Schweitzer said that man has become superman ... but superman suffers a fatal flaw. He has failed to rise to the level of superhuman reason which would match that of his superhuman strength."[36] Ava Helen repeated that the enemies of mankind were "war, ignorance, disease, poverty, hunger, the pollution of the environment, the wasting of the world's resources by militarism." She refused to accept aggression as an innate instinct; instead, she again urged her listeners to recognize and nurture "man's ability to cooperate," and the "power of reason." She reminded her listeners of Schweitzer's call for humanitarian work to be done "as men [sic] not as members of any particular nation or religious body."

In January 1974 Ava Helen struggled with a chronic headache at the back of her head. Linus kept rough notes of her descriptions of pain and the treatments they attempted, basically changing the doses of vitamins that Ava Helen routinely took. In 1976, at age seventy-two, Ava Helen's health faltered again. Linus recorded that her headache had recurred in April. She had digestive troubles and lost energy. Then that most frightening moment: when she and Linus were at the ranch in July, she discovered a tender lump in her abdomen, "just to the left of the navel," as Linus recorded it. They returned to Portola Valley the next day. She was diagnosed with stomach cancer; two weeks later, surgeons removed three-fourths of her stomach. "The tumor, fist-sized ... [was] completely encapsulated and entirely removed during the surgery," Linus wrote to Charles Huggins of the Ben May Laboratory for Cancer in Chicago.[37]

For Linus it may have been a blessing that Ava Helen's cancer crisis ran right into research that he and the Scottish oncologist Ewan Cameron had been conducting into the effects of ascorbic acid intake on the course of cancer. The nature of Ava Helen's tumor—hard and encapsulated, rather than "'soft,' cellular, rapidly proliferating, [and] highly invasive"—seemed to bear out other studies of the effect of regular doses of ascorbic acid on the characteristics of tumors. In his letter to Huggins he guessed that it might even be worthwhile to conduct a "cautious test" of the effect of ascorbic acid intake on the tumors of pre-operative patients. Linus could stay optimistic about Ava Helen's future; he could be directly involved in her treatment; and he could allow his scientific interest to distract him from his worry and grief. In line with his and Cameron's findings, Ava Helen decided to forgo chemotherapy after the surgery, instead ingesting ten grams of Vitamin C daily. Her health improved, although from then on the ravages of the cancer were etched on her face, and she became thinner and more frail looking.

In 1977 *Nova* produced a documentary focused on Linus's work against nuclear weapons in the context of his career as a scientist. He and Ava Helen appeared on camera together, to the delight of their legion of friends; their correspondence is full of happy recognition of the couple, their enduring marriage, and their advocacy of Vitamin C. Many wrote with reminiscences. It was a time to look backward.

Ava Helen rallied her personal reserves and began traveling and speaking again. After moving to Santa Barbara and then much farther away to Palo Alto, the Paulings could no longer attend the Los Angeles Unitarian Church, but they occasionally visited several other congregations, including the one in Santa Barbara. In September 1977 she visited the Livermore Unitarian fellowship to offer her statement of faith: "Why I Am a Unitarian." Her reasons would not surprise anybody who knew her or had followed her career to that point: Unitarianism's reliance on rationality, its belief in human progress, its humility before the "vaster forces of the universe," its conviction that humanity could solve its problems, and its sense of human brotherhood. Like Linus, Ava Helen stood squarely in the humanist strand of Unitarianism: perhaps the strongest strand that reached, at that time, back into Unitarianism's roots in dissident Christianity in the early nineteenth century.

But perhaps the most incisive reasons Ava Helen offered for her Unitarian affiliation were autobiographical. When she went to the Los Angeles church, she stated, it was "not to find a creed or a means of salvation," but instead to find a community: "to join with a group of like-minded people to work for the betterment of society and for the eradication of the evils

Linus and Ava Helen at a fundraising Unitarian dinner held in their honor on March 6, 1976, at the Ambassador Hotel in Los Angeles. A note on the back says that the church netted $6,000: "not bad!"

and inequities of the world" — people who believed, in short, in "rationality, happiness, and love, and the power of the human mind and spirit."[38] She revealed Stephen Fritchman's part in bringing her to the Unitarian Church — an unusually personal insight into a moment of emotional and spiritual vulnerability. When Dr. Thomas Addis died suddenly in 1949, Ava Helen remembered, she had been plunged into "genuine despair and grief and a sense of total and irreparable loss." Addis had been Linus's doctor, the man who guided and supported Ava Helen in saving Linus's life, and who also helped Linus develop a vision, in the early to mid-1940s, of the role of science and medicine in achieving a just world. For Ava Helen, there would be no comfort in appeals to heaven or a better hereafter. But instead, Reverend Fritchman offered memories of the man: "to rejoice in his good, productive life and accomplishments, to remember the happiness that we had in knowing him, to listen to some music he loved (Bach), to hear favorite excerpts from the Bible he often read (Ecclesiastes), revere and cherish his great goodness, and to remember him with love and thanksgiving for his having lived." For Ava Helen, this was a new kind of memorial service and offered a new idea of what religion might be good for. Thus began, too, a friendship as well as a pastoral relationship that would last several decades. She quoted Fritchman's statement: "There is nothing more glorious in the world than a good man *thinking*." Now characteristically, she rejoined, "To that I would add that there is nothing more splendid in the world than a *good woman thinking*."

On March 7, 1978 Ava Helen was injured in a potentially disastrous auto accident. Shopping for a new dictation machine, she was offered a ride to the showroom by the chairman of the company's board, who sent his chauffeur. The chauffeur, Earl, sat Ava Helen in the front passenger seat, without a seatbelt. He seemed disoriented from the beginning of the drive, taking an unusually long way around from Portola Valley to Redwood City. On the 280, Ava Helen saw with alarm that he had drifted across the center line. Before she could decide whether to comment, Earl yanked the car violently to the right and smashed hard into two parked cars. Ava Helen did not initially feel her own injuries, but looked over and saw that the chauffeur had lost consciousness, so she loosened his collar. In the aftermath, Ava Helen decided that Earl must have lost consciousness before the impact. Passersby called the police; a woman brought Ava Helen a paper towel for the huge cut that had opened under her chin. Both victims were taken to Sequoia Hospital, where Linus met his wife, who had already been X-rayed. The chin laceration, the only visible injury, required thirty stitches. She had painful bruises; worst of all was a sore throat from the impact, and hoarseness. She ran a slight fever for several days. Linda came to stay with her parents. For a week Ava Helen consumed a soft diet. By March 19, however, not quite two weeks after the shock and injury, she and Linus flew to Cuba.[39]

Twice in 1979 she traveled to Eugene, Oregon: once to introduce a concert by exiled Chilean musicians and once as a guest speaker on the role of women in disarmament. Having visited Chile in 1970, she had made connections there that now tugged at her after the bloody U.S.-sanctioned Pinochet coup of 1973. Victor Jara, a nationally beloved folk singer, had been tortured and murdered by the regime. His widow, Joan Jara, was traveling to raise money and awareness for the Chilean resistance by talking about her husband's murder as well as the daily repression of intellectual and artistic activity in Chilean universities.[40] In her introduction to the musical performance of Quilapayan, Ava Helen recalled the Paulings' visit to Temuca, in southern Chile. "A bus load of students from the University met us at the airport and as we drove around the city sang and played their guitars in the bus. Many of the songs were Victor Jara's. I kept crying *Mas, mas*, and the students responded." She remembered, too, with pride their visit to Pablo Neruda's house on the ocean. "I had taken off my shoes to wade in the sea. He gave me a book of poems with the inscription[:] to Ava without shoes[,] from your friend Pablo Neruda."[41]

Two months later Ava Helen returned to Eugene to speak on "The Role of Women in Disarmament" for the Third Annual Women's Symposium at the University of Oregon. Her friend Nelly Macon Link, who had brought her to Eugene for the Chilean concert, also appeared on the program, talking about the plight of Chilean women.[42] Besides her talk on disarmament, Ava Helen joined the local chapter of WILPF for a "fireside chat" at the Cottage Grove Methodist church. In her talk, Ava Helen referred to the budget figures she had taken to Australia in 1973, when she protested Nixon's defense budget. Today, she stated, under President Carter, the defense budget had ballooned yet again, to $120 billion.

Ava Helen's trademark speech was thesis bolstered by numbers and followed by recommendations for action. Very much as Linus had promised in the 1950s to discuss world peace in every speech from then on, Ava Helen seems to have pledged to herself to recommend action in every speech, no matter how grim the social and economic prospect. Even her most scholarly paper, a long essay on Bertha von Suttner and the history of the world peace movement, ended with an invocation to reject war as inevitable and man as inherently aggressive. These were her new mantras.

She prepared the von Suttner paper in honor of Otto Nathan, the economist and close associate of Albert Einstein. Nathan was Ava Helen's friend and colleague in WILPF, and also a friend of Evelyn Alloy, a correspondent with whom Ava Helen often let her hair down. It is not clear whether she intended the paper for a specific occasion; it was not a memorial, as Nathan still lived. She had been thinking about von Suttner for over a decade. To Alloy she had written in 1965 that von Suttner's work as an instigator of Nobel's endowment of the Prize for Peace was too little known in the United States. She had corrected WILPF when they wrote in 1960 that Jane Addams and Emily Greene Balch had been the first women recipients of the Nobel Peace Prize. Ava Helen had not been able to establish whether Addams had met, or even knew anything about, von Suttner. "It seems strange that Jane Addams would not have been influenced by Suttner and yet I think it is an error to talk about these two women having been great friends."[43] Finally, in a quiet interval at the ranch, she took the time to expand her meditation on the significance of von Suttner, whom she had been invoking in her speeches for almost twenty years. Von Suttner was the first woman to win the Nobel Peace Prize; she was briefly Alfred Nobel's assistant, and later his friend. Born Bertha Kinsky, she made a passionate love match with Arthur von Suttner. Dodging his family's disapproval, the couple ran away to the Caucasus.

Ava Helen tells the story of Bertha von Suttner's journey from novelist to social critic in the context of her personal happiness and fulfillment. *Die Waffen Nieder* was von Suttner's breakthrough novel of peace in 1889. Ava Helen pointed out that when Tolstoy congratulated von Suttner on her effect on the nineteenth-century peace movement, he called her novel "the Uncle Tom's Cabin of the peace movement." Ava Helen was fascinated by von Suttner's and Stowe's successes as social critics in an age of women's repression. She also repeated the history of von Suttner's persuading Alfred Nobel, still a friend, to contribute the funds for her peace conferences. In 1905 von Suttner herself was awarded the Peace prize, endowed by Nobel in his will.

Ava Helen concluded her paper with sections on Jane Addams and Emily Greene Balch. She speculated on why neither von Suttner nor Addams mentions having met the other, although both were speakers at the International Conference on Peace in 1904, and may have met elsewhere as well. We have seen that Ava Helen found Jane Addams's social philosophy rich and suggestive. She honored Emily Greene Balch as a pioneer in WILPF, as well as for having been fired by Wellesley for her peace activities. But she was ready to argue that "Bertha von Suttner in many ways is a more remarkable woman than Jane Addams. She is more scientific and not so religious in her outlook."[44] It may be that Bertha von Suttner appealed to her partly because, unlike Addams or Balch (at least in the public mind), von Suttner proved that a happily married woman could function as an independent agent, both in harmony with her husband and acting and thinking in her own right. This is most likely how Ava Helen imagined her own peace career, although she would not have admitted placing herself in the same ranks as von Suttner, Addams, or Balch.[45]

The later 1970s also brought continued family engagements, some worrisome, many joyful. In 1970 Linus, Jr., spearheaded building a bunkhouse at the ranch for visiting family members. The older Paulings welcomed this initiative. They loved to see their children and grandchildren, but they had a hard time with the conflicts that arose when willful people of several generations shared the same limited space. Ava Helen expected to organize and supervise the household, and her adult children, with growing youngsters and life transitions of their own, sometimes balked at her dictation. With Linus, Jr.'s encouragement, Linus bought the Lindal cedar kit and arranged for the pouring of the concrete foundation. Linus,

Jr., rounded up his brothers and Barclay Kamb, and together the men built the cabin. Called China Camp after earlier groups of Chinese workers who would come in by boat to harvest kelp, the little house created a separate private space at the ranch, particularly beneficial when Ava Helen was ill or low on energy.[46]

Ava Helen may have been a more attentive grandmother than she had been a mother. Among her grandchildren, perhaps Linda and Barclay's sons had the most frequent contact with their grandparents. Sascha and Barclay, or Barky, were the couple's oldest children, fraternal twin boys. They felt very close to their grandparents.

Crellin and Lucy moved from Seattle to the Bay Area around 1964, but that marriage did not survive. Peter and Julia stayed together into the 1960s, but finally divorced. Linus, Jr., too, went through the pain of telling his parents that he and Anita would divorce. He stayed in Honolulu, where he had built a solo practice in psychiatry. Throughout the 1960s he was chief of the psychiatric service at The Queen's Hospital, and for many years the sole psychiatrist at the University of Hawaii. Despite his success, Linus the younger carried the indelible impression that his career choice had been in his parents' eyes only second best: that a research-oriented Ph.D. was the requisite building block of professional achievement. This was an ironic legacy for a couple who repeatedly threw in their lot with pioneer medical professionals, among them Thomas Addis, Sam Kimura (Ava Helen's ophthalmic surgeon), the personnel of the Mount Sinai Medical School, Ewan Cameron (the crusading Scots oncologist), and of course Albert Schweitzer and his lieutenant, Frank Catchpool. Deeply influenced by Schweitzer's work in Africa as well as Linus's own researches in microbiology and medicine, both Linus and Ava Helen focused increasingly on the centrality of medical knowledge, and medical care, in creating a just and happy world. Linus's institute focused on medical issues. In 1978 both Paulings visited tiny Grenada, where Linus lectured on molecular diseases and Ava Helen on women in medicine. They were there to participate in a pioneer venture, an international Tele-Health Network designed to make medical and health-related information available in areas less well served by traditional medical facilities. Both Ava Helen and Linus were on the Board of Advisors.[47]

To be sure, Linus became embittered by the medical establishment's repeated dismissal of his Vitamin C work. Medical researchers rejected his and Ewan Cameron's protocols for cancer treatment with ascorbic acid. Journals turned down his papers, criticizing his research methodologies. The institute, unsuccessful in securing federal grants, depended on private

Linus and Ava Helen, 1977.

donations. And Arthur Robinson, once the enthusiastic collaborator whom Pauling had asked to take on the presidency, became a loose cannon in Pauling's eyes, taking the institute in directions that Pauling believed threatened its remaining claim to respectability. In July of 1978, Pauling asked Robinson to resign the presidency. Sadly, the last few years of Ava Helen's life coincided with the most tumultuous years of the institute, as Robinson filed multimillion-dollar lawsuits against Pauling and the trustees, lawsuits that would not be settled until 1983.

While carrying out his parents' medical mission despite their failure to acknowledge its importance, Linus, Jr., also carried on their political priorities. This was certainly not done to seek their acknowledgement, because his parents were not always aware of his activities, once learning of an important action through the news media. Ava Helen wrote to Fritchman in March 1965 that on returning from a trip to the ranch, where they were "frightfully busy" finishing the new house,

> *We saw in the paper that our son in Honolulu served as a doctor for the marchers in Selma. We had not known that he intended to take part and were quite happy and a bit dismayed. The paper said that the delegation from Hawaii carried a placard saying, We know integration works ... We have*

*never tried to influence our children with our ideas of a political nature but
I suppose that they cannot help but feel as we do. Certainly without our ever
telling them how they should approach the problems in the world, they all
share our interests and sympathies.*[48]

It is hard to believe that Ava Helen was as naïve about family dynamics
as this letter suggests, but she sincerely believed that the children had
found their own ways in the world—and that was the best outcome of an
upbringing that incorporated pushing them out of the nest.

The Paulings continued to plan what must have been exhausting trips
into 1981, as Ava Helen's health held steady. Her weight had settled to a
new normal about ten pounds less than through her adulthood. In the late
spring of 1981, as the couple prepared for another massive trip, to Japan and
China as well as Germany and England, Ava Helen suggested to Linus that
perhaps she should not go. For whatever reason, perhaps for Linus's sake,
perhaps hoping that her well-being would take an up-tick, she changed her
mind. From Tokyo the Paulings traveled to China for the second time. Linus,
Jr., was able to join his parents for part of that trip, a nutritional conference
in Tientsin, but then returned home. In Xian on June 19, Ava Helen was
hospitalized overnight for atrial fibrillation. She took drugs prescribed by
her Chinese physicians, but they nauseated her. She lost more weight.[49]

Despite her discomfort and the heart fibrillation scare, Ava Helen and
Linus continued on their journey, taking the twenty-seven-hour railway
journey to Shanghai on June 24-25 to arrive in Beijing the 26th. They flew
to Germany to spend a week, then to London July 4th and home to San
Francisco July 7th. The doctors identified a new lump in her abdomen,
which Ava Helen said that she had found several weeks before. Perhaps she
did not tell Linus to spare him, or perhaps she hoped it had an innocuous
explanation. Ava Helen was hospitalized and prepared for surgery. Linus,
Jr., Linda, and her husband, Barclay, arrived at the hospital. The next day
the surgeons found that the cancer was baseball-sized and could not be
removed. Crellin and his second wife, Kay, arrived on August 9.

From August through November, Ava Helen "hung in," as physician son
Linus would later note. Rejecting more invasive chemotherapy, she followed
a regimen of liquids, soft food when she could tolerate it, and a mixture
of ascorbic acid, selenite in the form of selenium yeast, copper chloride,
quinine, and a powdered nutritional mix called Vivonex. By adding an
artificial flavor, Ava Helen found she could tolerate the Vivonex. For pain,
she took as little Zomax as she could manage. For some patients Zomax
proved disastrous; Ava Helen found it a blessing because it controlled her
pain without causing the constipation produced by aspirin.[50]

In early September the Paulings spent a week at the ranch. Their niece Cheryl, Crellin's and Lucy's daughter, visited them from Humboldt State University. When they came home to Portola Valley her physician, Hal Holman, shared Ava Helen's cautious optimism, saying it seemed she was getting better rather than deteriorating—the lump felt about the same. Her pain continued fairly constantly, though, and every so often she took an anodyne in order to sleep.

The children came in and out. Peter arrived from London. Linda traveled to Portola Valley frequently. At the beginning of November the tribe gathered once more. The Monterey Chapter of the American Civil Liberties Union awarded Ava Helen the Ralph Atkinson Civil Liberties Award on Sunday, November 1, 1981. The award acknowledged Ava Helen's involvement in civil liberties particularly during the incarceration of the Japanese Americans during World War II, and the suppression of free and dissident speech in the 1950s. The whole family traveled to Monterey, where Ava Helen not only received the award, but also made a fifteen-minute speech, Linus recorded proudly. This was her last public appearance. Linus, Linus, Jr., and Crellin also spoke. On that occasion, as he typically did, Linus acknowledged Ava Helen's central influence in his life. "I have received awards in these fields from time to time, and each time I felt a mistake had been made, that she should be getting the award, not me. She has determined the course of my life and I attribute to her the fine life it has been my privilege to lead."[51] Francis Heisler, a prominent civil liberties and labor attorney, also spoke. The Monterey chapter also used the occasion to raise funds to fight contemporary battles during the early Reagan era assaults on civil liberties.

Ava Helen grew thinner, weighing just ninety pounds the week after the ACLU party. Linus was scheduled to fly to London and Madrid that week. On Wednesday, November 4, she asked him not to go—a sharply uncharacteristic gesture that must have signaled her sense of impending crisis. The next day, recovering her normal voice, she told Pauling to go, and Linus complied, perhaps with relief, perhaps trepidation. Linus and Peter took BOAC to London. Four hours after Linus checked into Brown's Hotel, he received a message that Ava Helen had experienced a massive hemorrhage and had been taken to Stanford University Hospital. He took the first available plane at 2 a.m. and returned to California. Ava Helen was stabilized and discharged November 15. A week later she had another hemorrhage, calling to Linus from the bathroom in the middle of the night. Linus, Jr., and his second wife, Stephanie, were staying at the guest cottage in Portola Valley. Linus pounded on their door, yelling "Momma! Momma!" and roused Linus, Jr., who wrapped his mother in a blanket and carried her to the station wagon so they could take her to the emergency room. She was stabilized and then transferred to Hoover Pavilion, part of the Stanford Hospital. Another hemorrhage followed.

For eight nights Linus slept in a cot by Ava Helen's hospital bed, while their children kept a twenty-four-hour vigil. When Linus was sleeping, away from the bedside, or unable to reach his book, Linda kept the log of her mother's intake of liquid and output of urine. The family agreed to stop intravenous feeding on Monday, November 26, in order to eliminate the discomfort of the tubes. Ava Helen continued to take liquids and some soft food — a few bites of mashed pear, soup, apple juice, eggnog. They all feared another hemorrhage and hoped that a soft food diet would reduce the chance of a recurrence.

Linus had been the major go-between in planning his wife's earlier treatment; now Linus, Jr., had an expanded role as family physician as well as tender nurse. He gave Ava Helen her bath and washed her hair at the end of the first week in the hospital, and cleaned his mother after subsequent bleeding episodes. (Ava Helen told him that he would have made a good nurse — again, even in these last weeks, a double-edged compliment to her physician son in an era when nurses were seriously undervalued.) He made sure that his father, who never left Ava Helen's side, got his nightly jigger of vodka. He was present during the most difficult conference between Dr. Holman and his parents, to decide against additional blood transfusions. "She agreed," Linus, Jr., now remembers, "with tears running down her cheeks. It must have been extremely difficult for my father."[52]

The family decided to move Ava Helen home a few days later, on Tuesday, December 1. Peter and Crellin were sent to buy sheets and medical supplies for what they all knew were Ava Helen's last days at home. Initially all the children were present at the Portola Valley house, but Linus seems to have ordered them to go home, even though the death watch had begun. Linda may have departed, but she returned to her parents' house. The family had twenty-four-hour nurses. Linus kept extensive notes both in the hospital and at home, sometimes in shaky handwriting on the backs of envelopes. Clear-minded throughout her final illness, Ava Helen tried to help the family arrange her affairs after her death. She asked Linus to collect her papers for Wellesley College, whose archivists had asked for them.[53] She also told Linus who should get her precious objects, and he tried to keep careful lists. In the final days she managed to tolerate one trip out to the garden in a wheelchair.

She had fears about the end; one was that she would have a stroke and linger on. Linus scribbled a note, probably after consulting with the doctors: "Tell AHP. You won't have a stroke (needs high BP [blood pressure])." He made a list of other hazards of her condition: low blood pressure, dehydration, coma. One day near the end, perhaps with whatever characteristic humor was left her, or perhaps after some nightmarish vision, Ava Helen suddenly said to Linus, "Paddy, be sure that I am really dead." At 12:20 p.m. on Monday, December 7, a few weeks short of her seventy-eighth birthday, Ava Helen died. Linda, Linus, and the nurse were in the room. Linus stayed by her side for another two hours, holding her hand.

Ava Helen Pauling, 1977.

"A very strong sense of what is right and of what is not right"[1]

Isabelle and I visited Ava Helen very recently, and she told us the story about the fish aquarium which had been empty, and she said something about its being empty, and that night Linus was a little late in getting home, and she wondered what on earth he was doing. He came in with two brimful sacks of fish to restock the aquarium, so she could see the fish. And she said, "I'll have to be careful that I don't say that I would want a horse."
—Unidentified woman at AHP's memorial service, December 12, 1981

Tears are on this page!
—Charles and Margaret Huggins to LP, December 1981[2]

I think that she was a wonderful woman, just about perfect.
—Linus Pauling, unmailed letter, March 1982[3]

The family had already planned the memorial service. Actually, as Linus, Jr., confirmed at the service, Ava Helen had planned it. Peter Christiansen, minister at the Unitarian Church in Los Angeles for seven years, and then at Walnut Creek, conducted the service at the Palo Alto Unitarian Church. (Stephen Fritchman, minister emeritus at Los Angeles, was also ailing and would die about the same time as Ava Helen.) The Stanford-based group the Mendicants sang. Frank Catchpool, the young doctor at Schweitzer's compound at Lambaréné so many years before, offered the eulogy. Catchpool had been a fan of Pauling's before he met the chemist and peace proponent in Africa. He had accepted Pauling's invitation to do a postdoc at Caltech, and had learned chemistry so he could work with Pauling on medical research. They ended up collaborating on the molecular basis of anesthesia. Catchpool had become a close friend and trusted associate of the Paulings. He remembered those days in Lambaréné in 1959: his own comfort with the Paulings, as he had been raised Quaker and grown up around people talking about peace and justice, and how Ava Helen had disliked and challenged the "macho" tone of the hospital. But he also remembered that, at that time as throughout her life, she had made her challenges in a soft, "somewhat shy" voice, though "the words were precise and the meanings always very clear."

Frances Herring, Ava Helen's peace colleague, took the floor for an astute and loving appraisal of Ava Helen's style of activism. Herring compared Ava Helen to Vietnamese women she had known: "small and delicate and frail-looking, but when they're defending the things they really believe in, just incredibly strong and brave." She recalled Ava Helen's activism in WILPF in the 1950s and into the 1960s, as she struggled against the red baiting of her organization colleagues. Herring also acknowledged Ava Helen's complexity: her devotion to Linus, and beside that, her bold activism.

> [S]he refused to be wholly defined by her role as a wife and a mother. Sometimes, on a social occasion, when I would look across at Linus and Ava Helen, usually sitting on a couch, with his arm on the sofa in back of her, and his hand resting lightly on her shoulder, I would see in my mind's eye her other roles — the way she worked so passionately with other independent women for the values they cherished most — human rights, economic justice, and peace. I remembered how she marched with Mary Clark[e] and the Women's Strike for Peace, and addressed a huge anti-government gathering, demonstration in Queens, where many people were arrested and beaten up, and how, with other thoughtful women, she bearded the officials of NATO in their lair, in the Hague, and reasoned with them about the folly of bringing nuclear weapons into Europe poised against the Soviet Union.

The memories drifted closer to home, to friends and family. An African American woman who described herself as a "live-in person" near the Paulings in Portola Valley told the assembly that Ava Helen had always invited her to pick the flowers from the Paulings' garden to share with people who otherwise might not have flowers. Martha Acevedo recalled in wonderment that Ava Helen planned picnics and other gatherings in the last week of her life; when asked if she ever cried, Ava Helen had said no — then remembered a letter from her grandson Sascha that had made her cry. Longtime friend Alice Richards remembered her courage, femininity, and sheer sense of fun, as well as her ability to focus on other people, even when she was ill.

There was in fact at least one more tearful episode in Ava Helen's last weeks, and poignantly, it speaks to her carrying memories and regrets for episodes long since past. Stephanie Pauling remembers Ava Helen weeping on a quiet afternoon over having left baby Linus, Jr., those many years before.[4]

Richard Morgan, Linus's young cousin, followed the couple from Portland to Caltech. He continued to visit the Los Angeles area when he transferred to Berkeley and then started work in Sacramento. Morgan had already written a valedictory letter, undoubtedly knowing Ava Helen was very ill. He filled it with memories: the waffle breakfasts he ate at the Paulings with Linus's shy graduate students, the camping trips to Painted Canyon, Linus sitting in the living room transfixed with a slide rule on his lap while Rich and Ava Helen fixed dinner. He thought Linus's wife was the most beautiful woman he had ever seen. "Did I ever tell you," he had written in an earlier letter, "that all through my undergraduate years at Tech and at Berkeley I kept your portrait photograph on the wall by my desk?"[5]

Linus, Jr., spoke of the quality of the nursing care Ava Helen had received at the Hoover Pavilion, and the delicate diplomacy of Dr. Hal Holman, who had helped Ava Helen help Linus to let go. "She was able," he said, "in these circumstances, to view the situation with clarity, to make absolutely rational, sensible, common-sense decisions, and to express them unequivocally to my father." She chose not to continue treatments or to take measures that would prolong life. It was her job, and now the children's job, to help rationalist Linus accept the emotions of the moment.

Crellin emphasized Ava Helen's decisive influence on his father, which came in phases: the phase of his great scientific breakthroughs, and then the phase of civil rights and peace activism, "in which we freely recognize that she raised his consciousness and he had the strength of character and integrity to put his reputation on the line in this behalf." And then there was ascorbic acid. "I'm willing to bet that the roots started with her, because she was talking up ascorbic acid to me when I started college, which was ten years before he jumped on the band wagon."

Crellin pointed out that his mother's final cause was the environment. In fact she had requested that memorial contributions go to the Sempervirens Foundation.[6] In the 1970s she was compelled by the efforts made to save the California redwoods. Sempervirens had a long history of conservation efforts aimed at the Santa Cruz Mountains redwoods, which in the 1960s had culminated in the founding of Big Basin Redwoods State Park. One of her last outings, in October 1981, was to Big Basin, with Linus, Peter, and two fellows of the Institute. She had also joined efforts to establish the Anza-Borrego desert reserve.

If Ava Helen had a younger woman's conflicts and difficulties over being a mother, being a grandmother was easy and natural for her. Tributes poured in to her affection, her generosity, her ability to personalize her attention and make each child feel special. "When I was younger," said Barky, Linda and Barclay's son, "Ava Helen was what a grandmother is to every child — she visited me on holidays, she brought presents, she was unreserved in her kindness." Barky went on at the service:

> *Since then I've grown, and I've had the fortune that not every grandson has of growing up in her presence — of maturing, of learning who she is, and from this I've found quite a lot of the things that I hold valuable, hold to be true … are things she represented to me in many ways: my love of music, my interest in art, my interest in politics are all things that she represented to me. But I think the foremost thing that stands out in my mind is her great concern — her concern for me as a child when I would be hurt by various family members; she's concerned for the people of the world and all the great suffering, as we all know; she's concerned for the little bird which every day hits its head against the windows in the living room.*

Crellin's daughter Cheryl remembers dancing for joy as a small child when she and her sister were going to her grandmother's house. She remembers Ava Helen finding games for her to play, and planning special activities for the children. Stephanie Pauling, Linus's second wife, remembers Ava Helen's special kindness to Stephanie's small daughter when they visited the older Paulings at the ranch and stayed in China Camp, the house that the boys had built for their visits. Each morning Ava Helen would hoist a dish towel on the flagpole, signaling that she welcomed little Carrie's visit to the big house.[7]

After Ava Helen's death, Linus was distraught. He wept through the miserable Christmas season of 1981. Somehow the usual boxes of pears had gone out to a list of friends and family. The family engaged a press agent to send out an obituary to newspapers around the world. Condolence cards strangely mixed with thanks and season's greetings filled the mailbox at Golden Hills Road and at the institute, where Linus's secretary also fielded calls and telegrams. Ava Helen's brother Clay, still living, and her sisters, Dickie, LuGorgo, and Nettie, all sent cards to Linus, as did his sisters, Lucile and Pauline. Grandchildren unable to return for the service sent loving notes. Many peace colleagues wrote. Linus's colleagues and friends from Caltech, Stanford, and the institute wrote, as well as friends and colleagues from around the world. A few sent religiously inflected comfort. Some sent poems. Some shared the loss of their own spouses. Some asked him about their own cancers, and Vitamin C, and his scribbled notes at the top of those letters suggests that he responded to them. To one correspondent who asked about whether the ascorbic acid was pointless, he wrote that he believed Ava Helen had not taken *enough* Vitamin C in her final illness. Many offered help. Some reminisced. Some just admitted they did not know what to say.

The survivors—family, friends, colleagues, and neighbors—knew that when they said goodbye to Ava Helen, they also said goodbye to that extraordinary marriage, a living thing in itself. The Paulings' marriage certainly figures among a relative handful in its longevity, its passion, and its productivity. At the same time, their union reflects many others of adjacent generations in the complexity and plasticity of the woman's role compared to the man's. Despite a difficult and emotionally complicated relationship to his own mother, Linus entered his lifelong romance with Ava Helen with ardor and grace that did not diminish over time. It is true that he accommodated her changing priorities, but because she was primarily devoted to him over any other person or activity—including their children—to some extent he got *more* of her when she turned to political activism and encouraged him to do the same. For her, though, the inner journey must have required a fair amount of nimble stepping to manage the nurturing of Linus's *two* careers along with the taming of her growing sense that, in a world in which women were increasingly claiming space, her own claim to recognition far outstripped her public profile.

An extraordinary essay collection, *Creative Couples in the Sciences,* captures a number of similarly fraught marriages. Even in dual-career partnerships in which the wives were equally or more productive, they often took it on themselves to protect and promote their husbands. Thus it was in the marriage of Pierre and Marie Curie—one in fact particularly significant to the Paulings, as Marie Curie was, like Linus Pauling, a dual Nobelist (though once with Pierre). Despite Pierre's lacking the drive to advancement and recognition, Marie "did her best to shield her husband from distractions," as Helena Pycior notes.[8] While her marriage to Pierre helped her gain access to laboratories, standing, and opportunity, his marriage to Marie gained Pierre a brilliant collaborator *and* a happy home. Further, or more explicitly, as Pycior points out, his partnership with Marie made him lead scientist in a research team for the first time. In the remarkable Curie story, when their daughter Irene married Frédéric Joliot, a second marital collaboration was born and a second shared Nobel won in 1935, for the discovery of artificial radioactivity. As that marriage went on, Irene Joliot-Curie continued to be productive scientifically, but also withdrew to some extent from the public stage she had occupied near the start of World War II, to nurse her own tuberculosis and protect her children during the Nazi occupation. Nonetheless, she paid a price for the political leftism she shared with Frédéric. Like many others, the Joliot-Curies joined the resistance from the left and then were caught in the Cold War persecution of Communists and left sympathizers. (Linus Pauling joined some other scientists in strong protest when Irene Joliot-Curie was denied foreign membership to the American Chemical Society in 1953 on the basis of her Communist associations.[9]) As Bernadette Bensaude-Vincent argues, Irene Joliot-Curie created a "role of her own" that integrated "multiple constraints as a scientific heiress, spouse, and mother," and that allowed her to stay, despite her Nobel-worthy scientific career, "at home."[10]

Of course there are multiple examples of "creative couples" whose female members were simply held back or pushed back, either from participation or from recognition: Carl and Gerty Cori, also Nobelists, are one such couple. There were also couples who, like the older Curies, forged a more equal collaboration, though sometimes at the expense of their children. Gunnar and Alva Myrdal — strikingly like Linus and Ava Helen — left their two-year-old with relatives during their 1930-31 field research trip to the United States from Sweden. Like Linus Pauling, Jr., and his younger brother, Crellin, Jan Myrdal carried a lifelong bitterness about that parental abandonment.[11]

Another kind of model of couple collaboration, and one in some ways closer to the way the Paulings worked things out, is offered by Willard and Dorothy Whitney Straight, who founded *The New Republic* in 1914. In his wonderful merger of intimate and intellectual history, *The Refuge of Affections*, Eric Rauchway analyzes that marriage in the context of the Straights' shared commitment to Progressive reform. Like Ava Helen Pauling, Dorothy Whitney Straight was able to stand on a public stage with, though a bit behind, her husband. But Whitney had money — and she had reform and social work experience before she married. And in the early years of their marriage, they quite self-consciously sought a nontraditional balance of private life and public commitment that included opportunities for Dorothy and Willard to work together on shared projects. The Paulings, by contrast, almost stumbled into their public partnership through years of private interaction in a more traditional relationship.[12]

Helen and Scott Nearing offer another comparative marital career. Like Linus Pauling, Scott Nearing suffered political persecution for his socialism and pacifism; unlike Pauling, he paid the price of his academic career as an economist. Thus his and Helen's partnership, unusually close and loving, did not have to breach barriers of conventional career expectations. They forged their own career as twentieth-century rural simple-life philosophers. Interestingly, as Linus pursued his popular writings in health and Vitamin C, he and the Nearings began appearing on the same bookstore shelves.[13]

Though much more conventional in the social structure of their lives, the Paulings certainly do not fit any model of oppressively patriarchal marital relations. Ava Helen's bulldog protection and defense of Linus, her putting him before all other people or things, and her young self's ready relinquishment of plans for a career of her own, resemble the relationship of Véra and Vladimir Nabokov, so poignantly recreated by Stacy Schiff.[14] Like Véra Nabokov, Ava Helen Pauling chose her role. Would she have done so if society had offered more sharply delineated options?

As I suggested earlier in this book, it was quite common for middle-class wives in the mid-twentieth century, as earlier, to make their public and political contributions through "housekeeping" activities, including the not negligible roles of volunteer agencies, women's clubs, and church groups, not to mention well-established activist groups like WILPF, the WCTU, and others.[15] Ava Helen Miller, from an aspirational middle-class family with ties to state government, with a mother interested in woman suffrage and a liberal-leaning father, would have been very aware of club activities as a springboard to exercising social responsibility. But we have also seen that she did not like to be just a cog in the organizational wheel. That role bored and frustrated her after a while. So to move from acting as Linus's "silent partner" to sharing the stage with him was a natural trajectory for Ava Helen. But these parallel, unpaid careers were a tricky business psychologically and emotionally, and Ava Helen's later interviews and speeches dealt increasingly honestly, if impersonally, with the price that generation paid.

A darker, but understandable, motive for sticking close to Linus was Ava Helen's underlying anxiety that she might not be able to withstand a tide of work or eros that could sweep him away at any moment. It had long been understood among the Pauling children that Ava Helen was a jealous spouse, worried and angry when Linus seemed to pay attention to another woman, even concerned that he not grow too close to Linda, as if his love for his daughter might cut into his devotion to herself. But it was also clear to the children, as to the Paulings' friends, that the jealousy was wholly unnecessary—that Linus "adored" Ava Helen, as Linda would later recall.[16]

In March Linus wrote a letter to his children that he apparently never sent: a "report" to them on how he was "getting along" after Ava Helen's death.

My evaluation of my situation is that I get along by managing to forget that Ava Helen has died. … [W]hen I am traveling I think that she is at home in Portola Valley waiting for me. When I am in the Institute I think that she is at home and that I shall soon see her. When I am in our house in Portola

Valley working at a table, I think she is in another room. When I am at the
ranch too I think that she is in another room. But then several times a day
something happens to make me realize that these thoughts are not true, and
that my dear companion is indeed dead.

He found himself crying, moaning aloud, in public, unpredictably. "I think that she was a wonderful woman, just about perfect." The depth of his uncomplicated, radical grief shook Pauling, and his emotional journey shocked him.[17] This was the overwhelming, traumatic grief of the rational humanist, who had prided himself on controlling his feelings, and now found to his amazement that his feelings could not even be predicted, much less controlled.[18]

When he could, Linus sat down with his big book of medical records and details of Ava Helen's final days, and wrote the things he remembered: the order of medical events; the details of her diet, supplements, and elimination; Ava Helen's fears and concerns—there were few that she admitted to, or that he committed to writing—and the memories that she shared. "Ava Helen talked to me about our trip through Italy, April 1926, especially the day when we took the tram to the end of the line and then walked out the Appian Way; we climbed up on top of a large ruined old tomb and ate our lunch of bread and cheese; two mounted carbinieres [sic] road up [sic], looked up at us, and then rode on." In her last days, her mind went back to that first trip to Europe, fifty-five years earlier, that had brought them such joy. For Linus, it had been an affirmation of scientific passion and discovery; for Ava Helen, a *Wanderjahr* during which she could forget that she would return to the rigors of parenthood and the routines of a faculty wife.

Poignantly, Linus also made lists of which friend, child, or grandchild should receive which memento, and whether it had been sent out. Linda received many of Ava Helen's cherished jewelry pieces, and she as well as her father delivered other pieces of jewelry, silver, and clothing that her mother had given as gifts.

For Linus himself, as he wrote on December 17, Ava Helen intended the MG. "She once said that of all of the presents that I had given her she liked the MG best. We had driven it to Stillwater, Oklahoma and back and had made other trips in it." He wrote that the battery was dead and he was now charging it.

Linus's last entry devoted to Ava Helen was dated the first of May 1982. "Last month I charged the battery of the MG. Today for the first time since Ava Helen's death I drove it. I went around the neighborhood, and washed it (the MG)."

Ava Helen would have enjoyed the inadvertent word play and the vision of Linus washing the neighborhood. One hopes that Linus heard it that way and managed a little smile.

Notes

Introduction

1. I use her first name throughout this book, though I usually avoid in my work what feels like a presumptuous practice. The difficulty is — appropriately to the subject — that convention generally recognizes her husband Linus as "Pauling," and so the way I clarify *which* Pauling I refer to at any time is contextually determined.
2. *Daily American*, May 13-14, 1964. Clipping. Ava Helen Pauling Papers (hereafter AHP), Box 3.003, Ava Helen and Linus Pauling Papers, Special Collections, Oregon State University.
3. Frank Catchpool, "Transcription of the tape recording of part of the memorial meeting for Ava Helen Pauling at the Unitarian Church of Palo Alto, December 12, 1981." AHP, Box 4.008.
4. Jenny Perry, "Mrs. Pauling's analysis: 'any work done happily is contribution to the whole world,'" Santa Barbara *News-Press*, August 16, 1964..AHP, Box 3.003.
5. Thomas Hager offers a wonderful narrative of the Paulings' Vitamin C era in *Force of Nature: The Life of Linus Pauling* (New York: Simon and Schuster, 1995).
6. Ms., black notebook, Ava Helen Pauling, 1927. AHP, Box 3.001.
7. AHP, interview with Lee Herzenberg, September 1977. AHP, Box 3.002, Folder 2.6.
8. "She campaigns with husband," *The Advertiser*, November 10, 1963. AHP, Box 3.003, Folder 3.13.
9. "Mrs. Pauling's analysis: 'any work done happily is contribution to the whole world," Santa Barbara *News Press*, August 16, 1964. AHP, Box 3.003, Folder 3.12.
10. Richard Morgan, interview with Thomas Hager, LP, hager2.003.3.

Chapter 1

1. AHM to LP, June 1, 1922. LP, Personal Safe, Box 1.002.

2. Quoted by Tim Ryan, "Walking Tall in the Shadow of her Husband," *The Cambrian*, November 8, 1979.

3. "So they were married and I suppose that he homesteaded a 160-acre farm. And that's where all 10 children were born. It's about 4 miles from Beaver Creek at a place called Four Corners. The farm is one of the corners of Four Corners. That's half a mile or a mile perhaps from Highland. The Highland school perhaps is still there. And the farmhouse that Nora Gard built I think after the divorce is still there. It's on the southwest corner of Four Corners, where two roads cross at right angles." Linus Pauling, interview with Thomas Hager, March 27, 1991. AHP, Box 2.003.

4. Thomas Hager, *Force of Nature: The Life of Linus Pauling* (New York: Simon and Schuster, 1995), 69.

5. The Pauling Blog, October 6, 2008, Special Collections, Oregon State University. http://paulingblog.wordpress.com/2008/10/16/the-ancestry-of-ava-helen-pauling/.

6. Personal communication, Pauling descendant, March 2012.

7. *The HIM Book*. AHP, Box 3.001.

8. LP interview with Thomas Hager, March 27, 1991. AHP, Box 2.003.

9. AHP family letters, G.R. Miller, Miller Family folder. AHP, Box 3.023.

10. AHP, note on back of photograph, 191?.i.169.

11. Mae Perks, *The HIM Book* (New York: Dodge Publishing Company, 1912). Ava Helen's copy of this book is in AHP, Box 3.001.

12. Linus Pauling (LP) to Ava Helen Miller (AHM), July 25, 1922. LP, Personal Safe.

13. AHM, *HIM Book*.

14. AHM, *HIM Book*.

15. Photographs, 191?i.45.

16. LP to AHM, November 21, 1922. LP, Personal Safe.

17. General Catalogue, Oregon Agricultural College, 1922-23, with List of Students for 1921-1922, Oregon State University Archives.

18. I have not determined whether Mrs. Miller purchased or rented this house, and what kind of relationship she maintained with her college-aged children. A clause in the 1923 catalogue warns that all incoming women students are expected to reside in the dormitories unless their parents live in the city, and that may have been part of the reason for Mrs. Miller to relocate to Corvallis. Men students, by contrast, might bypass the dormitories to board privately in the city — as Linus Pauling had done two years earlier — although all private boarding houses were supposed to be approved by campus authorities. See also LP to his children, January 16, 1982, read into an interview by Thomas Hager. LP, hager2.006.6.

19. Ava Helen Miller unofficial transcript, Oregon Agricultural College. AHP, Box 3.001.

20. More acreage lay south of town, and eight hundred acres were leased for farm purposes, according to the catalogue.

21. *Oregon Agricultural College General Catalogue, 1922-23; Student Handbook: A Compilation of General Information.* ([Corvallis:] Forum, 1921).

22. Interview with Linus Pauling and Ava Helen Pauling, January 12, 1977, NOVA transcripts. AHP, Box 3.002.
23. Chemistry Assignment, LP-AHM correspondence, January-May 1922, LP, Personal Safe.
24. The Pauling-Miller experience suggests that some kind of inhibition may commonly have been imposed by supervisors anxious to carry forward the general collegiate promise to parents to take care of female students' virtue. But in general, it seems that institutional scrutiny of professor-student relationships really followed the grassroots feminist movement of the 1960s and 1970s, in which among other things romantic and sexual relationships between instructors and students were often identified as sexual harassment, based on the power differential between instructors, with the power to manipulate grades and evaluations, and students, with little real-life power to retaliate. See for example Billie Wright Dziech and Linda Weiner, *The Lecherous Professor: Sexual Harassment on Campus* (Boston: Beacon Press, 1984).
25. AHM-LP love letters, about 1 May 1922. LP, Personal Safe.
26. Linus Pauling, Diary 1917-1918. LP, Personal Safe.
27. Hager, 53-54.
28. LP to Peter Pauling, June 10, 1960. LP Biographical, Box 5.044.
29. Hager, 56-57.
30. Linus Pauling, Diary, Friday, October 5, 1917, LP Biographical, Box 1.001.
31. Linus Pauling, Diary, Monday, October 29, 1917, LP Biographical, Box 1.001.
32. Linus Pauling, "Children of the Dawn," typescript, LP Biographical, Box 1.002. Pauling's mature handwriting notes that he won only second place with this submission.
33. Transcript, NOVA interviews, January 12, 1977, AHP, Box 3.002.
34. See NOVA interviews, January 12, 1977.
35. LP to AHM, [about 1 May 1922], AHP-LP correspondence Jan-May 1922. LP, Personal Safe.
36. LP to AHM, June 18, 1922. LP, Personal Safe.
37. LP to AHM, June 12, 1922. LP, Personal Safe.
38. LP to AHM, June [19] 1922. LP, Personal Safe.
39. LP to AHM, various, June 1922; quotes from June 23, 1922, and June 24, 1922. LP, Personal Safe.
40. He seems to have destroyed most of her half of their intimate correspondence after her death, while preserving his own. Relatives report that in 1982, the year after her death, he burned many papers, but he never told them which ones. Interview, Kay Pauling, March 13, 1982. Pauling Papers.
41. LP to AHM, June 26, 1922. LP, Personal Safe.
42. See, e.g., LP to AHM, June 20, 1922. LP, Personal Safe.
43. LP to AHM, August 6, 1922. LP, Personal Safe.
44. LP to AHM, [June 20, 1922]. LP, Personal Safe.
45. LP to AHM, July 26, 1922. LP, Personal Safe.
46. This stipend would have been for the academic year. However, oddly, there are varying reports of the fellowship amount among Pauling scholars. Thomas Hager reports it as $350 per month plus tuition — assuming graduate teaching

(*Force of Nature*, 71). Dr. Robert Paradowski's Pauling Chronology on the Ava Helen and Linus Pauling Papers site at Special Collections, OSU, mentions a figure of $750 plus tuition for the first year. In any case, the amount was small enough to persuade Linus and Ava Helen that it would be almost impossible for two of them to live on that amount.

47. LP to AHM, July 26, 1922. LP, Personal Safe.
48. LP to AHM, July 26, 1922 [2]. LP, Personal Safe.
49. Because we don't have her letter, but only his response, we don't know if she meant that she would work in Oregon or in California. His reply emphasized her staying in school for the coming year, and living at "Doc's." LP to AHM, July 29, 1922, LP, Personal Safe.
50. LP to AHM, August 8, 1922.LP, Personal Safe.
51. LP to AHM, August 6, 1922. LP, Personal Safe.
52. LP to AHM, August 7, 1922. LP, Personal Safe.
53. LP to AHM, August 7, 1922; LP to AHM, August 24, 1922. LP, Personal Safe.
54. LP to AHM, August 12, 1922. LP, Personal Safe.
55. LP to AHM, September 6, 1922. LP, Personal Safe.
56. LP to AHM, September 16, 1922. LP, Personal Safe.
57. LP to AHM, September 20, 1922. LP, Personal Safe.
58. LP to AHM, September 21, 1922. LP, Personal Safe.
59. For just one of probably hundreds of instances, see LP to AHM, September 16, 1922. LP, Personal Safe.
60. LP to AHM, August 1, 1922,. LP, Personal Safe.
61. LP to AHM, November 4, 1922. LP, Personal Safe. Robinson's *Woman: Her Sex and Love-Life* was first published in 1917 and extended to over twenty editions by the early 1930s. See also n. 77 below.
62. LP to AHM, November 4, 1922. LP, Personal Safe.
63. It is difficult to imagine what young man would be contented with this prescription.
64. LP to AHM, November 4, 1922. LP, Personal Safe.
65. AHM to LP, November 6, 1922. LP, Personal Safe.
66. Interestingly, in February he commented to Ava Helen that he was reading Upton Sinclair's *Mind and Body*, which recommended that he not rush through intercourse, but pause along the way, "wait, you know, for the time when we hold one another so very tightly." LP to AHM, February 14, 1923. LP, Personal Safe.
67. Paula Fass, *The Damned and the Beautiful: American Youth in the 1920s* (New York: Oxford University Press, 1977), 264-65.
68. Helen Lefkowitz Horowitz, *Campus Life: Undergraduate Cultures from the End of the Eighteenth Century to the Present* (New York: Alfred A. Knopf, 1987), 125-31.
69. Linda Gordon, *Woman's Body, Woman's Right: A Social History of Birth Control in America* (New York: Grossman Publishers, 1976), 192-193. One study sampled "middle-class married New York City women," while the second sampled college women. A Kinsey study of the same cohorts of women confirmed these findings. Gordon published an updated version of her history

of the birth control movement as *The Moral Property of Women: A History of Birth Control Politics in America* (Champaign: University of Illinois Press, 2002).

70. This summary of Mosher's findings is thanks to Marilyn Yalom, *A History of the Wife* (New York: HarperCollins Publishers, 2001), 296-97.

71. Gordon, 173-79. Robinson published over thirty editions of his *Fewer and Better Babies: Birth Control or the Limitation of Offspring by Prevenception*, between 1916 and his death in 1936. In it he tackled the common arguments against birth control. He clarified that he could not *legally* offer the public a handbook of birth control methods, which in itself necessitated the philosophical and sociological treatise he offered instead.

72. On July 20, 1922, for example, Linus wrote to Ava Helen, "The article on birth control [not specified] seemed good. I'd not thought of it much. I believe in it though. They said the simplest methods were best. I believe that the harmless methods of contraception should be told to all married couples, as well as the best method for helping conception in the childless. Birth control signifies both." LP to AHM, July 20, 1922. LP, Personal Safe.

73. LP to AHM, November 21, 1922. LP, Personal Safe.

74. LP to AHM, May 1, 1923. LP, Personal Safe.

75. LP to AHM, March 20, 1923. LP, Personal Safe.

76. LP to AHM, April 30, 1923. LP, Personal Safe.

77. LP to AHM, November 22, 1922. LP, Personal Safe.

78. LP to AHM, January 30, 1923. LP, Personal Safe.

79. LP to AHM, November 4, 1922. LP, Personal Safe.

80. LP to AHM, November 4, 1922. LP, Personal Safe.

81. LP to AHM, May 20, 1923. LP, Personal Safe.

82. MIT admitted its first woman in 1871, but the floodgates did not exactly open. Harvard and Radcliffe gradually merged undergraduate classrooms and degrees between 1943 and the early 1970s.

83. LP to AHM, November 4, 1922. LP, Personal Safe.

84. AHM to LP, November 6, 1922. LP, Personal Safe.

85. AHM to LP, November 6, 1922. LP, Personal Safe.

86. AHM to LP, around October 6, 1922. LP, Personal Safe.

87. AHM to LP, November 6, 1922. LP, Personal Safe.

88. AHM to LP, November 6, 1922. LP, Personal Safe.

89. LP to AHM, January 19, 1923. LP, Personal Safe.

90. AHM to LP, November 12, 1922. LP, Personal Safe.

91. LP to AHM, November 24, December 3, 1922. LP, Personal Safe.

92. LP to AHM, January 30, 1923. LP, Personal Safe.

93. Los Angeles Sunday *Times*, February 4, 1923, p. 1; clipping enclosed in LP to AHM, February 4, 1923. LP, Personal Safe.

94. LP to AHM, February 6, 1923. LP, Personal Safe. In March Linus referred to Ava Helen teaching the "senseless girls" chemistry. It is unclear which senseless girls she was teaching. The best guess may be that formally or informally she was tutoring classmates and other home economics majors. See LP to AHM, March 16, 1923, LP, Personal Safe.

95. See, for example, LP to AHM, February 6, 1923. LP, Personal Safe.
96. LP to AHM, February 16, 1923. LP, Personal Safe.
97. LP to AHM, November 17, 1922. LP, Personal Safe.
98. LP to AHM, November 17, 1922. LP, Personal Safe.
99. LP to AHM, December 31, 1922. LP, Personal Safe.
100. LP to AHM, January 10, 1923. LP, Personal Safe.
101. LP to AHM, January 6, 1923. LP, Personal Safe.
102. LP to AHM, March 15, 1923. LP, Personal Safe.
103. LP to AHM, March 11, 1923. LP, Personal Safe.
104. For about a week after March 22, Linus's letters to Ava Helen were forwarded from 445 South 15th Street in Corvallis to 1630 Court Street in Salem.
105. LP to AHM, March 19, 1923. LP, Personal Safe.
106. LP to AHM, April 26, 1923. LP, Personal Safe.
107. LP to AHM, May 20, 1923. LP, Personal Safe.
108. LP to AHM, May 17, 1923. LP, Personal Safe.
109. AHM to LP, "Tuesday," [after May 14, 1923]. LP, Personal Safe.

Chapter 2

1. Pauling Papers Online, safe 1.014.14.
2. Hager, *Force of Nature*, 103.
3. Hager, *Force of Nature*, 105-7; Robert Paradowski, "Pauling Chronology," Pauling Papers Online. http://osulibrary.oregonstate.edu/specialcollections/coll/pauling/chronology/page7.html.
4. AHP, *The HIM Book*. AHP, Box 3.001.
5. Robert Paradowski, one of Pauling's major biographers, elaborates on this decision-making process. In his account, Linus continued to be doubtful about the wisdom of leaving the baby in Portland for the year, even up through their departure from Portland. In addition, his family members were shocked and there was reportedly much conversation about Ava Helen's mothering style. See Paradowski, "An American in Munich: Truth and Controversy in the Life and Work of Linus Pauling during the Golden Years of Physics," address during Linus Pauling Centenary Celebration, February 28, 2001, Pauling Papers Online. http://osulibrary.oregonstate.edu/specialcollections/events/2001paulingconference/video-s2-2-paradowski.html.
6. AHP [and LP], entry on February 25, 1926, Black travel booklet: AHP travel diary, 1926 trip to Zurich. AHP, Box 3.008, (Hereafter cited as AHP travel diary.)
7. AHP, Box 3.001.
8. AHP travel diary, March 4, 1926.
9. Paradowski, "An American in Munich"; AHP travel diary, March 7, 1926. There is a fleeting reference in one of Linus's letters to Ava Helen to a "note" from her father before their wedding. That is the only evidence I have found that Richard Miller was in touch with Ava Helen after he left Oregon – except that somehow she had contact information to enable the young couple to meet Miller in Chicago. LP to AHP, February 18, 1923. LP, Personal Safe.

10. LP, AHP travel diary, March 9, 1926.
11. See Hager's account, *Force of Nature*, 105-9.
12. AHP [and LP], Black travel booklet: AHP travel diary, 1926 trip to Zurich. AHP, Box 3.008.
13. AHP travel diary, March 21, 1926.
14. AHP travel diary, March 23, 1926.
15. AHP travel diary, March 24, 1926.
16. AHP travel diary, April 1, 1926.
17. AHP travel diary, April 3 and April 5, 1926.
18. AHP travel diary, April 11, 1926.
19. AHP travel diary, April 4, 1926.
20. AHP travel diary, April 7, 1926.
21. AHP travel diary, April 16, 1926.
22. AHP travel diary, April 11, 1926.
23. Ava Helen and Linus Pauling to A.A. Noyes, May 22, 1926, corr278. 1-lp-noyes-19260522.
24. AHP travel diary, April 3, 1927.
25. AHP travel diary, April 3, 1927.
26. AHP travel diary, April 8, 1926.
27. Paradowski, "An American in Munich."
28. AHP to Sarah Fell Yellin, n.d. AHP, Box 3.020.
29. AHP travel diary, April 3, 1927.
30. Paradowski, "An American in Munich."
31. Lucile Pauling to LP, September 10, 1926. LP Biographical, Box 5.053.
32. LP to AHP, April 25, 1929. LP, Personal Safe.
33. For some of these details, see Linus Pauling, Jr., oral history, recorded September 23, 2011, Pauling Papers.
34. Oral History of Linus Pauling, Jr., Honolulu, Hawaii, June 3-8, 2012, 14. Transcription in Linus and Ava Helen Pauling Papers, Oregon State University.
35. LP to AHP, April 26, 1929. LP, Personal Safe.
36. Robert Paradowski, "Chronology," Linus Pauling Day-by Day, Special Collections, http://osulibrary.oregonstate.edu/specialcollections/coll/pauling/calendar/1932/index.html
37. Kevin Starr, *Endangered Dreams: The Great Depression in California* (New York: Oxford University Press, 1996), esp. vii-viii, 121-55.
38. LP to AHP, April 27, 1929. LP, Personal Safe.
39. LP to AHP, March 16, 1929. LP, Personal Safe.
40 LP to AHP, April 27, 1929. LP, Personal Safe.
41. LP to AHP, March 16, 1929. LP, Personal Safe.
42. LP to AHP, March 16, 1929. LP, Personal Safe.
43. AHP to LP, April 29 [1929]. LP, Personal Safe.
44. LP's account of his dream, April 28, 1929. LP, Personal Safe.
45. LP to AHP, May 2, 1929. LP, Personal Safe.
46. Hager, 151-52. See also Oral History of Linus Pauling, Jr., 15. Linus, Jr., even traces his father's signature beret to the Oppenheimer episode, speculating

that his father changed his hat to differentiate hist style from Oppenheimer's slouched hat.

47. LP to AHP, April 29, 1929. LP, Personal Safe.
48. AHP to LP, April 30, 1929. LP, Personal Safe.
49. AHP to LP, April 28 [1929]. LP, Personal Safe.
50. AHP to LP, April 30, 1929, LP, Personal Safe.
51. AHP to LP, April 28, [1929]. LP, Personal Safe.
52. LP to AHP, May 3, 1929. LP, Personal Safe.
53. Robert Paradowski, Pauling Chronology, Linus Pauling Papers on line. http://oregonstate.edu/specialcollections/coll/pauling/calendar/1930/index.html.n See also Thomas Hager, *Force of Nature*, 155.
54. AHP to LP, [March 1931]. LP, Personal Safe.
55. LP to AHP, Sunday [April 12, 1931]. LP, Personal Safe.
56. AHP to LP, [April 10, 1931]. LP, Personal Safe.
57. LP to AHP, May 23, 1923. LP, Personal Safe.
58. LP to AHP, December 16, 1935. LP, Personal Safe.
59. On this association, see for example Oral History of Linus Pauling, Jr., 23.
60. Oral History of Linus Pauling, Jr., 6-8.
61. Linus Pauling, Jr., "Life with Father … And Mother," "A Liking for the Truth," February 28, 2001, Pauling Online; Oral History of Linus Pauling, Jr., 37-38
62. "My parents, being good parents, insisted that the family be together at meals whenever possible, which meant virtually every supper, every weekend meal, and most breakfasts. Sunday breakfasts were especially elaborate, often with Pop mixing the batter and cooking waffles to the accompaniment of Mom's running criticism, especially when the waffles stuck to the iron and had to be pried off crumb by crumb. Other weeks, Mom made what we called "Pauling Omelets," but which really should have been called "Miller Omelets," because it came from that side of the family. It was an amazing Yorkshire pudding-like concoction served with sugar and milk. Or we had crepes, cooked at the table and rolled up with butter and sugar, sometimes sprinkled with lemon juice. Just thinking about these breakfasts makes my mouth water. Of course, in later years I cooked them for my own family. So meals were times for sharing news, making plans, and for us children, picking up information about our parents' attitudes as we listened to them discuss matters across the table—as long as they weren't speaking German, which was their secret language back then." Linus Pauling, Jr., "Life with Father … And Mother."
63. See, e.g., LP to Mrs. John Van N. Dorr, August 17, 1938. Pauling Papers Online, corr128.4-lp-dorr-19380915.
64. LP to Leslie E. Sutton, September 11, 1939. Pauling Papers Online, corr370.8-lp-sutton-19390911.
65. Thomas Hager, *Force of Nature*, 248-249.
66. LP to Arthur Compton, May 14, 1940. LP Peace, Box 4.009.
67. Clipping, Pasadena *Star-News*, July 11, 1940, LP Scrapbooks 1936-1940; LP, Box 6.003.
68. Nichols Medal acceptance speech. LP Speeches, 1941.

69. Among other references see "Thomas Addis: The Man Who Saved Pauling," in the Pauling Blog, March 11, 2010, Pauling Papers Online.
70. See, e.g., Joseph Koepfli, interview, April 14, 1992, hager2.002.5-addis.
71. AHP to Thomas Addis, April 29, 1941. LP Correspondence, Box 2.
72. AHP to LP, [November 1937?]. LP, Personal Safe.
73. AHP to LP, Thursday, November 11, 1937, LP, Personal Safe. She also told Linus, "Peter is the most amazing. You should see him ride a bike." The school had called home while the Paulings were away, and begged them not to help Peter with his reading because he was already so far ahead, they couldn't keep him busy. To do the school justice, on another occasion they told Ava Helen to just let Peter work at his own pace through the math book, whether he was ahead or not. AHP to LP, November 12, 1937. "I think he is our genius, all right," she reported to Linus the next day.
74. AHP to Peter, Linda, and Crellin Pauling, July 10, 1941. LP Biographical, Box 5.048.
75. Crellin Pauling to AHP, December 7, 1949. LP Biographical, Box 5.048.
76. AHP to LP, December 4, 1937. Personal Safe.
77. AHP to LP, November 16, 1937. Personal Safe.
78. AHP to LP, November 24, 1937. LP, Personal Safe.
79. LP to AHP, December 3, 1937. LP, Personal Safe.
80. AHP to LP, December 3, 1937. LP, Personal Safe.
81. AHP to LP, December 4, 1937. LP, Personal Safe.
82. Linda Pauling, interview with Thomas Hager; "RULES for others," [August 1951]. LP Biographical, Box 1.
83. "The Human Side of Linus Pauling," in "The Life and Work of Linus Pauling (1991-1994): A Discourse on the Art of Biography," February 28-March 3, 1995, Special Collections, Oregon State University Library. http://osulibrary. oregonstate.edu/specialcollections/events/1995paulingconference/video-s3-3-hedberg.html.
84. Crellin Pauling to AHP, Wed. night, [n.d.]. LP Biographical, Box 5.048.
85. Interview, Kay Pauling, March 13, 2012. Pauling Papers.
86. Interview, Linus Pauling, Jr., [fall 2011], Pauling Papers; Oral History of Linus Pauling, Jr., 11, 16
87. Linus Pauling, Jr., to Peter Pauling, July 28, 1941. LP Biographical, Box 5.041, Folder 41.2.
88. See, e.g., Oral History of Linus Pauling, Jr., 2.

Chapter 3

1. Transcript by Linus Pauling of letter received March 9, 1945. Pauling Papers Online, bio2.001.2-anonymous-lp-19450309.
2. Twenty-five years later Ava Helen did not recall feeling fear at the time, even after Linus left on his travels. But she did recall her horror and shock at the internment, after she had assured the people who had worked for her (presumably her gardeners) that nothing would happen to them. AHP to Dr. and Mrs. Harvey Itano, November 5, 1970. AHP, Box 1.001.

3. AHP handwritten account of garage vandalism, March 7 [& 10] 1945. AHP,
    Box 2.001. [Original in AHP, Box 5.001.]. See also Ted Goertzel and Ben
    Goertzel, *Linus Pauling: A Life in Science and Politics* (New York: Basic Books,
    1995), 109-10; Hager, *Force of Nature*, 297-98.
4. AH to Annalee [Stewart], November 1, 1960. AHP,Box 1.002. "Of course,"
    Ava Helen recalled to a reporter in the 1970s, "we sometimes had pickets and
    people sometimes wrote bad things to us, but no real suffering." Interview
    with Lee Herzenberg, September 1977. AHP, Box 3.002.
5. In Chapter 6 I will examine their relationship to the L.A. Unitarians and their
    minister, Stephen Hole Fritchman, in detail.
6. AHP to Annalee [Stewart], November 1, 1960. AHP, Box 1.002.
7. Ava Helen Pauling was elected to the board of the Southern California branch
    of the ACLU in December 1956, for a two-year term. See Eason Monroe to
    AHP, December 14, 1956. AHP, Box 1.004, Folder 4.3.
8. LP to AHP, [March 1958], Love Letters, 1958x.03.31.LP.wpd.
9. LP to AHP, September 7, 1945. LP, Personal Safe 1.017.33.
10. LP to AHP, September 4, 1945.LP, Personal Safe 1.017.32.
11. Linus Pauling, "An Episode that Changed my Life," in *Linus Pauling: Scientist
    and Peacemaker*, ed. Clifford Mead and Thomas Hager (Corvallis: Oregon State
    University Press, 2001), 193-94.
12. Linus Pauling, typescript, May 1, 1982. LP, Box 1982a. See too Oral History of
    Linus Pauling, Jr., 74.
13. M. J. Heale, *McCarthy's Americans: Red Scare Politics in State and Nation, 1935-
    1965* (Athens: The University of Georgia Press, 1998), 10.
14. Heale, 11-15. Heale argues that U.S. federalism facilitated anti-Communist
    inquisitions by offering scope to local politicians to make names for
    themselves often ahead of federal agencies investigating the same issues
    and individuals. See Heale, xv. See also Ellen Schrecker, *No Ivory Tower:
    McCarthyism and the Universities* (New York: Oxford University Press, 1986), an
    exhaustive and energetically written exploration of the damage done to higher
    education and the professoriat by Cold War-era inquisitions.
15. "Radio Group Officials Linked to Communists," Los Angeles *Times*,
    December 20, 1946. Clipping in LP, bio6.005-19461220.
16. George Pepper to LP, November 3, 1945. Pauling Papers, peace4.012.7-
    pepper-lp-19451103.
17. "Minutes of Meeting of Scientists and Educators [Pasadena area]," typescript.
    Pauling Papers, peace4.009.2-minutes-19451109.
18. Linus Pauling, "I.C.C. A.S.P.? Yes." Typescript, November 5, 1946. 5 pp.
    LP, 1946a.7. For the ICCASP episode in the Paulings' lives, see Thomas
    Hager, *Force of Nature*, 306-8, 312-14. See also Minutes of a Conference on
    Atomic Energy, Independent Citizens' Committee of the Arts, Sciences and
    Professions, December 3, 1945, LP, safe1.032.30.
19. Hager, *Force of Nature,* 308.
20. "Linus Pauling and the International Peace Movement," Special Collections,
    Oregon State UniversityLibrary. http://osulibrary.oregonstate.edu/
    specialcollections/coll/pauling/peace/narrative/page8.html.

21. Andrew J. Falk, *Upstaging the Cold War: American Dissent and Cultural Diplomacy, 1940-1960* (Amherst: University of Massachusetts Press, 2010), 75, 78-80.
22. Falk, *Upstaging the Cold War*, 104-11.
23. Stephen H. Fritchman, minister at the First Unitarian Church of Los Angeles, gave a characteristically impassioned speech to the "Hollywood Council of the Arts, Sciences and Professions" in September 1951. See ms., "Remarks," LP Peace Section, Box 4.001. People like Edwin Meese, one of Ronald Reagan's core advisors, asserted as late as 2002 that ICCASP was a Communist front group whose nefarious goals and methods were critical in educating Reagan in the dangers of Communism when he was president of the Screen Actors Guild in 1947. See Meese, "A Salute to Freedom," June 12, 2002. http://www.reagansheritage.org/html/reagan_cruise_meese.shtml.
24. Linus Pauling, "The Threat to Academic Freedom in California," January 21, 1946. Speech sponsored by ICCASP, Masonic Temple, Hollywood, California. LP, safe1.032.48.
25. Pauling, "Threat to Academic Freedom in California."
26. Expressing his concerns about his Berkeley colleagues to Peter in 1950, he admitted, "I myself am having a little difficulty with our own Institute." LP to Peter Pauling, July 20, 1950. LP Biographical, Box 5.041.
27. David H. Price writes a wonderful analysis of the effect on the discipline of anthropology of McCarthy-era repression and harassment by both government bodies and academic administrators. "One of the problems," he argues, "in tracking and measuring assaults on academic freedom is that in few instances can one find a smoking gun firmly establishing acts of reprisal on individuals for specific actions. … There were few instances during the 1940s and 1950s in which tenured professors were explicitly fired for political actions; more often than not, accusations of repression involve the gray areas of contractual relationships." Price, *Threatening Anthropology: McCarthyism and the FBI's Surveillance of Activist Anthropologists* (Durham: Duke University Press, 2004), 107. This would hold true for Linus Pauling in 1958, when President DuBridge pressured him to give up his chairmanship of the Caltech Division of Chemistry and Chemical Engineering.
28. In fact, most academics in the late 1940s and early 1950s agreed ideologically that Communists, presumably acting under party discipline, were inappropriate teachers for American youth. Further, to understand the jeopardy faced by Pauling and his internationalist colleagues, it helps to revisit the nature of the self-repression Schrecker uncovered in interviews several decades later. This phenomenon has also been described by Noam Chomsky at Harvard, on the other side of the country. While his faculty associates roundly criticized the USSR's brutal invasion of Hungary in 1956, they recoiled from any suggestion that parallel critiques might be offered of British or United States actions in Africa or Latin America. Kenya—Guatemala—Vietnam—all posed examples of European or United States interference in another nation's self-determination. None were viewed as comparable to the Soviet Union's suppression of self-government in Eastern Europe. The Cold

War campaigns against Communism calcified the anti-Soviet cast of western imperialism forged after the First World War and shifted the boundaries of acceptable speech and opinion. See Noam Chomsky et al., *The Cold War & the University: Toward an Intellectual History of the Postwar Years* (New York: The New Press, 1997), esp. 175-78.

29. Schrecker, 117-25.

30. Schrecker identifies the holdout as Russell Fraser, English instructor at UCLA.

31. Linus Pauling, "Should Communist Party Membership be Grounds for Dismissal from a College Faculty?" Town Hall Debate, Los Angeles, June 13, 1949. LP, 1949s.9.

32. AP, "Budenz Names 30 as Commies," 1950, unnamed periodical. Pauling Newspaper Clippings, 1950n.18.

33. See Pauling's account of this episode in Griffin Fariello, *Red Scare: Memories of the American Inquisition. An Oral History* (New York: W. W. Norton & Company, 1995), 426-28. See too Hager, *Force of Nature*, 360-65. "Linus Pauling and the International Peace Movement," a narrative in Pauling Papers Online, contains a detailed account of Pauling's tangles with loyalty screening committees. http://osulibrary.oregonstate.edu/specialcollections/coll/pauling/peace/narrative/page22.html.

34. Hager writes a stirring chapter on the alpha helix discoveries and their publicity. Hager, *Force of Nature*, esp. 368-87.

35. Hager, 387-90.

36. Shipley was a strong Cold Warrior and took seriously her outsized privilege to deny passports to anyone deemed unfriendly or a threat to the United States. For a contemporary profile of her style and her power, see "Sorry Mrs. Shipley," *Time* 58, Issue 27 (December 31, 1951), 15. For an extensive review of the twentieth-century history of U.S. passports and Mrs. Shipley's key position in that dynamic, see Jeffrey Kahn, "The Extraordinary Mrs. Shipley: How the United States Controlled International Travel Before the Age of Terrorism," *SMU Dedman School of Law Legal Studies Research Paper No. 60*, Social Science Research Network. http://papers.ssrn.com/sol3/papers.cfm?abstract_id=1604602.

37. LP to Peter Pauling, January 14, 1954. LP Biographical, Box 5.042.

38. Pauling Papers, ID 1954i.36. Copyright Svenskt pressfoto, Stockholm, Sweden. AHP, Diary "My Trip," 1954. Linus Pauling Safe Contents Drawer 4, Folder 4.036.

39. See, e.g, LP to Linda Pauling, 22 October 1952, 4 June 1954. LP, Personal Safe. Pauling gave the commencement address again in 1959, on the occasion of Crellin's graduation, by invitation of Crellin's classmates.

40. Peter Pauling to LP and AHP, August 10, 1954. LP Biographical, Box 5.042.

41. Linda Pauling to LP and AHP, February 9, 1955. LP Biographical, Box 1.

42. Linus Pauling, Jr., to AHP, September 26, 1956. LP Biographical, Box 5.037. Linus, Jr., also warned Crellin against modeling himself after their father.

43. Linus Pauling to Peter Pauling, February 8, 1956. LP Biographical, Box 5.042.

44. Peter J. Pauling to Linus Pauling, February 13, 1956. LP Biographical, Box 5.042.

45. LP to Linda Pauling, February 7, 1956. LP Biographical, Box 1.
46. LP to Peter Pauling, July 20, 1950. At that time Linus misspelled Kamb's name as "Kand." Kamb was also apparently using his last names interchangeably, sometimes going by "Ray" and sometimes by "Kamb."
47. Linus Pauling Day-by-Day, 1956. Pauling Papers Online. http://osulibrary. oregonstate.edu/specialcollections/coll/pauling/calendar/1956/index.html.
48. Eleanor Ray and Barbara Maranacci, *Vineyards in the Sky: The Life of Legendary Vintner Martin Ray* (Aptos, California: Mountain Vines Publishing, 1993).
49. Martin Ray to Chairman, House Un-American Activities Committee, June 18, 1957. Pauling Papers, LP Biographical, Box 1.
50. Jeanne Augé to AHP, n.d., Box 1.0001, General Correspondence, Personal, A-M. Augé was longtime assistant to the Caltech graduate dean.
51. Linus Pauling, Jr., "Life with Father ... and Mother," transcript, "A Liking for the Truth: Truth and Controversy in the Work of Linus Pauling," Oregon State University, February 28, 2001. http://osulibrary.oregonstate.edu/events/2001paulingconference.video-s2-3-pauling.html. See also Hager, *Force of Nature*, 317.
52. Linus Pauling, Jr., to LP, September 26, 1956. LP Biographical, Box 5.037.
53. Peter Pauling to Linus Pauling, Jr., September 19, 1959. LP Biographical, Box 5.043.
54. Linus Pauling, Jr., to Peter Pauling, September 25, 1959. LP Biographical, Box 5.038.
55. AHP to Peter Pauling, September 23, 1960, LP Biographical, Box 5.044.
56. Peter Pauling to Linus Pauling, Jr., September 19, 1959. LP Biographical, Box 5.043.
57. LP to Peter Pauling, September 29, 1959. LP Biographical, Box 5.043.
58. Peter Pauling to Linus Pauling, Jr., September 19, 1959. LP Biographical, Box 5.043.
59. Peter Pauling to LP and AHP, January 20, 1959. LP Biographical, Box 5.044.
60. LP to Peter Pauling, April 4, 1960; quote from June 10, 1960. Pauling also admits that he and Ava Helen faced financial problems the first few years of marriage, "but nothing quite so bad as this earlier three months for me." LP Biographical, Box 5.044.
61. In addition to destroying or omitting from the family donation virtually all Ava Helen's letters to him, Linus seems to have pulled many of his wife's letters to her children. It is also possible that the children themselves did not save many of these letters, since most of the ones we have from Linus, Sr., are transcribed Dictaphone stencils.
62. AHP to Peter Pauling, September 23, 1960. LP Biographical, Box 5.044.
63. Interview with Cheryl Pauling, March 9, 2012; interview with Kay Pauling, March 13, 2012; Pauling Papers.
64. LP to LP Jr., June 15, 1954. LP Biographical, Box 5.037.
65. Crellin Pauling to LP, AHP, Linda Pauling, October 12 [1954]. LP Biographical, Box 5.048, Folder 48.5.
66. Crellin Pauling to AHP, [1955]. LP Biographical, Box 5.048, Folder 48.5.
67. Crellin Pauling to AHP, May 7, 1956. LP Biographical, Box 5.048.

68. Crellin Pauling to AHP, Wednesday [1955]. LP Biographical, Box 5.048.
69. Crellin Pauling to AHP, LP, and Linda Pauling, Friday [November 23, 1956]. LP Biographical, Box 5.048.
70. Patsy Mills to AHP and LP, December 11, 1956. AHP, Box 1.001.
71. Hager, *Force of Nature*, esp. 453-55.
72. "An Appeal by American Scientists to the Governments and People of the World." LP Peace, Box 5.001.
73. Edward Teller weaves in and out of the Pauling story from 1926, when they first encountered each other in Europe, pursuing the siren song of quantum physics, through the American fallout debates of the 1950s and 1960s. Teller, a Hungarian Jewish émigré, worked on the Manhattan Project. He became an outspoken advocate of nuclear deterrence and building a nuclear arsenal. In 1952 he signed a letter protesting Pauling's denial of a passport, but two years later he testified against granting J. Robert Oppenheimer a renewed security clearance. Having alienated many colleagues by betraying Oppenheimer in that fashion, Teller continued to rise in federal defense circles. He became director of the Lawrence Livermore National Laboratory in 1958. Also in 1958, he and Pauling debated the safety of nuclear testing on television—a debate that many believed Teller won, not because of sound argumentation, but because of his polished, relaxed delivery on camera. Among other commentary, see Hager, *Force of Nature*, 482-87. For a larger introduction to the political debates roiling the nuclear scientists' world, see Gregg Herken, *Brotherhood of the Bomb: The Tangled Lives and Loyalties of Robert Oppenheimer, Ernest Lawrence, and Edward Teller* (New York: Henry Holt and Co, 2002).
74. "Linus Pauling and the International Peace Movement," Pauling Papers Online. http://osulibrary.oregonstate.edu/specialcollections/coll/pauling/peace/narrative/page27.html. See also Hager, *Force of Nature*, 475-91.
75. Linus Pauling, "Every Test Kills," pamphlet reprinted from an article in *Liberation*, February 1958. Swarthmore College Peace Collection, CDGA Pauling, Linus and Ava Helen.
76. For Ava Helen's reflections see Red booklet: AHP travel diary, 1957 trip to Europe. AHP, Box 3.008.
77. AHP travel diary, 1957 trip to Europe.
78. Ava Helen Pauling, "The Australian and New Zealand Congress for International Cooperation and Disarmament and Festival of the Arts," November 7-14, 1959, AHP, Box 2.001.
79. Ava Helen Pauling, Memo book: AHP diary of trip to Lamboréné … 1959. AHP, Box 3.008. Subsequent quotes about the trip from the same source.
80. Linus Pauling, "Our Choice: World Peace or Nuclear Annihilation," Linus Pauling Online, 1959s2.6-notes.
81. In an interview with Tom Hager, Linus recalled that the Nobel Prize brought him $35,000, and they paid $35,000 for the ranch. But Linus also remarked that, since the success of *General Chemistry* in 1947, the family finances had been "reasonably good." LP, Hager2.006.8.
82. William Trombley, "What Are They Doing to Big Sur?" *Saturday Evening Post*, v. 237, issue 6 (February 15, 1964), 24-29.

83. LP to LP Jr., Peter, Linda, and Crellin re: historical account of purchase of Deer Flat Rance property, May 25, 1986. LP Biographical, Box 4.051.
84. LP to Peter Pauling, November 7, 1960. LP Biographical, Box 5.043.
85. LP to Karl W. Kenyon, May 19, 1958. LP Biographical, Box 4.051.
86. Linus, Jr., remembers another caretaker named Phil who lived in a tent on the property. Oral History of Linus Pauling, Jr., 79.
87. Michael Hall to AHP, n.d., Personal correspondence E-H. AHP, Box 1.001. There is also a letter much later from John Sprungman to the Paulings, mingling thanks for the Paulings' wedding present with musings on the couples' various misunderstandings regarding caretaking at the ranch. John Sprungman to LP and AHP, October 22, 1970. AHP, Box 1.002.
88. AHP to R.D. "Dick" Morgan, March 20, 1965. AHP, Box 1.001.
89. LP to Dr. Campbell, Dr. Lippman, and Dr. Niemann, June 4, 1957. LP Biographical, Box 4.051.
90. LP to Mrs. John F. Hardham, March 21, 1958. LP Biographical, Box 4.051.
91. LP to LP, Jr, Peter, Linda, and Crellin re: historical account of purchase of Deer Flat Ranch property, May 25, 1986. LP Biographical, Box 4.051.
92. AHP to Catherine, November 2, 1960. AHP, Box 1.002.
93. E.g., LP to Dr. Campbell, Dr. Lippman, and Dr. Niemann, June 4, 1957. LP Biographical, Box 4.051.
94. LP to Luther Williams, June 4, 1957. LP Biographical, Box 4.051.
95. LP to Peter Pauling, February 20, 1959 and March 17, 1959. LP Biographical, Box 4.053.
96. AHP to Mrs. Freda Malherbe, April 22, 1971. AHP, Box 1.001.
97. AHP to Mrs. Walter Knapp, May 4, 1971. AHP, Box 1.001.
98. AHP, WILPF diary, 1960, AHP, Box 3.006; LP to [children], February 12, 1960; Crellin Pauling to LP and AHP, February 10, 1960. LP Biographical, Box 5.048.

Chapter 4

1. [See letter Janet Stevenson to AHP, October 10, 1963, quoted later in chapter.]
2. AHP, Box 1.002.
3. AHP, Box 1.004.
4. Personal communication, November 2011. Richards explores AHP's legacy to WILPF and peace work in Linda Richards, "Human Dynamos vs. Nuclear Weapons: A Tribute to Ava Helen Pauling and WILPF's Disarmament Work," *Peace and Freedom: Magazine of the Women's International League for Peace and Freedom,* 69 (Winter 2009), 4-5ff.
5. AHP to Claire Walsh, October 26, 1959. AHP, Box 1.004, Folder 4.5.
6. Bess Butcher to AHP. AHP, Box 1.001.
7. Jan Symons to AHP, March 27, 1961. AHP, Box 4.001.
8. AHP to Ruth, November 1, 1960. AHP, Box 1.002.
9. The Washington *Post,* June 22, 1960.
10. Thomas Hager's account of the Pauling hearings is excellent; see *Force of Nature,* 512-22. See also AHP, Annotated WILPF Engagement Calendar, 1960. AHP, Box 3.006.

11. The Washington *Star*, June 22, 1960.
12. Thea Gould to AHP, July 15, 1960. AHP, Box 1.001.
13. Jean Dan to AHP, October 11, 1960.
14. AHP to "Dear" Eleanor, September 23, 1960. AHP, Box 1.002.
15. AHP to Dorothy Crowfoot Hodgkin, September 23, 1960, AHP, Box 1.001.
16. Willard Uphaus to AHP, February 27, 1960, AHP, Box 1.004.
17. AHP to Mrs. James Pittman, December 8, 1960. AHP, Box 1.004.
18. Quoted in "Linus Pauling and the International Peace Movement," Pauling Papers Online, Oregon State University. http://osulibrary.oregonstate.edu/ specialcollections/coll/pauling/peace/narrative/page39.html.
19. AHP to Lady Jessie May Street, November 2, 1960; Lady Jessie May Street to AHP, October 24, 1960. AHP, Box 1.004.
20. Hager, *Force of Nature*, 524-25.
21. AHP to Catherine, November 2, 1960, AHP, Box 1.002.
22. AHP to Lola Boswell, November 2, 1960. AHP, Box 1.004.
23. Ava Helen Pauling, Review, *Children of the A-Bomb*, typescript, n.d.. AHP, Box 2.001. See too Jean Dan to AHP, October 11, 1960.
24. Rochelle Girson, *Saturday Review* Book Review Editor, September 19, 1960. AHP Papers, Box 2.001.
25. AHP to Eleanor, September 23, 1960. AHP, Box 1.002.
26. AHP to Anne Frey, November 1, 1960. AHP, Box 1.004.
27. Milton S. Katz, *Ban the Bomb: A History of SANE, the Committee for a Sane Nuclear Policy, 1957-1985* (New York: Greenwood Press, 1986), 45-64. For a broader review of the history of Communist-infiltration fears in the American peace movement, see Robbie Lieberman, *Communism, Anticommunism, and the U.S. Peace Movement, 1945-1963* (Syracuse: Syracuse University Press, 2000). Lieberman dispassionately analyzes the agonies of American peace and social justice groups in confronting accusations of Communist infiltration. There are sections on SANE and on WILPF (discussed below).
28. Katz, *Ban the Bomb*, 49-52.
29. Quoted by Katz, *Ban the Bomb*, 52.
30. AHP to Catherine, November 2, 1960. AHP, Box 1.002.
31. AHP to Ruth, November 1, 1960. AHP, Box 1.002.
32. AHP to Lola Boswell, November 2, 1960. AHP, Box 1.004.
33. AHP to Anne Frey, November 1, 1960. AHP, Box 1.004.
34. AHP to Ray Goodman. AHP, Box 1.001.
35. Information on the disarmament conference may be found in AHP, Box 2.001.
36. Both Addams and Balch had paid dearly for their peace advocacy: Addams in a tumble from her status as cultural icon in the 1920s, when American Legion reactionaries implicated her in the "spider web" charts of subversive Americans, and Balch when she was fired from her position as economics professor at Wellesley College because of her peace activities during the World War I.
37. Catherine Foster, *Women for All Seasons: The Story of the Women's International League for Peace and Freedom* (Athens: The University of Georgia Press, 1989), 22-25. Another helpful history of the early decades of the U.S. Section of

WILPF is Carrie A. Foster, *The Women and the Warriors: The U.S. Section of the Women's International League for Peace and Freedom, 1915-1946* (Syracuse: Syracuse University Press, 1995). Foster's account makes clear the palpable difficulties of maintaining a consistent and forceful pacifist stance in the interwar years, and the challenges of neutrality as Nazi aggression progressed through the 1930s.

38. Harriet Hyman Alonso, *Peace as a Women's Issue: A History of the U.S. Movement for World Peace and Women's Rights* (Syracuse: Syracuse University Press, 1993), 185. Alonso deals extensively and evenhandedly with WILPF's Cold War McCarthy-era divisions in chapters 6 and 7. For these episodes, see also Joyce Blackwell, *No Peace Without Freedom: Race and the Women's International League for Peace and Freedom, 1915-1975* (Carbondale: Southern Illinois University Press, 2004), 156-72.

39. Alonso, *Peace as a Women's Issue*, 169.

40. Ibid., 173.

41. "Women's International League for Peace and Freedom, Los Angeles Branch." AHP, Box 1.004, Folder 4.3.

42. AHP to LP, November 22, 1937. LP, Personal Safe.

43. "You Are Cordially Invited to a Garden Party," AHP, Box 4.001, Folder 1.1; "Notice," AHP, Box 4.001, Folder 1.1.

44. Andrea Andreen to AHP, July 20, 1960, AHP, Box 4.001, Folder 1.1.

45. Ibid.

46. [Sarah Lampin???] to AHP, October 4, 1960. AHP, Box 4.001.

47. Marjorie Avery to AHP, September 17, 1960. AHP, Box 4.001.

48. Mary Phillips to AHP, October 28, 1960. AHP, Box 4.001.

49. Gertrude Baer to AHP, November 19, 1960. AHP, Box 4.001. Ava Helen seems to have been absolutely right about Orlie Pell's views. In September 1961, Mildred Scott Olmsted passed around a long letter from Ava Helen among other WILPF leaders. Orlie Pell scribbled on the top that it was a nice letter, but she disagreed with Ava Helen's idea that U.S. peace workers should emulate the British in working with Communists as well as non-Communists for peace. See AHP to Mildred Scott Olmsted, September 22, 1961, DG043: WILPF. Part III: U.S. Section, Series A, 2. Papers of Non-Staff Leaders: Pauling, Linus & Ava, Box 36.

50. Margaret Hope Bacon, *One Woman's Passion for Peace and Freedom: The Life of Mildred Scott Olmsted* (Syracuse: Syracuse University Press, 1993), 281.

51. AHP to Mildred Scott Olmsted, November 1, 1960. DG043: WILPF. Part III: U.S. Section, Series A, 2. Papers of Non-Staff Leaders: Pauling, Linus & Ava, Box 36.

52. AHP to Annalee [Stewart?], November 1 1960. AHP, Box 1.002.

53. Lieberman, *The Strangest Dream*, 121-34.

54. Katherine Arnett to AHP, November 14, 1960. AHP, Box 4.001.

55. AHP to Katherine Arnett, December 8, 1960. AHP, Box 1.004.

56. Mildred Scott Olmsted to AHP, December 19, 1960. AHP, Box 4.001.

57. Mildred Scott Olmsted, December 19, 1960. AHP, Box 4.001. In fact the WILPF national board did issue a strong statement backing Linus Pauling and

condemning the action of SISS in demanding his correspondence about the petition. See "Linus Pauling Statement," June 21, 1960. DG043: WILPF. Part III: U.S. Section, Series A, 2. Papers of Non-Staff Leaders: Pauling, Linus & Ava, Box 36.

58. Andrea Andreen to AHP, January 1, 1961. AHP, Box 4.001.

59. AHP to Hannah Bernheim-Rosenzweig, June 23, 1961. AHP, Box 4.001.

60. The full list: Karl Barth, Max Born, Boyd Orr, Brock Chisholm, Mrs. Cyrus Eaton, Erich Fromm, J. Heyrovsky, Johan Hygen, Robert Hutchins, Hugh Keenleyside, Francois Mauriac, Alexander Meiklejohn, Lewis Mumford, Gunnar Myrdal, Arne Naess, Mrs. Rameshwari Nehru, Philip Noel-Baker, Marcus Oliphant, Alan Paton, Jean Rostand, Bertrand Russell, Albert Schweitzer, Albert Szent-Gyorgyi, and Hideki Yukawa.

61. Jan Symons to AHP, March 27, 1961. AHP, Box 4.001.

62. "La Grande Medaille de Vermeil de la Ville de Paris."

63. AHP to Mildred Scott Olmsted, June 13, 1961. DG043: WILPF. Part III: U.S. Section, Series A, 2. Papers of Non-Staff Leaders: Pauling, Linus & Ava, Box 36.

64. Ava Helen Pauling, "Oslo Conference Stresses Responsibility of Individuals," *Four Lights* v. 21, no. 3, July 1961, n.p.

65. Frances W. Herring, "A Personal Journal of the Oslo Conference" [A gift to Swarthmore College Peace Collection by the author: Dr. Frances W. Herring]. [Need reference to SCPC file – under WILPF, non-staff etc.] This extraordinary document, sleeping peacefully in the Pauling folder at the Swarthmore College Peace Collection, details Herring's experiences and responses to the conference and her colleagues from the time she left the United States to her return and subsequent reflection on the conference. It is a priceless record of the event that, perhaps more than any other single action, earned Pauling the Nobel Peace Prize for 1962.

66. LP to Joan Harris and Linda Hopkins, May 8, 1961. Pauling Papers Online, corr168. 1-lp-harris-19610508.

67. Else Zeuthen, E. Z. Circular letter No. 4/1961. AHP, Box 4.002.

68. AHP to Peter Pauling, May 11, 1961. LP Biographical, Box 5.044.

69. Women's International League for Peace and Freedom, New Jersey Branch, Bergen Chapter, May 19, 1961. AHP, Box 4.001.

70. Linus Pauling to Gunnar Jahn, October 8, 1961. LP, Box 14.043.

71. Anne Braden to Virginia Foster Durr, December 14, 1962. AHP, Box 4.003, folder 3.1.

72. LP to AHP, September 9, 1962, 1962x.09.09.LP.

73. Nancy Reeves to AHP, May 4, 1961.AHP, Box 4.001, Folder 1.1.

74. Lenore Job to AHP, Sunday [1961]. AHP, Box 4.001, Folder 1.1.

75. Nancy Reeves to AHP, May 24, 1961.AHP, Box 4.001, Folder 1.1.

76. AHP notes, Monday June 26. AHP, Box 4.002.

77. Olive Mayer to AHP, July 15, 1961. AHP, Box 4.002.

78. Stella Polya [Acting President of WILPF Palo Alto chapter] to Dorothy Hutchinson, July 25, 1961. AHP, Box 4.002.

79. Olive Mayer to AHP, July 25, 1961. AHP, Box 4.002.

80. Gertrude Baer to AHP, June 28, 1961. AHP, Box 4.001, Folder 1.1.

81. Gertrude Baer to AHP, July 25, 1961. AHP, Box 4.001, Folder 1.1.

82. Else Leuthen to AHP, July 28, 1961. AHP, Box 4.001, Folder 1.1.

83. AHP to Mildred Olmsted, August 14, 1961. AHP, Box 4.001, Folder 1.1.

84. AHP to Orlie Pell, October 2, 1961. AHP, Box 1.004.

85. AHP to Virginia Foster Durr, July 18, 1962. AHP, Box 4.003.

86. AHP to Evelyn Alloy, June 21, 1963. CDGA. Alloy, Evelyn. Collected Papers. SCPC.

87. Mildred Law Olmsted had been one of the early WILPF leaders who had insisted on the organization expending significant energy getting black women to join and to extend peace ideals into black communities. She had been a founder of the Interracial Extension Committee active in Philadelphia in the 1920s. It is possible that Ava Helen was not aware of Olmsted's credibility or commitment in this regard.

88. AHP to Virginia Foster Durr, July 18, 1962. AHP, Box 4.003.

89. See, e.g., Minnesota "Branch Letter," July 1961, with reflections on the St. Paul Annual Meeting, at which Durr gave a report on the Freedom Riders. AHP, Box 4.001, Folder 1.1.

90. Virginia Foster Durr to AHP, August 31, 1962. Virginia Foster Durr Collection, Schlesinger Library, Radcliffe Institute, Harvard University.

91 Virginia Durr detailed this history to Ava Helen in 1963. Though they never felt themselves in physical danger because of their activism, she wrote, they shared with the Paulings a different kind of danger: "[T]oday a friend sent us a letter from the head of the Alabama Commission of Civil Rights, in which he said Cliff could not be considered as a member of the Advisory Committee as he COULD NEVER BE CLEARED BY THE FBI. This kind of derogation, this kind of smear, this kind of ghost, this kind of dirty business has followed us now for twenty years, ever since Cliff took on Hoover and refused to pay any attention to those secret dossiers … Cliff simply refused to look at them and made a big fight on Hoover for sending them around." Virginia Foster Durr to AHP, July 23, 1963. Virginia Foster Durr Collection, Schlesinger Library, Radcliffe Institute, Harvard University.

92. Virginia Foster Durr, *Outside the Magic Circle: The Autobiography of Virginia Foster Durr* (Tuscaloosa: University of Alabama Press, 1985), 234-35.

93. Virginia Foster Durr to AHP, July 22, 1961. Durr Papers, Schlesinger Library, Radcliffe Institute, Harvard University.

94. Virginia Foster Durr to AHP, July 22, 1961. Durr Papers, Schlesinger Library, Radcliffe Institute, Harvard University.

95. Virginia Foster Durr to AHP, May [n.d.], 1962. Virginia Foster Durr Collection, Schlesinger Library, Radcliffe Institute, Harvard University.

96. Virginia Foster Durr to AHP, July 23, 1962. Virginia Foster Durr Collection, Schlesinger Library, Radcliffe Institute, Harvard University.

97. Virginia Foster Durr to AHP, May [n.d.], 1962. Durr Collection.

98. Virginia Foster Durr to AHP, July 23, 1962. Virginia Foster Durr Collection, Schlesinger Library, Radcliffe Institute, Harvard University.

99. Virginia Foster Durr to AHP, August 31, 1962. Virginia Foster Durr Collection, Schlesinger Library, Radcliffe Institute, Harvard University.

100. Ibid.

101. Virginia Foster Durr to AHP, October 11, 1962. Virginia Foster Durr Collection, Schlesinger Library, Radcliffe Institute, Harvard University.

102. AHP to Leroy Collins, September 23, 1960. AHP, Box 1.004, Folder 4.1.

103. Ava Helen also sent a check in 1962, through James Dombrowski, to bail out Cordell Reagon after one of his many civil rights-related arrests. Reagon was a founder of Freedom Singers and married for a time to Bernice Johnson Reagon, still active as a member of Sweet Honey in the Rock. Their daughter, Toshi Reagon, is also a singer-songwriter. See James Dombrowski to AHP, August 30, 1962. AHP, Box 1.00x, Folder 3.2.

104. AHP to Evelyn Alloy, September 11, 1963. SCPC, CDGA Alloy, Evelyn. Collected Papers.

105. AHP to Barbara Dodds, July 13, 1963. AHP, Box 4.004.

106. Melinda Plastas, *A Band of Noble Women: Racial Politics in the Women's Peace Movement* (Syracuse: Syracuse University Press, 2011), 3. Plastas' account weaves together a history of the early decades of WILPF with an analysis of racial thinking and activism among both black and white women up to the end of World War II. She also reminds us of the deliberate quality of both black and white women's thoughts about the linkage of international conflict and race.

107. One of the most important African American leaders of the 1920s Philadelphia IEC was Addie Dickerson, while leadership on the "white" side was provided by Mildred Law Olmsted, by the 1950s the national administrative secretary of WILPF and one of Ava Helen's correspondents. See Plastas, 145-62.

108. Joyce Blackwell, *No Peace without Freedom: Race and the Women's International League for Peace and Freedom, 1915-1975* (Carbondale: Southern Illinois University Press, 2004), esp. 160-63.

109. Virginia Foster Durr to AHP, October 11, 1962. Virginia Foster Durr Collection, Schlesinger Library, Radcliffe Institute for Advanced Study, Harvard University.

110. Virginia Foster Durr to AHP, December 28, 1962. Virginia Foster Durr Collection, Schlesinger Library, Radcliffe Institute For Advanced Study, Harvard University.

111. AHP to Virginia Foster Durr, July 25, 1963. AHP, Box 4.003.

112. Virginia Foster Durr to AHP, February 18, 1963. Virginia Foster Durr Collection, Schlesinger Library, Radcliffe Institute for Advanced Study, Harvard University.

113. Virginia Foster Durr to AHP, April 12, 1963. Virginia Foster Durr Collection, Schlesinger Library, Radcliffe Institute for Advanced Study, Harvard University.

114. AHP to Virginia Foster Durr, August 13, 1963. AHP, Box 4.003.

115. Virginia Foster Durr to AHP, July 23, 1963. Virginia Foster Durr Collection, Schlesinger Library, Radcliffe Institute for Advanced Study, Harvard University.

116. AHP to Eleanor Fowler, April 5, 1963. SCPC, DG 043, WILPF, Part III: U.S. Section. Box 36: Pauling, Linus and Ava.

117. LP, note. LP, Personal Safe, 4.094.

118. AHP, Notes on White House dinner, Sunday, April 29, 1962. AHP, Box 3.001.

119. Virginia Foster Durr to AHP, August 7, 1963, and August 27, 1963, Virginia Foster Durr Collection, Schlesinger Library, Radcliffe Institute for Advanced Study, Harvard University.

120. Virginia Foster Durr to AHP, September 20, 1963. Virginia Foster Durr Collection, Schlesinger Library, Radcliffe Institute for Advanced Study, Harvard University.

121. For more planning about the visit, see AHP to Mrs. Harry J. Nielsen, July 26, 1963, and AHP to Mrs. Gussie Sitkin, July 26, 1963. AHP, Box 4.004.

122. Virginia Foster Durr to AHP, October 24, 1963. Virginia Foster Durr Collection, Schlesinger Library, Radcliffe Institute for Advanced Study, Harvard University.

123. Janet Stevenson to AHP, October 10, 1963. AHP, Box 1.002.

Chapter 5

1. AHP, Box 1.004.

2. AHP, Box 1.003.

3. AHP to Mrs. James Patrick Murphy, October 25, 1963. AHP, Box 1.001.

4. AHP to Madame Stanislawa Zawadecka, [November 29, 1963]. AHP, Box 3.020.

5. AHP to J. Stuart Innerst, October 25, 1963. AHP, Box 1.001.

6. AHP to Catherine Colburn, November 20, 1963. AHP, Box 1.004.

7. Linus Pauling, oral history, interviewed by John L. Greenberg, Archives, California Institute of Technology, May 10, 1984.

8. E.g., LP to Kees Van Niel, 19 November 1963.

9. AHP to Mr. and Mrs. Rudolph Pastor, October 25, 1963. AHP Box 1.004, Folder 4.4.

10. Linus Pauling, oral history, California Institute of Technology.

11. AHP to Evelyn Alloy, June 21, 1963, DG043: WILPF. Part III: U.S. Section, Series A, 2. Papers of Non-Staff Leaders: Pauling, Linus & Ava, Box 36

12. AHP to Otto Nathan, n.d. AHP, Box 3.020.

13. Dagmar Wilson to AHP [form letter], n.d. AHP, Box 4.004.

14. Evelyn Alloy to AHP, May 29, 1962, CDGA. Alloy, Evelyn. Collected Papers. SCPC.

15. Amy Swerdlow, "Ladies' Day at the Capitol: Women Strike for Peace versus HUAC," in U.S. Women in Struggle: A Feminist Studies Anthology, ed. Claire Goldberg Moses and Heidi Hartmann (University of Illinois Press, 1995), 219.

16. Virginia Foster Durr to AHP, April 12, 1963. Virginia Foster Durr Collection, Schlesinger Library, Radcliffe Institute for Advanced Study, Harvard University.
17. Herblock, *The Washington Post,* December 13, 1962. Quoted by Swerdlow, "Ladies' Day," 225.
18. AHP to Ethel [Taylor?], October 15, 1961. AHP Box 4.004.
19. See the account of this White House protest/dinner in the previous chapter.
20. Anne Bloom and Bessie Jordan to AHP and LP, August 18, 1962. AHP, Box 4.04.
21. Margaret [Russell] to Linus and Ava Helen Pauling, November 8, 1963. AHP, Box 4.004.
22. Amy Swerdlow, *Women Strike for Peace: Traditional Motherhood and Radical Politics in the 1960s* (Chicago: The University of Chicago Press, 1993), 187.
23. See Swerdlow's fascinating portrait of Ruth Gage Colby in *Women Strike for Peace,* 188-92.
24. Swerdlow, *Women Strike for Peace,* 194-98.
25. "Women chart peace drive at conference in Montreal," *National Guardian,* October 1, 1962.
26. Gertrude Bussey and Margaret Tims, *Women's International League for Peace and Freedom, 1915-1965: A Record of Fifty Years' Work* (London: George Allen & Unwin Ltd., 1965), 246.
27. AHP to Helen Tucker, October 11, 1962, AHP, Box 4.004.
28. AHP to Mildred Scott Olmsted, October 16, 1961. DG043: WILPF. Part III: U.S. Section, Series A, 2. Papers of Non-Staff Leaders: Pauling, Linus & Ava, Box 36.
29. Los Angeles Women Strike for Peace and Washington, D. C., Women Strike for Peace, [Statement to the Oxford Conference], read by Ava Helen Pauling on January 4, 1963, AHP, Box 2.001, Folder 1.16.
30. AHP to Stephen Fritchman, October 30, 1963. AHP, Box 4.008.
31. Jessica Mitford was Mrs. Robert Treuhaft, with whom Ava Helen had some correspondence. She had recently read Mitford's book and in fact had received from her a contribution for the Durrs' October 1963 visit to California. "This puts us out of the red in regard of them," she wrote gratefully. AHP to Mrs. Robert Treuhaft, November 20, 1963, AHP Box 1.004, Folder 4.5.
32. AHP to Ethel Taylor, November 6, 1963. AHP, Box 1.006.
33. See, too, Ron Theodore Robin for a critique of Friedan's position on Korean POWs, in *The Making of the Cold War Enemy: Culture and Politics in the Military-Intellectual Complex* (Princeton: Princeton University Press, 2001), 165.
34. See, for example, Swerdlow, *Women Strike for Peace,* 205.
35. Corda D. Bauer to AHP, February 21, 1964. AHP, Box 1.004. The photograph Bauer describes was taken by Arthur Dubinsky, a gifted photographer and friend of the Paulings. Though Special Collections at OSU holds a copy of the photo, copyright remains with Dubinsky's family.
36. Linus Pauling, Jr., oral interview, [Fall 2012].

37. Wallace Thompson, "Remarks introducing Mrs. Ava Helen Pauling," Second Birthday Celebration, Women Strike for Peace, Beverly Hilton Hotel, November 1, 1963.
38. Bauer to AHP, February 21, 1964.
39. See Swerdlow, *Women Strike for Peace*, 206.
40. Lorraine Gordon to AHP, March 15, 1964. AHP, Box 1.004.
41. Anne Eaton to AHP, March 31, 1964. AHP, Box 1.002; see also Anne [Eaton] to AHP, March 17, 1964.
42. LP to Fred P. Osborn, April 15, 1964. AHP, Box 1.002.
43. Swerdlow, *Women Strike for Peace*, 208ff. In addition, a long memo went out to subscribers and friends of WSP, describing the situation; that account on May 12 is substantively identical to Swerdlow's retrospective narrative. "Special Bulletin to Memo Subscribers and Friends of WSP," May 12, 1964. LP Manuscripts, Box 1964i.12.
44. "Holland Admits Peace Marchers," *The Gazette and Daily*, York, PA, May 13, 1964. LP Manuscripts, Box 1964i.12.
45. AHP to LP, May 15, 1964; AHP to LP, May 18, 1964. LP, Personal Safe.
46. LP to Editor, New York *Times*, May 21, 1964. LP Manuscripts, Box 1964i.12.
47. AHP to LP, May 18, 1964. LP, Personal Safe.
48. *Pomoi*, May 17, 1964. AHP, Box 3.003.
49. AHP to LP, May 18, 1964. LP, Personal Safe.
50. Ava Helen Pauling, "You Can Beat the Dutch," *The Minority of One*, 6 (August 1964), 22. AHP, Box 2.002.
51. "...da sagten die Frauen NEIN!" *Frau und Frieden*, 13 Jahrgang, no. 6, June 1964. Clipping in AHP, Box 3.003.
52. Ava Helen Pauling, "You Can Beat the Dutch," typescript; also article by the same title, *The Minority of One*, August 1964, p. 22. AHP, Box 2.002.
53. AHP to Olive Mayer, April 1, 1964. AHP, Box 1.004, Folder 4.3.
54. Ruth [Gage-Colby] to AHP, [March 27] 1964. AHP, Box 1.008, Folder 8.2.
55. Stephen H. Fritchman, *Heretic: A Partisan Autobiography* (Boston: Beacon Press, 1977), 290.
56. Jenny Perry, "Mrs. Pauling's Analysis: 'any work done happily is contribution to the whole world,'" Santa Barbara *News-Press*, August 16, 1964.

Chapter 6

1. AHP, "More About Women," Talk at Los Angeles Unitarian Church, 11 April 1965. AHP, Box 2.002.
2. AHP to Evelyn Alloy, [n.d.], Swarthmore College Peace Collection, CDGA, Alloy, Evelyn. Collected Papers. Correspondence with Ava Pauling 1962-1965.
3. Robert Paradowski, "Chronology," Linus Pauling Day-by-Day, Pauling Papers Online, Oregon State University.
4. AHP to Mrs. Gertrude Klause, March 30, 1965. AHP, Box 1.004.
5. Linus Pauling, "Science and Peace," Nobel Lecture, Oslo, Norway, December 11, 1963. Pauling Manuscripts and Typescripts of Speeches, 1963s.22.

6. Hager summarizes the libel suit outcomes in *Force of Nature*, 558-564. See also "Linus Pauling and the International Peace Movement," Pauling Papers Online, Special Collections, Oregon State University. http://osulibrary. oregonstate.edu/specialcollections/coll/pauling/peace/narrative/page40. html. On *Sullivan*, see Kermit L. Hall and Melvin I. Urofsky, *New York Times v. Sullivan: Civil Rights, Libel Law, and the Free Press* (Lawrence: University Press of Kansas, 2011).

7. AHP to Gloria Stern, April 7, 1965. AHP, Box 1.004.

8. In the 1980s and 1990s, Carol Gilligan and colleagues at the Harvard Graduate School of Education developed a multifaceted project on gender in intellectual and moral development. This work seeded efforts to identify, understand, and erase differences in girls' and boys' levels of achievement in math and science. Gilligan's signature work was *In a Different Voice: Psychological Theory and Women's Development* (Cambridge: Harvard University Press, 1982). Four years later, Mary Field Belenky, Blythe McVicker Clinchy, Nancy Rule Goldberger and Jill Mattuch Tarule collaborated on *Women's Ways of Knowing: The Development of Self, Voice, and Mind* (New York: Basic Books, 1986). This work moved from Gilligan's social and moral focus on gender development to an inquiry into cognitive development as reported in interviews with 135 women. The American Association of University Women took the gender difference issue into the school systems, commissioning a poll of girls and boys aged 9-15 that managed, as the summary put it, to "link the sharp drop in self-esteem suffered by pre-adolescent ad adolescent American girls to what they learn in the classroom" (*Shortchanging Girls, Shortchanging America: Executive Summary* [Washington, D.C.: American Association of University Women, 1991, 1994), 4. Peggy Orenstein then wrote an influential, popular book that brought the AAUW findings down to earth with a close study of students and their families in two California schools: *Schoolgirls: Young Women, Self Esteen, and the Confidence Gap* (New York: Doubleday, 1994).

9. Having fled the Nazis with her family, Mann Borgese became an American citizen in 1938 and then a Canadian citizen in 1983. She had an extraordinary career as an editor, feminist theorist, and expert in ocean conservation and maritime law.

10. Stephen H. Fritchman, *Heretic: A Partisan Autobiography* (Boston: Beacon Press, 1977), 229-47.

11. Stephen Hole Fritchman, March Sermon of the Month, "Your Conscience and the Hydrogen Bomb," March 12, 1950. LP Peace, Box 4.001.

12. A good, brief account of these encounters may be found on http://uua.org/ re/tapestry/adults/resistance/workshop9/workshopplan/handouts/182553. shtml.

13. LP to Dean Acheson, November 4, 1952. LP Peace, Box 4.001.

14. For the origin of his humanist philosophy, see Fritchman, *Heretic*, esp. 42-45.

15. Linus Pauling, "Science and Peace." Pauling acknowledged Kennedy, as well, in claiming that the loss of even one human life, or "malformation of even one baby," was of "concern to us all."

16. On Fritchman's respect for the Paulings, see Fritchman, *Heretic*, 45, 257-58, 290.

17. Oral History of Linus Pauling, Jr., 94.

18. The correspondence between LP and Stephen H. Fritchman may be found in LP Peace Section, Box 4.001, Folder 1.1. Ava Helen's correspondence with Fritchman, and her committee correspondence in connection with First Unitarian, is located in AHP, Box 4.008.

19. AHP to Mr. and Mrs. John Hoffman, March 18, 1965. AHP, Box 1.004.

20. Jeanne Sollen to AHP, October 17, 1965. AHP Box 1.004.

21. AHP to Dr. Albert Szent Gyorgyi, April 7, 1965. AHP, Box 1.006.

22. AHP to Gloria M. Stern, April 7, 1965. AHP, Box 1.004.

23. Jeanne Sollen to AHP, April 17, 1967. AHP, Box 1.004.

24. AHP, Typescript, "High-Energy Radiation and the Human Race," n.d. [1960s], AHP Papers, Box 2.002, Folder 2.10.

25. AHP to Elsa Peters Morse, March 30, 1965. AHP, Box 1.004.

26. See, e.g., AHP to Richard Drinnon, April 27, 1965. AHP, Box 1.004.

27. AHP to John and Hattie Hoffman, August 16, 1966. AHP, Box 1.004.

28. In addition to family reminiscences and photographs in the Pauling Papers, a two-part article illustrated with photographs by Tim Ryan in *The Cambrian*, November 8 and 15, 1979, offers glimpses of the ranch's décor. AHP, Box 3.004.

29. LP, Typescript, Notes: *Biographical Information - Hospitalization of Ava Helen Pauling*, by Linus Pauling, December 4, 1967. AHP, 3.018.

30. Manuscript notes, … [re: student unrest and the nature of revolution], speech by Ava Helen Pauling, 1968. AHP, Box 2.002, Folder 2.8.

31. Typescript, "San Diego City College, 14 May 1970." AHP Papers, Box 2.002, Folder 2.12.

32. "Go placidly amid the noise and the haste, and remember what peace there may be in silence." Max Ehrmann wrote this popular piece in 1927. It would conclude Ava Helen's memorial service in December 1981.

33. Manuscript, Typescript, Itinerary: "Is Woman Really Number Two?", speech by Ava Helen Pauling. AHP, Box 2.002, Folder 2.12.

34. For a detailed history of the Linus Pauling Institute, there are a number of sources. The most readable may be found in Thomas Hager's *Force of Nature*. In addition, the Chronology by Robert Paradowsky on the Special Collections web page (http://osulibrary.oregonstate.edu/specialcollections/coll/pauling/chronology/) offers an excellent and reliable account of Pauling's career.

35. AHP, manuscript fragment, "Women and World Peace," Australia, May 12, 1973.

36. AHP, "The Enemies of World Peace: What They Are and How We Can Vanquish Them," speech, delivered at "Dr. Albert Schweitzer's Centennial Birth Anniversary Commemoration Symposium," September 1975. AHP, Box 2.002, Folder 2.23.

37. LP to Charles Huggins, August 3, 1976. AHP, Box 3.018, Folder 18.8.

38. AHP, "Why I Am a Unitarian," typescript, September 18, 1977. AHP, Box 4.008, Folder 8.7.

39. AHP, manuscript account of car accident and subsequent health, March 7-19, 1978. AHP, Box 2.003.

40. Jara and others condemned the recent visit to Chilean universities of Robert MacVicar, then president of Oregon State University. This incident must have been very much on the mind of OAC alumna Ava Helen.

41. AHP, dedication address for "A Tribute in Concert to Victor Jara," February 20, 1979. AHP, Box 2.003, Folder 3.5.

42. For insight into Macon Link's relationship with Ava Helen and Linus, as well as some biographical information, see Nelly Macon Link to LP, January 14, 1989. AHP Box 1.004, Folder 4.3.

43. AHP to Evelyn Alloy, April 27, 1965. CDGA Alloy, Evelyn. Collected Papers. SCPC.

44. AHP to Evelyn Alloy, April 27, 1965. CDGA Alloy, Evelyn. Collected Papers. SCPC. In fact this evaluation of Jane Addams as "religious" in her outlook is a misreading of Addams's animus, and it is not clear where this evaluation came from.

45. AHP, "Bertha von Suttner and the World Peace Movement," paper prepared in honor of Otto Nathan, 1978. AHP, Box 2.003, Folder 3.4.

46. On the building of the cabin, see Oral History of Linus Pauling, Jr., 20-21.

47. AHP, "Women in Medicine," manuscript, April 1978. AHP, Box 2.003.

48. AHP to Stephen Fritchman, March 27, 1965. AHP, Box 4.008.

49. These details were meticulously recorded by Linus in August, after the couple's return home. See AHP, Box 3.019.

50. Linus glued the ingredients panel of a Vivonex box to a page of the lined ledger book in which he kept treatment notes.

51. LP, quoted in Ken Peterson, "ACLU Honors Ava Helen Pauling's Dedication to Peace, Civil Liberties," *Monterey Peninsula Herald*, November 2, 1981. AHP, Box 3.004.

52. Linus Pauling, Jr., personal communication, March 16, 2012; Oral History of Linus Pauling, Jr., 89.

53. Special Collections at Oregon State University ultimately received Ava Helen's papers along with Linus Pauling's.

Afterword

1. Crellin Pauling at AHP memorial service. This and subsequent references to the memorial service may be found in "Transcription of the tape recording of part of the memorial meeting for Ava Helen Pauling at the Unitarian Church of Palo Alto, December 12, 1981." AHP, Box 4.008.

2. Condolence Cards and Letters, A-H. AHP, Box 1.010.

3. Thomas Hager, record of Pauling's unmailed letter. LP, Hager2.006.8a.

4. Transcript, Oral History Interview of Stephanie Pauling, [interviewed by Chris Petersen], June 5, 2012. Pauling Papers.

5. Richard Morgan to AHP, December 4, 1981. AHP, Box 1.011.

6. The scientific name for the California coastal redwood is *Sequoia sempervirens*.

7. Transcript, Oral History Interview of Stephanie Pauling, [interviewed by Chris Petersen], June 5, 2012. Pauling Papers.

8. Helena Pycior, "Pierre Curie and 'His Eminent Collaborator Mme Curie,'" *Creative Couples in the Sciences*, ed. Helena M. Pycior, Nancy G. Slack, and Pnina G. Abir-Am (New Brunswick, New Jersey: Rutgers University Press, 1996), 48.

9. Hager, 435; LP to Farrington Daniels, December 17, 1953, sci14.007.1-lp-daniels-19531217.

10. Bernadette Bensaude-Vincent, "Star Scientists in a Nobelist Family: Irene and Frederic Joliot-Curie," *Creative Couples*, 71.

11. Pnina G. Abir-Am, "Collaborative Couples Who Wanted to Change the World: The Social Policies and Personal Tensions of the Russells, the Myrdals, and the Mead-Batesons," *Creative Couples*, 274.

12. Eric Rauchway, *The Refuge of Affections: Family and American Reform Politics, 1900-1920* (New York: Columbia University Press, 2001), 31-60.

13. See Helen Nearing, *Loving and Leaving the Good Life* (White River Junction, Vermont: Chelsea Green Publishing Company, 1992).

14. Stacy Schiff, *Véra (Mrs. Vladimir Nabokov)* (New York: Modern Library, 2000).

15. Gwen Athene Tarbox writes about the expansion from nineteenth-century women's club work to representations of girls' and young women's collective activities in *The Clubwomen's Daughters: Collectivist Impulses in Progressive-era Girls' Fiction* (New York: Garland Publishing, Inc., 2000). A study closer to home in terms of possible influences on Ava Helen Miller as she grew up is Sandra Haarsager's *Organized Womanhood: Cultural Politics in the Pacific Northwest, 1840-1920* (Norman: University of Oklahoma Press, 1997). Stephanie Coontz reminds us of the myth making that has surrounded the "traditional" image of marital roles, and the real-life complexity of jibing intimate partnership with marketplace valuations of household and non-household labor. See *The Way We Never Were: American Families and the Nostalgia Trap* (New York: Basic Books, 2000), esp. 42-67. Marilyn Yalom reviews the great changes in marital roles in the last half of the twentieth century in *A History of the Wife* (New York: HarperCollins Publishers Inc., 2001), esp. 352-400. The classic study of interactive, interdependent marital partners is Phyllis Rose, *Parallel Lives: Five Victorian Marriages* (New York: Alfred A. Knopf, Inc., 1983). There are many more possible citations. Mary Catherine Bateson, for example, writes about her own parents' collaborative, unique marriage in *With a Daughter's Eye: A Memoir of Margaret Mead and Gregory Bateson* (New York: William Morrow & Co, 1984). A recent biography of the great photographer Dorothea Lange by Linda Gordon, *Dorothea Lange: A Life Beyond Limits* (New York: W. W. Norton & Company, 2009), offers a poignant narrative of Lange's *two* longterm marriages – the second, with the agricultural economist Paul Taylor, more satisfying both emotionally and professionally. For Lange, both driven and diffident as an artist, balancing love, work, and childrearing never really happened. Like Ava Helen and Linus Pauling, she and her first husband Maynard Dixon colluded in boarding their

young boys with another family in order to pursue professional goals that seemed incompatible with nurturing children.

16. Thomas Hager interview with Linda Pauling Kamb [hager2.006.8a]; see also Linus Pauling, Jr., interview, September 23, 2011. Pauling Papers.

17. Pauling's imagining of Ava Helen in order to carry on a somewhat "normal" life suggests not only the natural course of grief, survival, and recovery, but also the phenomenon discussed by Ruth Perry and Martine Watson Brownley in *Mothering the Mind: Twelve Studies of Writers and Their Silent Partners* (New York: Holmes and Meier, 1984). They introduce this collection of studies of writers and their "silent partners" by suggesting that according to some developmental theory, "the capacity to be alone ... can develop only in the presence of another (who reflects the self back to one); it thus grows along with a complicated contrapuntal recognition of what is Other and external to the self" (7). The editors cite D. W. Winnicott among others to support this not unreasonable theory.

18. Insight into the "humanist" approach to emotions in human relationships was offered me by the Reverend Joel M. Miller, familiar with the tradition and personnel of the twentieth-century humanist movement within the Unitarian-Universalist Church. Personal communication, May 30, 2012.

INDEX